Praise for Clay Clark
(A Man Who Has Quasi-Successfully Been a Father for Over 21 Consecutive Years)

"Over the last decade, Clay Clark has served—quite unintentionally, I suspect—as a corrective to our national epidemic of impatience. In an age of microwave ambitions and TikTok attention spans, Clay stands like a granite monument to that old-fashioned notion: sustained, unglamorous diligence. It is a principle he teaches not with the airy abstraction of a theorist but with the muscular conviction of a man who has lived it, bled for it, and—yes—prospered by it. He reminds us that excellence is never the result of a single, brilliant spasm but a symphony of disciplined habits conducted over years. Clay Clark has, in short, taught me that consistency is the ultimate disruptor.

What Clay embodies—and what he has impressed upon me repeatedly—is the radical idea that intentionality is not a slogan but a science. He is gloriously intolerant of drift, allergic to half-measures, and convinced (correctly) that success bends only to those who pursue it with a kind of cheerful relentlessness.

Most mentors dispense platitudes about focus; Clay practices it, preaches it, and insists upon it with a vigor that borders on the evangelical. He has shown me that the future is not predicted; it is engineered. And the engineer, as Clay tirelessly argues, must rise every morning with the explicit intention to improve, to refine, to execute. Anything less is mere wishful thinking masquerading as ambition.

Over time—and here is the lesson that separates Clay from the common herd of motivational peddlers—he has demonstrated that diligence, practiced daily and without fanfare, compounds with the quiet ferocity of interest on a well-invested fortune. Clay has taught me that while talent glitters, diligence endures; while inspiration flickers, routine burns steadily; and while most men overestimate what one year can deliver, they catastrophically underestimate what ten years, guided by clear intent, can achieve. His stewardship of my thinking has been akin to intellectual weight training: repetitive, demanding, occasionally uncomfortable, and absolutely transformative.

And so, after a decade under his tutelage, I can say this without hesitation: Clay Clark is one of the rare figures in American entrepreneurial life who not only preaches the gospel of long-term intentionality but lives it with an almost monastic rigor. He has taught me the indispensable truth that greatness is not an accident, nor is it bestowed; it is built brick by tedious brick, day after unspectacular day—through the disciplined application of purpose. In a culture drunk on shortcuts and intoxicated by instant gratification, Clay restores sanity. He restores proportion. And, in no small measure, he restores hope. If diligence and intentionality are indeed the twin engines of achievement, then Clay Clark is one of their most accomplished modern pilots."

— Michael Levine

(5X New York Times Best-Selling author and public relations expert of choice for 58 Academy Winner, 61 New York Times Best-Sellers 36 Grammy Award Winners and celebrities including: Michael Jackson, Barbara Streisand, George Carlin, Sam Kinison, Rodney Dangerfield and countless top level celebrities. Michael Levine has been referred to in different publications as the "Michael Jordan of entertainment P.R.)

"We've met some of the biggest CEOs in the world, guys that run the biggest Fortune 500 companies and Clay Clark has 100 times the backbone of the toughest person that you will see."

— Eric Trump

(The Executive Vice President of The Trump Organization who is responsible for managing the $8 billion business, thousands of employees, the Trump Organization's real estate and the Trump brands.)

"Five years ago, I just felt like we were stuck, so I reached out to Clay Clark. Clay Clark helped me to build the systems we have now!"

— Gabe Salinas

(Founder of WindowNinjas.com)

"Clay, you've become an influencer. More than anything else, you have evolved into an influencer where your word has more and more power. As you know, there are a lot of fake influencers out there. I'm glad that you and I agree so much. You are on it, man! Everybody listen to this guy. He knows what he's talking about."

— Robert Kiyosaki

(The best-selling author of The Rich Dad Poor Dad book series and a man who has sold over 40 million copies of his entrepreneur books.)

"We have grown 5X! We have grown from 60 to 300 employees. Before we teamed up with Clay Clark, we didn't have any systems or processes!"

— Kevin Thomas

(Founder of MultiClean.com)

"Clay Clark is an entrepreneur extraordinaire."

— David Robinson

(NBA Hall of Basketball Player, former NBA MVP, NBA Championship Winner & Investor.)

"Clay Clark has helped us grow from 2 locations to now 6 locations. Clay has done a great job of navigating anything that has to do with running the business, building the systems, the checklists, the workflows, the audits, how to navigate lease agreements, how to buy property, how to work with brokers and builders. This guy is just amazing."

— Charles Colaw

(Founder of ColawFitness.com)

"He's like Steve Martin meets Steve Forbes."

— Jim Stovall

(New York Times best-selling self-help writer best known for his bestselling novel The Ultimate Gift. The book was made into the movie The Ultimate Gift, distributed by 20th Century Fox. The Ultimate Gift has a prequel called The Ultimate Life and a sequel called The Ultimate Legacy.)

"He helped us to grow 4,000% from February to February! In the last two and a half days we have bettered our entire month of last year's February. The phone is blowing up. And everything is just blowing up! It's like a rocket ship and we are just pitching ourselves actually!"

— Juliana Grimnes

(Co-Founder of www.GiveADerm.com)

"Clay Clark has been recognized nationally by the White House as Oklahoma's Small Business Entrepreneur of the Year, and he still hasn't reached the seasoned age of forty. He has learned to leverage his business acumen and now finds himself in multiple successful business partnerships. So I was not surprised at all when he set out to launch Thrive15.com – the place to get what you need to know to get you where you want to go. Those are his words. This book extends his winning talks beyond sold-out conferences to an audience of thousands more nationwide and around the world. And through Thrive15. com, he will open up passageways for others to live beyond the "just surviving" mentality. He celebrates success wherever it is found. He understands the hard work and dedication required. He really does admire Napoleon Hill and fills his life with Mr. Hill's actionable quotes. They are all through this book. As I look at Clay's success and his larger-than-life vision for his future, he is well on his way to emulating the man he so admires. And quite frankly, he is placing him in a similar position to be admired and quoted as his life and businesses continue to THRIVE. Oftentimes, people offering advice simply trust that the message is understood and move on, but not Clay Clark. He is committed to being in your face for your success. Not afraid of repetitious conversation and in-your-face humor, he is committed to each reader getting the message and more importantly, implementing the action steps set forth in this book and those voiced at Thrive15.com. Embracing and implementing the action steps in his books and training. Clay Clark is obsessed with implementing the action steps around your "big idea." This man gets emotional over your business success – maximizing your talents and potential. He remembers his dorm-room start and fully celebrates yours. Quoting Clay, "My friend, as you can tell by now, running a successful business is about so much more than just having a 'big idea.'

Your BIG IDEA is important, but the overwhelming majority of what will make your business succeed or fail has little to do with the "big idea" itself and everything to do with the execution of the "big idea." Clay leaves us no doubt that action on our part matters. His life as well as his insightful consulting encounters become a clear window through which we can look and see what is possible in many of our lives if we are willing to put in the time and effort necessary to turn ideas into reality. Clay clearly points out that our "want to" becomes the driver of our actions or lack of actions. Yes, I could have failed had I not embraced the notion that execution of a plan matters. Clay is right. His life challenges us to not settle, but to THRIVE. In doing so, we place ourselves in a position to light the darkness for others. It is in our reach to others that we truly maximize our existence on this planet. If I were still home in the Delta doing the same thing all those around me were doing, I seriously doubt if I would be able to light the pathway for myself or others. Today I am lighting the darkness as a businessman and writer, telling others what is possible for their lives. Clay's passionate plea for others to move beyond merely surviving comes from an honest place of caring. Why fail when you can THRIVE? Thank you, Clay, for not being afraid to step out beyond the ordinary and for inviting us along on your remarkable journey."

— Clifton L. Taulbert

(The first African American west of the Mississippi to found a bank, a Pulitzer-Prize Nominated and Best-selling Author, long-time Clay Clark mentor and the President of the Building Community Institute President & CEO.)

"We definitely feel the growth. It's been amazing. Clay Clark has really helped us to expand. It was scary at first. I know I needed someone to guide us through this, through employees, through income, through spending. There are a lot of problems when you have a business and you can become very overwhelmed very fast. It's the best decision we've ever made!"

— **Ginny Mingioni**

(NewConcept.Healthcare)

"Train up a child in the way he should go; even when he is old he will not depart from it."

— Proverbs 22:6

(Proverbs was written by King Solomon. King Solomon prayed relentlessly that God would give him wisdom. Under King Solomon's leadership Israel reached the peak of its wealth. However, King Solomon also did not listen to everything God told him because he went on to have 700 wives and 300 concubines. If you are reading this, I would encourage you to not have 700 wives and 300 concubines.)

"Let us hear the conclusion of the whole matter: Fear God, and keep his commandments: for this is the whole duty of man."

— Ecclesiastes 12:13

(At the end of King Solomon's life after having achieved enormous success and wealth he wrote the book of Ecclesiastes.)

HOW TO BECOME THE 2ND BEST FATHER IN THE HISTORY OF THE PLANET EARTH

Clay Clark

A Man Who Has Attempted to Be a Father for
Over 21 Consecutive Years

My father, Thomas Clayton Clark gave me priceless gifts that forever changed my life. He co-created me, he instilled in me the love of Jesus Christ as my Lord and Savior, he gave me a sense of humor, he taught me how capitalism works, he pushed for me to have a love of sports and entrepreneurship and my father BELIEVED IN ME.

ISBN: 979-8-9925935-2-5

HOW TO BECOME THE 2ND BEST FATHER IN THE HISTORY OF THE PLANET EARTH

Pictured from left to right:
My mentor and adopted-father (although we never did the paperwork), Doctor Robert Zoellner, Aubrey Napoleon-Hill Clark (my son) and me (Clay Clark), getting ready for Aubrey's first official DJ Show as Aubrey prepared himself to DJ the annual company Christmas Party that Dr. Z and I hosted for our employees.

When my father died after losing his long battle with Lou Gherig's Disease, my long-time mentor and friend Doctor Robert Zoellner called me and said something like, "Son, I know you just lost your father...and I could never replace him...but if you ever need a father I am here for you."

I said, "I do."

So without any further ado, I want to dedicate this book to my father (Thomas Clayton Clark), to my mother (Mary Clark), to my wife (Vanessa Clark), to my five incredible children (Havana, Aubrey Napoleon-Hill, Angelina, Scarlett & Laya) and to the man who has been there for me long after my earthly father got called up to meet Jesus, Doctor Robert Zoellner! Thank you for being you and I hope that this book inspires you the way you all inspire me!

Pictured above is my father Thom Clark and my father-in-law Rick Moore attending our wedding at Tarp Chapel in Broken Arrow, Oklahoma at: 1401 West Washington St S, Broken Arrow, OK, 74012.

Table of Contents

Pictured from left to right:
Laya Clark (Daughter), Clay Clark (Father / Son), Vanessa Clark (Wife and Mom), Angelina Clark (Daughter), Aubrey Clark (Son), Havana Clark (Daughter) and Scarlett Clark (Daughter) in Breckenridge, Colorado.

Behold, my incredible wife and the love of my life (Vanessa Clark).

Special Note to My Special Wife & Special Kids.

This book is dedicated to my 5 incredible children and my 1 incredible wife. My only regret is that my wife and I didn't have 22 children. I love our kids.

At the time I am writing this book:
Our daughter, Havana Ann Clark is 20 years old
Our son, Aubrey Napoleon-Hill Clark is 17 years old.
Our daughter, Angelina Lynn Clark is 16 years old.
Our daughter, Scarlett Kathleen Clark is 15 years old.
Our daughter, Laya Jane Clark is 15 years old.
I am 44 years old.

My wife, Vanessa Clark, is getting younger every day. She is so sharp I often almost cut my retina just looking at her.

When life gets tough and it's going to HECK, I always look forward to taking our family to Thanksgiving at Breck (Breckenridge, Colorado).

The Most Profound Job That You Will Ever Have Is Being THE 2ND BEST FATHER IN THE HISTORY OF THE PLANET

The Most Profound Job That You Will Ever Have Is Being THE 2ND BEST FATHER IN THE HISTORY OF THE PLANET

Greetings, Dad (or about to be dad, or man who has already been a dad and who has now transitioned into grandpa mode)!

It is my belief that being intentional as both a father to our kids and husband to our wives (I hope you have one wife) is the most important job that you and I will ever have as dudes on the planet Earth. I know that in the world we live in we are constantly being bombarded with Grant Cardone videos, Tai Lopez videos and Andrew Tate videos that are teaching us how to dominate life while making copious amounts of cash in route to mastering physical fitness, however this book is not about that. This book is about teaching you how to become the world's second best dad. I personally believe that God ("Our Father which art in heaven, Hallowed be thy name") is the best father in the history of the planet and thus you and I can strive to be the world's second best.

"7 But when ye pray, use not vain repetitions, as the heathen do: for they think that they shall be heard for their much speaking. 8 Be not ye therefore like unto them: for your Father knoweth what things ye have need of, before ye ask him. 9 After this manner therefore pray ye: Our Father which art in heaven, Hallowed be thy name. 10 Thy kingdom come, Thy will be done in earth, as it is in heaven. 11 Give us this day our daily bread. 12 And forgive us our debts, as we forgive our debtors. 13 And lead us not into temptation, but deliver us from evil: For thine is the kingdom, and the power, and the glory, for ever. Amen. 14 For if ye forgive men their trespasses, your heavenly Father will also forgive you: 15 But if ye forgive not men their trespasses, neither will your Father forgive your trespasses."

— Matthew 6:7-15

(This book was written by Matthew who was a former tax collector and who went on to wrie one of the most influential books of the New Testament.)

Having coached with thousands of business owners en route to helping them to achieve massive financial success, I want to encourage you that becoming a great father and a great business success story are not two opposing ideas. Yes! THIS JUST IN!!! BREAKING NEWS!!! Becoming a great father and becoming a great business success story are not mutually exclusive ideas.

Thus, this book is 100% focused on helping you and I to take our father game to the next level. I BELIEVE your kids need you to become the best dad that you can be! The world needs you to become the best dad you can be! You need to become the best dad that you can be! However, in order to motivate YOU about the importance and the necessity of choosing to become an intentional and great dad I wanted to share with you the following mind-blowing statistics and FUN FACTS about the importance of children having a great father in their lives.

Did your father ever teach you how to live in a way that will not cause you to be perpetually in prison and journeying to jail?

- According to a study done by the Fulton County Texas Department of Corrections, 85% of all youths in prison come from fatherless homes. Thus, kids who come from fatherless homes are nearly 20 times more likely to go to jail than kids who were raised in a home with their biological fathers.

- According to a September 1988 study by the United States Department of Justice, 70% of youths in state-operated institutions come from fatherless homes – 9 times the average.

Did your father ever tell you what it meant to be a man or a woman? Their fathers didn't.

- According to research conducted by the U.S. Census Bureau and posted on Fatherhood.org, nearly 24 million children in America (1 out of 3) live in homes where the biological father is absent.

Did you ever get in trouble with your parents for not studying hard and doing well on your tests? They never did.

- In a 2011 article written by Lory Hough, the Harvard School of Education found that over 50% of the 18-24 year old Americans surveyed by National Geographic couldn't find the state of New York on a map.

- In a Sept 14, 2011 article posted by Michael Winter for USA Today, the College Board now shows that just 40% of the high school seniors met benchmarks for college success.

Did your parents ever teach you about the consequences of your actions? Their parents never did.

- In a May of 2008 article published in USA Today, researchers in Chicago found that 1 in 4 teen girls have a sexually transmitted disease. Thus, approximately 3 million teens now have an STD.

- In a March 9th, 2012 article posted on Reuters by JoAnne Allen, about 16% of Americans between the ages of 14 and 49 are infected with genital herpes, making it one of the most common sexually transmitted diseases.

- In Newsweek's cover story entitled "iCrazy," it was revealed that one quarter of employees who use the internet during work visit porn sites. In fact, hits to porn sites are highest during office hours than at any other time of day.

Did your parents tell you not to lie? Their parents never did.

- 40% of the information on résumés is misrepresented (false, untrue, a lie) according to research conducted by American DataBank from 2008 - 2010.

Did your parents ever teach you that a quitter never wins and that a winner never quits? Their parents never did.

- Despite being in a deep economic recession, a July 7th, 2010 article published by the Harvard Business Review reported that more employees quit their jobs than were terminated, according to the US Bureau of Labor Statistics 3 month research.

Do you remember when college was supposed to make you more intelligent and more hirable? They don't.

- According to a USA Today Article written by Mary Beth Marklein, research shows students spent 50% less time studying compared with students a few decades ago. The research compared college students enrolled in 2001 versus college students enrolled in 2011.

Whatever happened to common sense?

- According to Gail Cunningham, In a 2011 Newsweek Article, research was conducted by asking 1,000 U.S. citizens to take America's official citizenship test. Twenty-nine percent (29%) couldn't name the Vice President. Seventy-three percent couldn't correctly explain why we fought the Cold War.

- The spokeswoman for the National Foundation of Credit Counseling, as quoted in a July 2012 article in Newsweek Magazine, 56% of U.S. adults admit they don't have a budget; one-third don't pay all their bills on time.

- According to an article written by Mary Beth Marklein in USA Today, nearly half of the nation's undergraduates show almost no gains in learning in their first two years of college. The report concludes this is because, in large part, colleges don't make academics a priority. Among their top activities, students report spending 24% of their time sleeping, 51% of their time socializing and just 7% actually studying.

Do you remember when childhood was supposed to be about exploration, love, and innocence? They don't.

- A study put together in 2006 by the Centers for Disease Control and Prevention showed that 1 in 4 women and 1 in 6 men were sexually abused before the age of 18. This means there are more than 42 million adult survivors of child sexual abuse in the United States.

Do you remember when 1 out of 5 of your co-workers wasn't insane? They don't.

- According to a disturbing article published by Harvard Health Publications in February of 2010, researchers analyzing results from the U.S. National Co-Morbidity Survey found a nationally representative study of Americans ages 15 to 54. In that study it was reported that 18% of those who were employed said they experienced symptoms of a mental health disorder in the previous month.

Do you remember when your father taught you how to start and grow a successful business? They don't.

- According to Inc. Magazine (as of 2015), 96% of businesses fail.

"Train up a child in the way he should go: and when he is old, he will not depart from it."

— Proverbs 22:6

(Proverbs is a book written by King Solomon and it is found in that controversial book known as The Bible.)

6 PRO-TIPS On How to Get the Most Out of This Book

As we sprint through the pages of this action-packed and practical guide book on How to Become the 2nd Best Father You Can Be I highly recommend that you take notes, highlight and wrestle with the content found in this ULTIMATE MAN BOOK. I encourage you to take copious amounts of notes as you mentally wrestle with the concept of How to Become the 2nd Best Father You Can Be. First off, I would encourage you to rate yourself on a scale of 1 to 10 with 10 being the highest in the following areas:

1. How highly would you rank yourself on a scale of 1 to 10 with 10 being the highest in the area of being a great husband?

   _____

2. How highly would you rank yourself on a scale of 1 to 10 with 10 being the highest in the area of being a great father?

   _____

"²³ And whatsoever ye do, do it heartily, as to the Lord, and

not unto men; ²⁴ Knowing that of the Lord ye shall receive the

reward of the inheritance: for ye serve the Lord Christ."

— Colossians 3:23-24

(Colossians is a book written by the Apostle Paul. Before discovering Christ, Paul was known as Saul where he previously spent his time rounding up Christians, persecuting them and feeding them to lions.)

As a husband, father, business owner, investor, consultant, song-writer, author, podcaster (and more), I always find myself wishing that I had more time to get things done. I typically go to bed at 9 PM and wake up at 3 AM because that is the best sustainable and daily flow for me and my life to get the most out of each day. However we all just have 24 hours per day in this great gift we call our God-given life. Thus, if you have an ounce of proactivity in the areas of your faith, family, finances, fitness, friendship, fun and focused attention, you and I are going to have to choose to find the time TO BECOME THE 2ND BEST FATHER IN THE HISTORY OF THE PLANET!

"No one lives long enough to learn everything they need to learn starting from scratch. To be successful, we absolutely, positively have to find people who have already paid the price to learn the things that we need to learn to achieve our goals."

— **Brian Tracy**

(Legendary best-selling author, trainer, speaker and investor.)

Pro-Tip #1

What gets scheduled gets done. If you don't schedule it, it won't be done. If you don't schedule a specific time to be with your family it will not happen. That is jackassery.

Pro-Tip #2

By default, you and I will become the world's worst fathers unless we are intentional about aiming to BECOME THE 2ND BEST FATHER IN THE HISTORY OF THE PLANET. I believe God has given us all the ability to choose to get better or worse in many areas of our life. Not choosing to become the best dad you and I can possibly be is not a move. That is jackassery.

Pro-Tip #3

Abdicating our fatherly duties and abandoning our role as dads in route to earning copious amounts of money "to provide for our family" is not a move. That is jackassery.

Pro-Tip #4

Not providing financially for your family as you attempt to find yourself and your path on HOW TO BECOME THE 2ND BEST FATHER IN THE HISTORY OF THE PLANET is not a move. That is jackassery.

Pro-Tip #5

Becoming a horrible husband while attempting to discover HOW TO BECOME THE 2ND BEST FATHER IN THE HISTORY OF THE PLANET is not a move. That is jackassery.

Pro-Tip #6

Knowledge without application is meaningless. If you read the words on this page and do not apply what you are learning, that is much like discovering that you have a flat tire, learning how to repair a tire and then not repairing your tire. That is jackassery.

I realize that you and I might not agree on every word of this practical guide on HOW TO BECOME THE 2ND BEST FATHER IN THE HISTORY OF THE PLANET, but I would encourage you to 100% AGREE to block out the uninterrupted 120 minutes that will be required to read this book from cover to cover and to really focus on HOW TO BECOME THE 2ND BEST FATHER IN THE HISTORY OF THE PLANET. The process of becoming THE 2ND BEST FATHER IN THE HISTORY OF THE PLANET is learnable but it does require an investment of time. Much like getting into great physical shape, learning a new skill, learning to shoot free throws or learning how to play a new instrument, I do believe that the skill of becoming a HIGH-QUALITY father is 100% trainable and learnable, but it does require an investment of your time.

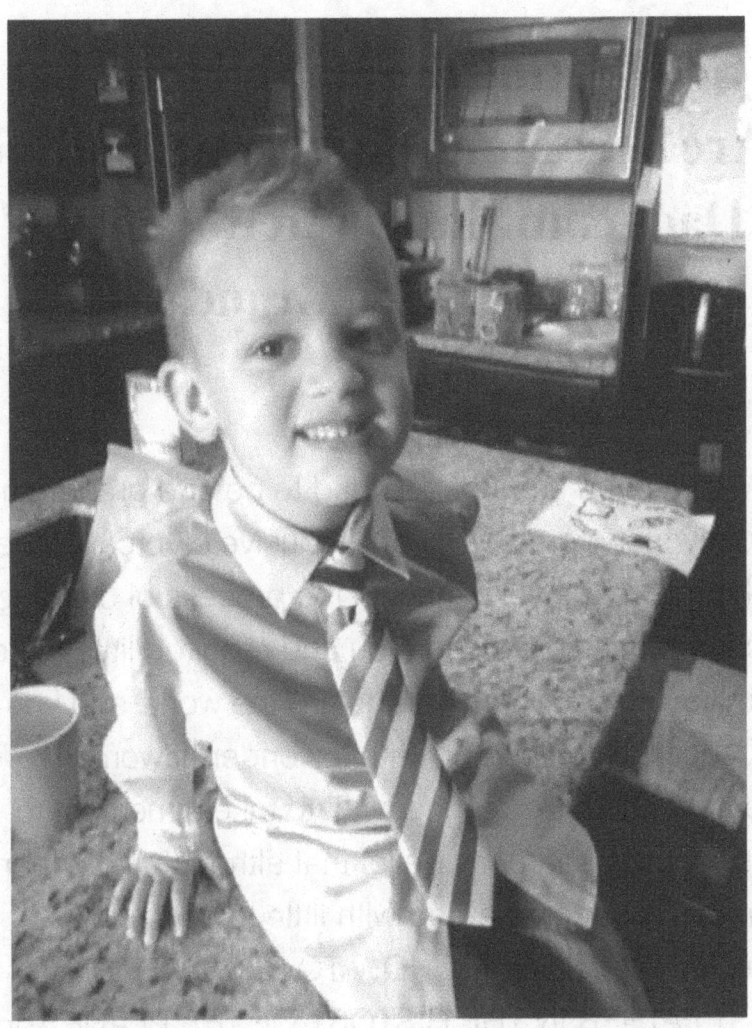

My son Aubrey Napoleon-Hill Clark wearing a tie for the first time. I named Aubrey Napoleon-Hill after my wife's grandfather Aubrey and Napoleon-Hill the best-selling author of *Think and Grow Rich* which forever changed my life and mindset.

Celebrating the Manly Men That Are Becoming First-Time Dutiful Dads & to Mature Men Who Are Now Grizzled Grandpas

Whether you are a dad, a dad to be or a grandfather, you my friend are part of an exclusive club called dads. Although your involvement in the process of creating a child was enjoyable for you and required little to no sacrifice on your part, you put in "the work" and you successfully teamed up with a wonderful woman to create a child. However, I want to take a moment to passionately share my belief that although most men can easily become a dad with little to no sacrifice, the process of learning HOW TO BECOME THE 2ND BEST FATHER IN THE HISTORY OF THE PLANET does require sacrifice, commitment, intentionality and the investment of both your time and your money.

"Children's children are the crown of old men; and the glory of children are their fathers."

— Proverbs 17:6

(Proverbs is a book of the Bible that is in favor of taking massive action. This book was written by King Solomon and it is found in that controversial book known as The Bible.)

Once your child arrives on the planet Earth via your wife's birth canal, the world, your family and your friends are going to shift their focus on to your wife for a while. Which makes sense, since she is the one who just pushed a baby human the size of a watermelon out of her birth canal. So don't whine about the world focusing on the mother of your child for a while. This just in...the world will focus more on the mother than on the father after the baby arrives, and it should. If you start to feel neglected, shut up and ponder how difficult it would be to push a baby human the size of a watermelon out of your body and then ask how you can help the mother of your child.

Pictured Left to Right: Laya Clark, Havana Clark, Aubrey Clark, Clay Clark, General Flynn, Vanessa Clark, Scarlett Clark and Angelina Clark in Washington, D.C. (2025).

Once Your Child Arrives Via the Birth, Things Will Get a Lil' Crazy On Earth (For You)

As you are reading this book you and I are up against the clock and need to move quickly. We only have 120 minutes together to learn HOW TO BECOME THE 2ND BEST FATHER IN THE HISTORY OF THE PLANET.

Pictured Left to Right: Havana Clark, Laya Clark, Angelina Clark, Aubrey Clark and Scarlett Clark.

Man Law #1
As An Intentional Father Remember, Acta Non Verba

"Acta non verba" is a Latin phrase meaning "actions, not words," and it happens to be the favorite phrase of the legendary best-selling author of the "Rich Dad Poor Dad" book series, Robert Kiyosaki. It doesn't matter what you say, it matters what you do. If you want your kids to have a good work ethic, you must demonstrate a good work ethic. Both fortunately and unfortunately, our kids are going to watch what we do and not what we say. If we want to teach our kids how to speak well, we must speak well. If we want to teach our kids to be organized, we must be organized. If we want to teach our kids to be kind, we must be kind. Remember when it comes to teaching our kids how to grow up to be successful, honest, and high-integrity productive people it always comes down to "Acta non verba," actions, not words.

"He that is good for making excuses is seldom good for anything else."

— Benjamin Franklin

(A man who had just 24 hours in every day just like you and I, yet became an American polymath: a writer, a scientist, an inventor, a statesman, a diplomat, a printer, a publisher and a political philosopher. Benjamin Franklin found the time to become one of the most influential intellectuals of his time, Franklin was one of the Founding Fathers of the United States, a drafter and signer of the Declaration of Independence, and the first postmaster general.)

Man Law #2

As an Intentional Father, Tell Your Child You Love Them All the Time

So much of our lives is going to be spent trying to find the kernels of corn (positivity) in the vomit of life (the reality of day to day life and the depravity of the human condition). Thus, your child needs to know that you love them. Tell your child you love them every time you see them and then tell them that you love them some more or your child will end up falling into the arms of a stranger, that couldn't be stranger.

"Ninety-nine percent of the failures come from people who have the habit of making excuses."

— George Washington Carver

(A man who was born a slave, yet went on to become an agricultural scientist and inventor who promoted alternative crops to cotton and methods to prevent soil depletion. He was one of the most prominent black scientists of the early 20th century.)

Man Law #3

As An Intentional Father, Don't Put a Chip In Your Head or a Whore In Your Bed

"We can do a full brain machine interface. Ultimately...sort of a symbiosis with artificial intelligence."

— Elon Musk (July 17th 2019)

(Elon Musk founded OpenAI in San Francisco in 2015 with Sam Altman, and others. OpenAI LP received a $1 billion investment from Bill Gates' and Microsoft. Musk owns the COVID-19 vaccine developer CureVac and is openly discussing using his Boring Company to dig the new CERN Hadron Collider. Elon Musk was listed on the 2008 World Economic Forum list of Young Global Leaders. Why did Elon Musk wear a Baphomet costume during Halloween of 2022? Musk produced three children with Grimes who released the SATANIC song "We Appreciate Power" which prophesied the COVID-19 / Great Reset / Transhumanism agenda. Why did Grimes use the Baphomet hand signal during her 2022 Vanity Fair photo shoot? Why did Elon Musk wear a white tuxedo jacket with the words 'NOVUS ORDO SECLORUM' (which means 'NEW WORLD ORDER') written on the back of it to the 2018 MET Gala while his guest Grimes wore a Vantablack crown? Why did Elon Musk post "Novus Ordo Seclorum" on November 6th 2024? Why did Elon Musk post "Deus X Machina" via Twitter on October 16th 2022?)

"22 And the voice of harpers, and musicians, and of pipers, and trumpeters, shall be heard no more at all in thee; and no craftsman, of whatsoever craft he be, shall be found any more in thee; and the sound of a millstone shall be heard no more at all in thee; 23 And the light of a candle shall shine no more at all in thee; and the voice of the bridegroom and of the bride shall be heard no more at all in thee: for thy merchants were the great men of the earth; for by thy sorceries were all nations deceived."

— Revelation 18:22-23

"12 And the ten horns which thou sawest are ten kings, which have received no kingdom as yet; but receive power as kings one hour with the beast. 13 These have one mind, and shall give their power and strength unto the beast."

— Revelation 17:12-13

(Revelation is the final book in that controversial book filled with the irrefutable word of God known as the Bible. This book was written by the Apostle John after God appeared to him during an open vision while the Apostle John was exiled on the island of Patmos.)

Pictured Left to Right: Havana Clark, Vanessa Clark, Clay Clark, Chloe Domeck, Eric Trump and Laya Clark visiting Eric Trump at Trump Tower (New York City, New York) in 2023.

Man Law #4

As An Intentional Father, Love Your Wife the Way Christ Loved the Church. Unless you Hate Your Life, You Need to Obsess About Loving Your Wife!

This part of the Bible has always really convicted me and caused me to realize how much better I can become as a husband and a father. God literally commands us to love our wives the way Jesus loved the church and Jesus died for the church. Jesus sacrificed his life for the church. Meanwhile, I have found myself getting frustrated about my wife wanting to turn the heat up in the car while we are driving on a road trip. What is wrong with me? I can do better. You can do better. We can do better. We must aim to love our wives the way that Christ loved the church. Our children are watching our every move like they work for a chinese spy agency. Our children are observing what we are doing and they are learning to copy what they see us doing. Over time you will discover that kids will do what you do and not what you say.

Pictured above is Aubrey Napoleon-Hill Clark (our son), Vanessa Clark (my wife) and myself at Metro Christian Fall Senior Night.

"[25] Husbands, love your wives, even as Christ also loved the church, and gave himself for it; [26] That he might sanctify and cleanse it with the washing of water by the word, [27] That he might present it to himself a glorious church, not having spot, or wrinkle, or any such thing; but that it should be holy and without blemish. [28] So ought men to love their wives as their own bodies. He that loveth his wife loveth himself. [29] For no man ever yet hated his own flesh; but nourisheth and cherisheth it, even as the Lord the church: [30] For we are members of his body, of his flesh, and of his bones. [31] For this cause shall a man leave his father and mother, and shall be joined unto his wife, and they two shall be one flesh. [32] This is a great mystery: but I speak concerning Christ and the church. [33] Nevertheless let every one of you in particular so love his wife even as himself; and the wife see that she reverence her husband."

— Ephesians 5:25-33

(Ephesians was written by the Apostle Paul. Before turning his life around and choosing to follow Jesus Christ, Paul used to go by the name Saul and he was THE WORST. Saul used to spend his day persecuting Christians, rounding up Christians and feeding Christians to lions. When in doubt. Don't feed your enemies to lions.)

Pictured from Left to Right: Scarlett Clark, Havana Clark, Laya Clark, Aubrey Clark and Angelina Clark.

Man Law #5
As An Intentional Father, Always Publicly Praise Your Wife

"Be devoted to one another in love. Honor one another above yourselves."

— Romans 12:10

(The book of Romans was written by the Apostle Paul. In fact 13 books in the new testament were written by the Apostle Paul.)

It's important that your kids hear you praising your wife, celebrating your wife and saying good things about your wife. Your kids need to have a reverence for their mother and they need to believe that their mom is the best! Your kids need to believe that their mother is on a God-inspired mission to raise them to become the best adults that they can be. When in doubt, tell your kids that your wife is the best! When you are really frustrated by something and when you and your wife are really not getting along well, tell your kids how great your wife is.

Man Law #6
As An Intentional Father, You Must Remember That You And Your Wife Are On the Same Team

"⁴ Haven't you read," he replied, "that at the beginning the Creator 'made them male and female,' ⁵ and said, 'For this reason a man will leave his father and mother and be united to his wife, and the two will become one flesh'? ⁶ So they are no longer two, but one flesh. Therefore what God has joined together, let no one separate."

— Matthew 19:4-6

(This book was written by the Apostle Matthew.)

During the heat of the battle of life and when life becomes intense, you must remember that you and your wife are on the same team. Pastor Jackson Lahmeyer of www.Sheridan.Church calls these times, "Moments of intense fellowship." During these challenging times you must remember that you and your wife are on the same team. Your kids need to know that you and your wife are on the same team. When you are on a hard-working goal-focused team of any kind there will be conflict and you must learn to have these arguments in private and away from the listening ears of your children as you remember that YOU AND YOUR WIFE ARE ON THE SAME TEAM.

Man Law #7

As An Intentional Father, Don't Abdicate the Process of Educating Your Kids

Our kids are the greatest gift that God can give us, so you and I must not abdicate our responsibility for educating our kids to a school system, to a day care or to some institution of higher learning.

"He that spareth his rod hateth his son: but he that loveth him chasteneth him betimes."

— Proverbs 13:24

(Proverbs is a book of the Bible that is in favor of taking massive action. This book was written by King Solomon and it is found in that controversial book known as The Bible.)

It is very important that you are personally involved in educating your children, because if you do not educate your children someone else will. I am not writing this to attack all teachers that are working in the profession of education, however, I do want to point out the following disturbing facts when it comes to the people that are educating America's children:

- "Overall, 70% of U.S. teachers are engaged in their work, matching the national average for all workers. A majority, 57%, of full-time K-12 teachers in the U.S. are "not engaged" (https://news.gallup.com/poll/180455/lack-teacher-engagement-linked-million-missed-workdays.aspx).

- "In 2025, researchers at the University of Missouri released a study in which they surveyed around 500 public school teachers. They found that 78 percent have thought about quitting their profession since the pandemic" (https://www.nea.org/nea-today/all-news-articles/whats-causing-teacher-burnout).

I don't know about you, but I don't want my children to be taught by the 70% of the teachers that are not engaged and by the 78% of teachers that are thinking about quitting their profession. There is no higher calling than educating our own children. Find a way to train your children or you will quickly find yourself dealing with the consequences of raising poorly disciplined, demotivated and uneducated children who were taught during 50% of their waking hours by teachers that are poorly disciplined, demotivated and uneducated.

Young Laya Clark celebrates life!

Young Aubrey Napoleon-Hill Clark celebrates life!

Man Law #8
As An Intentional Father, You Must Make Sure That Your Kids Gain Biblical Literacy

" I charge thee therefore before God, and the Lord Jesus Christ, who shall judge the quick and the dead at his appearing and his kingdom; 2 Preach the word; be instant in season, out of season; reprove, rebuke, exhort with all long suffering and doctrine. 3 For the time will come when they will not endure sound doctrine; but after their own lusts shall they heap to themselves teachers, having itching ears; 4 And they shall turn away their ears from the truth, and shall be turned unto fables. 5 But watch thou in all things, endure afflictions, do the work of an evangelist, make full proof of thy ministry."

— 2 Timothy Chapter 4:1-5

(2nd Timothy was written by Paul the Apostle as a letter addressed to Timothy who was a fellow missionary.)

We now live in a world where Elon Musk is rolling out Artificial Intelligence (AI) "companions," where your children have 24/7 evil content via their phone and where the moral decline of our nation is evident in our streets, on our television screens, in our schools and in the air everywhere via sexualized music, movies, advertising and more. Unless you want your kids to grow up as Biblically illiterate and morally reprehensible humans who have become masters of the dark art of jackassery, you must be intentional about scheduling time into your schedule to teach your children the Bible.

Man Law #9
As An Intentional Father, You Must Make Sure Your Kids Gain Financial Literacy

Although there are potentially thousands of high-quality self-help and success-focused books that may be of some value to your kids, as an award-winning entrepreneur who has successfully taught thousands of people how to start and grow a super successful business I would highly recommend that both YOU and your kids read and understand the following books:

1. "Think & Grow Rich," by Napoleon Hill

2. "Rich Dad Poor Dad," by Robert Kiyosaki

3. "How to Win Friends & Influence People," by Dale Carnegie

4. "Soft-Selling In a Hard World," by Jerry Vass

5. "The E-Myth Revisited," by Michael Gerber

6. "America's #1 Business Coach Provides the Proven Playbook on How to Build a Successful Business: The Ultimate Step-By-Step Guide for Growing a Sustainability Successful & Time-Freedom Creating Business," by Clay Clark

7. "Jackassery: Unfiltered Entrepreneurship," by Clay Clark

"⁸ But if any provide not for his own, and specially for those of his own house, he hath denied the faith, and is worse than an infidel."

— 1 Timothy Chapter 5

(1ˢᵗ Timothy was written by Paul the Apostle as a letter addressed to Timothy who was a fellow missionary.)

The Bible actually tells us that if you and I cannot provide for our family we have denied our faith and are worse than an infidel (an unbeliever). That is harsh. I would STRONGLY recommend that you block out time into your schedule to teach your kids "Think & Grow Rich," by Napoleon Hill; "Rich Dad Poor Dad," by Robert Kiyosaki; "How to Win Friends & Influence People," by Dale Carnegie; "Soft Selling In a Hard World," by Jerry Vass; "The E-Myth Revisited," by Michael Gerber; and my books, "America's #1 Business Coach Provides the Proven Playbook on How to Build a Successful Business: The Ultimate Step-By-Step Guide for Growing a Sustainability Successful & Time-Freedom Creating Business" and "Jackassery: Unfiltered Entrepreneurship."

Don't allow your kids to grow up being financially illiterate. If they do, it is our fault as fathers.

Young Scarlett Clark celebrates life!

Man Law #10
Being Present Is a Present & Every Day Is a Gift

"²⁴ This is the day which the Lord hath made; we will rejoice and be glad in it."

— Psalm 118:24

(King David is the most prominent, credited with 73 psalms. Other writers include Asaph, who is credited with writing 12 psalms; the sons of Korah are credited with writing 11; and other humans which include Solomon, Moses, Heman, and Ethan are also credited with contributing to the Book of Psalms.)

This is truly the day that the Lord has made and we should truly rejoice and be glad in it. Every day is a GIFT from God. Think about that? If every day that we have in this life on the planet Earth is a gift then what we do with every day on this planet is a gift to God. Marinate on that. Every day you and I must choose to be intentional about how and where we schedule our time and we must choose to work as unto the Lord as we work on raising our families and teaching our children to not grow up to become Godless low-energy, pro-abortion, gender-confused communists.

What does the Bible say about work?

- The word "work" means "worship" in Hebrew and the word "worship" means "work" in Hebrew.

- Genesis 2:15 — "And the Lord God took the man, and put him into the garden of Eden to dress it and to keep it."

- Colossians 3:23-24 — "Whatsoever ye do, do it heartily, as to the Lord, and not unto men; knowing that of the Lord ye shall receive the reward of the inheritance: for ye serve the Lord Christ."

Pictured from Left to Right: Aubrey Napoleon-Hill Clark, Havana Clark, Scarlett Clark, Thom Clark, Angelina Clark and Laya Clark. My children and my father's grandchildren gather around their dying grandfather to bring him life, encouragement and love. As Lou Ghehrig's Disease ravaged my father's body he never EVER lost his faith in Jesus Christ as his Lord and Savior and my mother never left his side! Dad, I am happy you are in heaven. I miss you sir!

Man Law #11
Attempt to Praise Your Wife Every Day

"Husbands, love your wives, and be not bitter against them."

— Colossians 3:19

(The Apostle Paul wrote this book of the Bible which was originally a letter to the Colossians.)

You and I must focus on publicly praising our wives and we must focus on publicly praising our wives in front of our children. Our children need to know that we sincerely view our wives as a gift from God. I cannot stress this enough. Block out time in your schedule to praise your wife on a daily basis, or plan on saving up $50 per day to pay a divorce attorney in the future.

As I objectively look at the situation and all self-deprecation aside, I am married to a "10." My wife is beautiful and smart and I am a solid "4.73." I will outwork anybody and I am the most consistent human I have ever met, however, I am still a solid "4.73." Thus, I have to sell this "product" (me) to my wife each and every day. And the best way to sell this "product" (me) to my beautiful wife is to sincerely praise her for the great work she has done and is doing to raise our wonderful children and the amazing job she has done as being a loyal helpmate and soulmate to me as my wife.

"He who finds a wife finds a good thing, And obtains favor from the Lord."

— Proverbs 18:22

(This book was written by King Solomon who should have known a lot about having a great wife because he actually had 700 wives and 300 concubines. Historians claim that King Solomon had 700 wives and 300 concubines as a political strategy to form alliances throughout the world, however I believe King Solomon had 700 WIVES AND 300 CONCUBINES FOR DIFFERENT REASONS!!!! I believe that "Dirty" King Solomon was a "Dirty Dog.")

Pictured above my father attempts to dance with his granddaughter (Havana Clark) one more time at his high school reunion using his wheelchair. While my dad could not stop smiling I could not stop crying. In this world of perpetual distractions, we must never forget what matters most.

Man Law #12
You Must Learn to Say No In Order to Grow Your Relationship With Your Children

"Blessed is the man that walketh not in the counsel of the ungodly, nor standeth in the way of sinners, nor sitteth in the seat of the scornful."

— Psalms 1:1

(The Psalms written by many different authors and not just one specific author, however King David is credited as being the man who wrote 73 of the psalms.)

In order to teach your children to become productive, successful and God-fearing people on the planet Earth that are destined to spend eternity with their Lord and Savior Jesus Christ, you must say no to the following unproductive people, events and more:

1. You must say no to bad influences in your life as a father in order to be a good influence to your children.

2. You must say no to bad influences in your children's lives in order to be a good influence to your children.

3. You must say no to investing copious amounts of time into playing video games in order to be a good influence to your children.

4. You must say no to filling your home with foul music in order to be a good influence to your children.

5. You must say no to watching hate-filled and evil video content in your home.

6. You must say no to investing your time mindlessly watching television, Netflix, scrolling through social media and endless online jackassery in order to be a good influence to your children.

7. You must say no to investing your time at the local bar in order to be a good influence to your children.

8. You must say no to investing your time at the local casino in order to be a good influence to your children.

9. You must say no to _____ (fill in the blank) in order to be a good influence to your children.

10. You must say no to _____ (fill in the blank) in order to be a good influence to your children.

11. You must say no to _____ (fill in the blank) in order to be a good influence to your children.

12. You must say no to _____ (fill in the blank) in order to be a good influence to your children.

13. You must say no to _____ (fill in the blank) in order to be a good influence to your children.

Clay and Vanessa Clark. In this picture I am celebrating the fact that I have successfully tricked my wife into marrying me...and I keep tricking her into staying married to me each and every year. You may want to pray for my wife that her vision would be restored...I don't have proof, but she may be legally blind. That's a pro-tip for all the "4.73 men" out there looking for your dream woman. Find a "10" that has little to no vision.

Man Law #13
You Must Establish Boundaries

"[13] Ye are the salt of the earth: but if the salt have lost his savour, wherewith shall it be salted? it is thenceforth good for nothing, but to be cast out, and to be trodden under foot of men. [14] Ye are the light of the world. A city that is set on an hill cannot be hid. [15] Neither do men light a candle, and put it under a bushel, but on a candlestick; and it giveth light unto all that are in the house. [16] Let your light so shine before men, that they may see your good works, and glorify your Father which is in heaven."

— Matthew 5:13-16

(The book of Matthew was written by the Apostle Matthew who died as a martyr in Ethiopia. Matthew was put to death by a swordsman who was commanded by a king to kill Matthew because Matthew rebuked the king who wished to marry a virgin who was converted to Christianity by the Apostles.)

Movies, music, advertising, social media and the internet all provide gateways and opportunities for your children to gain access to a world of dystopian evil and a Satanic agenda, thus you as a parent must set the boundaries for the activities that you will impose on your family in order to protect your marriage and to protect your children.

As the father of your children, you must make a list of the items that you will not let your children be exposed to in order to protect their hearts, their minds and their futures:

Boundary #1: You will not allow your children to have access to: _____

Boundary #2: You will not allow your children to have access to: _____

Boundary #3: You will not allow your children to have access to: _____

Boundary #4: You will not allow your children to have access to: _____

Boundary #5: You will not allow your children to have access to: _____

Boundary #6: You will not allow your children to have access to: _____

Boundary #7: You will not allow your children to have access to: _____

Boundary #8: You will not allow your children to have access to: _____

Your kids are going to attempt to get what they want and when you let them know that you are not going to give them what they want, children have developed three moves that they will use in an attempt to motivate you to give them what they want.

1. They will act extremely nice and polite and they will praise you in an attempt to amaze you so much that you give them what they want.

2. They will act as though you are killing their soul, ruining their life and ruining their entire future if you do not give them what they want.

3. They will beg, plead, whine, cry, grovel and nag you if you do not give them what they want.

Angelina Clark, Laya Clark, Grandma Mary, Aubrey Clark, Scarlett Clark and Havana Clark jamming out and celebrating life!

Man Law #14
Don't Fight With Your Wife
In Front of Your Kids

"A friend loveth at all times, and a brother is born for adversity."

— Proverbs 17:17

(Proverbs was written by King Solomon. King Solomon was the successor of his father David, and has been described as being the wealthiest man to have ever lived. The Bible states that King Solomon prayed relentlessly for wisdom and an "understanding mind" so that he could rule his people successfully while being able to discern clearly between both good and evil.)

You should seek to make sure that your wife is your best friend and your source of comfort during times of need. Thus, when things are not going well you want to grow together through it as you go through it. Be intentional about sincerely seeking to love your wife the way Christ loves the church and to not go to bed angry, because remember, your children are always watching what you do and not what you say.

As I sincerely think back on our nearly 25 years of marriage I wish I had a time-machine that would allow me to travel back in time and slap myself with a big wet fish anytime that I even thought about arguing with my wife.

Man Law #15
Make Sure Your Kids Occasionally Catch You Hitting On Your Wife & Making Out With Your Wife

"²⁷ So God created man in his own image, in the image of God created he him; male and female created he them. ²⁸ And God blessed them, and God said unto them, Be fruitful, and multiply, and replenish the earth, and subdue it: and have dominion over the fish of the sea, and over the fowl of the air, and over every living thing that moveth upon the earth."

— Genesis 1:27-28

(The book of Genesis was inspired by God and written by Moses. In the Bible Moses is a key Hebrew prophet and leader who was actually trained and raised within the Egyptian elite leadership. Moses was the man who directly received the Ten Commandments from God while on top of Mount Sinai. Moses is also considered to be the founder of the nation of Israel. Moses is known to be the author of five books which are found within the Bible which include: Genesis, Exodus, Leviticus, Numbers, and Deuteronomy.)

Your wife is a gift from God. My wife is a gift from God. You and I must celebrate this great gift and our children must see us celebrating the gift of marriage. In a world that is filled with negativity about the God-ordained husband and wife relationship you and I must be intentional about creating the pattern, the momentum and the culture of celebrating marriage.

Man Law #16
Make Sure to Celebrate Your Wife for All of Your Life

"Whoso findeth a wife findeth a good thing, and obtaineth favour of the Lord."

— Proverbs 18:22

(The book Proverb, pro-verbs is a book in favor of taking God-inspired action. Proverbs was written by King Solomon. King Solomon was the successor of his father David, and has been described as being the wealthiest man to have ever lived. The Bible states that King Solomon prayed relentlessly for wisdom and an "understanding mind" so that he could rule his people successfully while being able to discern clearly between both good and evil.)

We live in a culture where we celebrate new cars, new shoes, new houses, new songs, new clothes, new ideas, new products and new girlfriends. The divorce statistics are bad and they are getting worse. If you want to achieve marital success in a world that is filled with endless causes of marital stress you must decide to be intentional about living your best and celebrating your wife for all of your life. Am I perfect at this? No. However, I am intentional about celebrating the gift that is my wife.

As an example, every year, I round up my five kids and we devote copious amounts of time into buying my wife a massive variety of Christmas gifts. In fact, each and every year, my wife's stack of gifts is 10X the size of everybody else's gift pile. My children and I start our weekly trips into "The Belly of the Beast" (what I call the heavily congested shopping center areas in Tulsa) to find the perfect gifts for mom during late August and September. What?! Yes! Why do we do this? I do this because I want my children and my wife to see that I am being intentional about celebrating my wife for all of my life.

If you are needing additional inspiration, listen to the 1997 R&B smash hit, "All My Life" by K-Ci & JoJo.

Pictured from Left to Right: My brother (Carson Clark), my dad (Thomas Clayton Clark), my Mom (Mary Clark), myself (Clayton Thomas Clark), my grandfather (Thomas Clayton Clark), and my grandmother (Dorothy Clark).

Great Grandmother Alice Cooper with Havana Clark (our daughter).

Man Law #17
FINANCIAL PRO-TIP:
Do Not Get Divorced

"²⁵ Husbands, love your wives, even as Christ also loved the church, and gave himself for it; ²⁶ That he might sanctify and cleanse it with the washing of water by the word, ²⁷ That he might present it to himself a glorious church, not having spot, or wrinkle, or any such thing; but that it should be holy and without blemish. ²⁸ So ought men to love their wives as their own bodies. He that loveth his wife loveth himself. ²⁹ For no man ever yet hated his own flesh; but nourisheth and cherisheth it, even as the Lord the church. ³⁰ For we are members of his body, of his flesh, and of his bones. ³¹ For this cause shall a man leave his father and mother, and shall be joined unto his wife, and they two shall be one flesh. ³² This is a great mystery: but I speak concerning Christ and the church. ³³ Nevertheless let every one of you in particular so love his wife even as himself; and the wife see that she reverence her husband."

— Ephesians 5:25-33

(The Apostle Paul wrote the book of Ephesians and thirteen books of the New Testament. Paul was so committed to his faith that he was willing to be martyred for it. Paul was beheaded around 67 AD in Rome under the orders of Emperor Nero.)

As a business coach, I am constantly approached by business owners that tell me that they have a strong desire to DOUBLE the size of their business. In fact, just today I spoke with a man who is taking over running the day-to-day operations of his family's business, which has been around since the 1960s.

During our first consultation with me today, he told me during the coaching call that his goal was to "Double the Size of My Business" within the next 18 months and I am excited about helping him to achieve his goal! However, I want to point out that one great way to DOUBLE your net worth or to avoid cutting your net worth in half is to choose to stay married. Statistically speaking, the divorce rates in America are alarming, at best, but anecdotally I can also tell you that divorce has wrecked the lives of countless people and clients that I know. Thus, if it is possible, I would strongly recommend that you do what you can do to put in the work and stay married.

FUN FACT: "Research shows that 41% of first marriages end in divorce. By contrast, 60% of second marriages and 73% of third marriages end the same way" (https://www.usatoday.com/story/life/health-wellness/2024/09/05/marriage-divorce-rate/74899214007/).

In order to keep your marriage healthy, strong and growing in the right direction I highly recommend taking your wonderful wife on at least one date per week before and after you have kids. It's important you build your family on a solid foundation based upon a stable and sustainable marriage.

When you take your wonderful wife on that weekly date ask her sincerely if there is anything that you can do better and if there is anything you can do to better support her. A marriage is like a garden. It's a process and not an event. When you are growing a garden you must intentionally pull the weeds every week or marital weeds will grow and they will eventually overtake your garden and then you are going to end up getting a divorce and living in a van down by the river. Don't let divorce happen by default. You must be intentional about cultivating, growing and creating a happy marriage.

"Drifting, without aim or purpose, is the first cause of failure."

— Napoleon Hill

(The best-selling author of Think & Grow Rich, which is a book that changed my life so much that I named my son, Aubrey Napoleon-Hill Clark.)

Man Law #18
Be the First to Apologize

I am sure that you are never going to make a mistake within your marriage, so this chapter is probably just written for somebody else. But, hypothetically, perhaps this portion of the book will be of some value for someone else that you know that occasionally messes up and makes a mistake within his marriage so you can share this portion of the book with him. You must learn how to apologize or you will learn how to eulogize the demise of your marriage.

As you start raising children and the energy, urgency and demands on your time begin to increase, there is a potential for your home to become edgy, chippy, intense and a place where bitterness builds unless you become a master at a apologizing and taking the blame for any strife that occurs within the your home. I don't care whether you started the "intense fellowship" with your beautiful bride or not, it is absolutely important that you become a master of apologizing quickly, taking 100% of the blame, owning the conflict and deescalating the situation quickly.

"Confess your faults one to another, and pray one for another, that ye may be healed. The effectual fervent prayer of a righteous man availeth much."

— James 5:16

(The book of James was written by the actual brother of Jesus! Think about that for a second. James was a very relevant and prominent leader in the early church; his book is filled with very specific and practical encouragement and wisdom about how to live life that demonstrates your faith in Jesus Christ as your Lord and Savior.)

"³ Take heed to yourselves: If thy brother trespass against thee, rebuke him; and if he repent, forgive him. ⁴ And if he trespass against thee seven times in a day, and seven times in a day turn again to thee, saying, I repent; thou shalt forgive him."

— Luke 17:3-4

(The book of Luke was written by the Apostle Luke who was also a good friend and companion of the Apostle Paul. Luke was martyred for his faith by hanging on an olive tree in Greece.)

"And be ye kind one to another, tenderhearted, forgiving one another, even as God for Christ's sake hath forgiven you."

— Ephesians 4:32

(The book of Ephesians was written by the Apostle Paul while he was imprisoned in Rome. Before converting to Christianity, Paul's name was Saul of Tarsus. Saul of Tarsus was well known for persecuting Christians, rounding them up and feeding them to Lions. Most Bible scholars agree that fourteen of the twenty seven books found in the New Testament were written by Paul.)

Pictured from Left to Right: Havana Clark, myself (Clay Clark), Angelina Clark, the newly born twins, Aubrey Napoleon-Hill Clark and Mary Clark (My Mom).

Man Law #19
Find Funny

If you are able to successfully become the world's second best father you are going to have to learn how to find funny. When bad things happen you must discover how to find funny. When horrible things happen and you run out of money you must discover how to find funny.

"A merry heart doeth good like a medicine: but a broken spirit drieth the bones."

— **Proverbs 17:22**

(King Solomon is the principal author of the book of Proverbs. King Solomon's father was King David. He brought massive amounts of wealth and trade to his kingdom. King Solomon had 700 wives who were often princesses from foreign nations. King Solomon also had 300 concubines. In total King Solomon had "relations" with 1,000 women at the same time. Think about that. If King Solomon wanted to dedicate one day to spend with each woman it would only be possible for King Solomon to have this dedicated day with each woman once per 2.73 years. PRO-TIP: If you are a man and you want to become a good father only have ONE WIFE.)

I shall never forget the moment that I got the "the call." I was at our 1100 Riverwalk Terrace, Jenks Oklahoma, ThrivetimeShow.com office when I received a call from my dad. My dad told me that although he had successfully beat cancer, he was now feeling sick again so he went to some doctors to get some tests done and he wanted to share the results with me. I told my Dad that he was 100% important to me and my top priority and that I would 100% call him back as soon as a wrapped up actions items A, B and C. And so approximately 30 minutes later, I went outside and into my "Hummer of Love." The "Hummer of Love" was an H2 Hummer that I drove for years despite the fact that it had no practical utility as a vehicle. The H2 Hummer was designed to look like the original Hummer, however it had almost no horsepower to speak of, it had virtually no storage space, it had little to no acceleration capacity and it typically averaged 7 miles per gallon. However, I thought it was good marketing as an autowrapped vehicle, so I kept driving it until it stopped working.

Anyway...so I geographically relocated my body into the "Hummer of Love" because this was a place where I knew that I could cry. I don't allow myself to cry in front of people I know or people I don't know. I typically like to cry in the parking lot of Atwoods (it's a farm and garden store where you can buy chicken food, tools, beef jerky, guns and man stuff). In fact Atwoods is where I love to cry. If I had to cry, I love crying at Atwoods in that beautiful and empty parking lot back near where they sell the sheds because nobody is over there.

So I'm in the hummer driving south on Riverside towards the Creek Turnpike in Tulsa and I call my Dad back. I said, "Dad, so what is the word?"

My Dad said, "Son, I have Lou Gherig's Disease and I am going to die."

I remember actually thinking, "Oh sh$% where is an Atwoods?! I've got to get to a f%$anding Atwoods! Where in the h$#% is Atwoods. D$@%it! The waterworks are starting and I'm not near an Atwoods!"

I said, "Dad, I love you." And then I couldn't talk. It couldn't stop crying, but I kept driving. I turned left and I got to the toll booth and the tears were really flowing. Then I pulled over on the shoulder of the road and I could not stop crying knowing that my father was going to be dying slowly of suffocation from Lou Gherig's disease.

I said something to effect of Dad, "I need to get my sh$% together and then I shall call you back. You are my top priority and I shall call you back."

My father said, "I'm proud of you son."

And then I started crying again as attempted to navigate to Atwoods despite the fact that I couldn't stop the tears from flowing.

Once I I got to Atwoods I tried to find funny. I looked around and I saw a billboard that had marketing that didn't make any sense and I thought that was kind of funny. But, then I thought, no, that is kind of sad! Somebody is paying for that advertisement on that billboard and that advertisement is definitely not going to work. There isn't a clear PROBLEM, SOLUTION, NO-BRAINER, CALL TO ACTION on that billboard and thus it is not going to work. Then I thought to myself, "You just found out that your father is dying of Lou Gherig's Disease and you are in the parking lot of an Atwoods trying to find funny and in the process of doing so you have found bad marketing and that is concerning to you. Now that is funny. Yes! I had found funny!"

"Thankfully, persistence is a great substitute for talent."

— Steve Martin

(Stephen Glenn Martin (born August 14, 1945) is an American comedian, actor, writer, producer, and musician. Known for his work in comedy films, television, and recording, he has received many accolades, including five Grammy Awards, a Primetime Emmy Award, and a Screen Actors Guild Award as well as nominations for eight Golden Globe Awards and two Tony Awards.)

I remember taking out my to-do-list and writing down fun things that my father (Thom Clark, may you rest in peace Dad!) and I could do together with a renewed sense of urgency. I thought to myself, maybe we could throw Dad a massive-ass going away party. When most people die, all of their friends and family go to their funeral to say nice things about them, but most people don't typically gather around a person to say nice things about them, encouraging words about them and the impact they made on lives of others until they are dead. But what if I could organize a massive-ass going away party for my father where we could bring his friends and family to his house so that they could say great things about my dad directly to my dad while my dad was actually slowly dying from Lou Gherig's Disease? I called my Dad back!

"Dad, I have a plan. Can I come and meet you at your house?!" (I always talk kind of loud so I need to put in more explanation points to be true to form).

My Dad said, "Sure son." (I feel like I need to find an Atwoods right now as I type this).

I sat sound with my Mom and Dad and I laid out the plan, "Dad, I"ll pay for it, but here is the plan. I'll get on the phone and call everyone in your life that matters to you and invite them over to visit you for a massive-ass going away party that I'll throw on your behalf. We'll have great food, great people and you then I'll organize one-on-one time with and each guest. Vanessa's best friend Sharita can keep the line moving and I'll keep it fun."

My Dad said, "Son this sounds incredible."

I said, "Dad, you and mom can make a list of people you want me to invite and I'll call them all until they cry, buy or die."

My Dad said, "Son, I love you. Thank you for doing this."

And then I had to go back to Atwoods because I couldn't stop crying again.

"Despite a lack of natural ability, I did have the one element necessary to all early creativity: naïveté, that fabulous quality that keeps you from knowing just how unsuited you are for what you are about to do."

— **Steve Martin**

(Stephen Glenn Martin is an American comedian, actor, writer, producer, and musician. Known for his work in comedy films, television, and recording, he has received many accolades, including five Grammy Awards, a Primetime Emmy Award, and a Screen Actors Guild Award as well as nominations for eight Golden Globe Awards and two Tony Awards.)

Finding funny is what you need to do if you want awkward conversations and miscarriages to go well. What the hell? Yes, I meant what I just wrote. If you want awkward conversations and miscarriages to go well you must find funny.

When my wonderful wife Vanessa and I discovered that she had a miscarriage that was not good. We had to schedule an urgent time to have the dead baby removed and it was 100% terrible. However, back in the day Saint Francis hospital would give you FREE ice cream if you were in the hospital delivering a baby, having a miscarriage or somehow paying copious amounts of money to have doctors help you to deliver a live or dead baby. Amidst the tears and issues that were causing a heavy use of tissues I remember actually thinking, "I wonder how much ice cream I am truly allowed to eat before they cut me off? I mean we are paying $500 per hour and we going to be here for at least 24 hours racking up a massive-ass bill...I wonder how much FREE ice cream I can actually eat before they cut me off and say, "Sir you cannot have any more delicious frozen ice cream and ice cream bar snacks because we only offer up FREE ice cream to THIS LEVEL and then we have to cut you off."

And so it began. Doctor Thompson came and and said, "How are you guys. Vanessa and Clay I'm sorry about this situation. But the baby is no longer living and I am going to have to remove the baby today. Do you have any questions?"

And the whole time I was thinking, "This doctor has no idea how much ice cream I can eat. I'm going to eat and then I am going to force myself to eat. I am going to gain 20 pounds today! I am going to crush that ice cream as soon as this procedure starts."

And that is what I did. I remember grabbing a box of ice cream sandwiches from the community freezer and getting a tremendous ice cream headache as I was watching the clock waiting for the procedure to be completed. Ice cream sandwiches one through eight were easy. No problem! But I had to eat more! I had to do it! I had to set a record! I had to go down as the man who ate the most ice cream in the history of Saint Francis. So I went back for another box of delicious frozen ice cream sandwiches. After eating my 16th ice cream sandwich I discovered that the nurses were clearly distracted from managing the ice cream consumption level of their patients. These hospital professionals were clearly too distracted by all of the babies, the births and the mothers to properly manage the frozen food section of the hospital. And it was then while feeling a little sick from having eaten two boxes of ice cream sandwiches that I found funny.

I remember after the procedures walking into the hospital room to check on my wife who was still groggy from the medication and telling her the good news. "Bird! We can truly have unlimited free ice cream at the hospital. The nurses are so distracted by all of the births, babies and moms that they have no idea what is going on with the frozen food section. I just crushed 16 ice cream sandwiches!"

"If a book about failures doesn't sell, is it a success?"

— Jerry Seinfeld

(Jerome Allen Seinfeld) is an American stand-up comedian, actor, writer, filmmaker, and television producer specializing in observational comedy. Seinfeld gained stardom playing a semi-fictionalized version of himself in the NBC sitcom Seinfeld (1989–1998), which he co-created and wrote with Larry David. Seinfeld earned a Golden Globe Award for Best Actor – Television Series Musical or Comedy in 1995.)

"Being funny is one of the ultimate weapons a person can have
in human society."

— Jerry Seinfeld

*(Jerome Allen Seinfeld) is an American stand-up comedian, actor, writer,
filmmaker, and television producer specializing in observational comedy.
Seinfeld gained stardom playing a semi-fictionalized version of himself in the
NBC sitcom Seinfeld (1989–1998), which he co-created and wrote with Larry
David. Seinfeld earned a Golden Globe Award for Best Actor – Television
Series Musical or Comedy in 1995.)*

Oftentimes throughout my life I have been told, "that
is not funny." Or have been asked, " why do you find
that to be so funny?" My response has always been to
let people that know that I am serious about not being
serious.

"For what is your life? It is even a vapor that appeareth for a
little time, and then vanisheth away."

— James 4:14

*(Most Bible scholars and Bible experts believe that James, who was the brother
of Jesus, wrote the book of James. James became a very important leader in the
early church found within Jerusalem after Jesus ascended into heaven. How
wild is that? James was the brother of Jesus!)*

"Deliver me from mine enemies, O my God: defend me from them that rise up against me. ² Deliver me from the workers of iniquity, and save me from bloody men. ³ For, lo, they lie in wait for my soul: the mighty are gathered against me; not for my transgression, nor for my sin, O Lord. ⁴ They run and prepare themselves without my fault: awake to help me, and behold.

⁵ Thou therefore, O Lord God of hosts, the God of Israel, awake to visit all the heathen: be not merciful to any wicked transgressors. Selah. ⁶ They return at evening: they make a noise like a dog, and go round about the city. ⁷ Behold, they belch out with their mouth: swords are in their lips: for who, say they, doth hear? ⁸ But thou, O Lord, shalt laugh at them; thou shalt have all the heathen in derision."

— Psalms 59: 1-8

(According to many Bible scholars , King Solomon's father (King David) is credited with writing 73 of the Psalms. Other Psalms are credited to Asaph, the Sons of Korah and Moses. I don't know if it is comforting or to know or not, but according to Psalms, God does actually LAUGH AT HIS ENEMIES.)

My friend and the legendary comedian Jim Breuer is one of the best people I've ever met when it comes to the quest of finding funny when life gets terrible or you runny out of money.

I mean this sincerely. When life gets terrible I tend to use the word "ass" alot. I think "ass" makes things a little more classy. In fact "ass" can be found in the word "classy" and that has always been helpful to me.

No, but seriously I mean this seriously. We have to get serious about not being so serious for a second. When life gets terrible and miscarriages, Lou Ghehrig's disease, car accidents, floods, theft, betrayal and horrible things happen you must find a way to find funny or life gets too heavy.

Pictured above is my son Aubrey Napoleon-Hill Clark. I love him and I could not be more proud of him for choosing to become the man he is. He is diligent, kind, an audio expert in the making, a solid drummer, a focused young man with a plan, a persistent person, and HE IS FUNNY!

Pictured: Jim Breuer and myself taking a quick photo together behind the scenes at the ReAwaken America Tour. James Breuer is an American stand-up comedian, and actor. He was a cast member on Saturday Night Live from 1995 to 1998 and starred in the film Half Baked (1998) with Dave Chappelle. He went on to host The Jim Breuer Show after leaving SNL. Breuer regularly tours as a comedian. Footage of his 2008 tour was used in his documentary More Than Me and in his four-hour DVD program The Jim Breuer Road Journals. In September 2021, he cancelled shows at venues requiring COVID-19 vaccination in New Jersey and Michigan and has stated that he will not perform at venues with such requirements.

Man Law #20
Bore Down & Make Your Marriage Great While the Rest of the World Struggles With Boredom

"⁶ Now we command you, brethren, in the name of our Lord Jesus Christ, that ye withdraw yourselves from every brother that walketh disorderly, and not after the tradition which he received of us. ⁷ For yourselves know how ye ought to follow us: for we behaved not ourselves disorderly among you;

⁸ Neither did we eat any man's bread for nought; but wrought with labour and travail night and day, that we might not be chargeable to any of you: ⁹ Not because we have not power, but to make ourselves an ensample unto you to follow us. ¹⁰ For even when we were with you, this we commanded you, that if any would not work, neither should he eat. ¹¹ For we hear that there are some who walk among you disorderly, working not at all, but are busybodies. ¹² Now those who are such we command and exhort by our Lord Jesus Christ, that with quietness they work, and eat their own bread."

— 2 Thessalonians Chapter 3:6-12

(This book was written by the Apostle Paul. This book addresses issues, and misunderstandings that were happening within the church and this book was written to provide encouragement and additional coaching / guidance amidst the massive amounts of persecution and suffering being faced by followers of Christ at this time.)

We live in a world that actually encourages people to get a divorce when things get tough, and there is a massive momentum to it. Once you see close friends of yours get a divorce then it almost seems ok for you to get a divorce. Years ago my wife and I were in a home fellowship group with many young couples. My wife and I had just gotten married and so we both thought it would be a good idea to be around other Christian couples. We both thought it would be a good idea to attend a Bible study with these people, and now, 20 years later, nearly all of the couples that were within that local home fellowship group are divorced. Nearly all of the couples cheated on each other and I am sincerely glad that I do not stay in touch with these toxic people and their toxic life choices, which I believe to be contagious. If you want to raise your children to be the best that they can be and you want to become the second best father in the history of the world you have to protect your marriage and you have to be intentional about who you and your family choose to be around. You must decide to withdraw yourselves from every brother that walketh disorderly, and not after the Christian traditions that God taught us in The Bible.

"The essence of the Purple Cow — the reason it would shine among a crowd of perfectly competent, even undeniably excellent cows — is that it would be remarkable. Something remarkable is worth talking about, worth paying attention to. Boring stuff quickly becomes invisible."

- SETH GODIN
(Best selling author and marketing guru)

Pictured: On Tuesday February 8th 2011, I teamed up with my son Aubrey Napoleon-Hill Clark, Havana Clark and the office team in a successful attempt to build the tallest snow man in Tulsa history. When the world was suffering from winter boredom, I chose to bore down and to make a memorable moment and snow man history.

Man Law #21
Choose to Provide for Your Family Well Every Day That You Don't Want to Burn In Hell

"⁸ But if any provide not for his own, and specially for those of his own house, he hath denied the faith, and is worse than an infidel."

— 1 Timothy Chapter 5:8

(This book was written by the Apostle Paul.)

The Bible is very clear that you and I are worse than an unbeliever if we intentionally choose not to provide for our family. This is more intense than if we were out camping. Think about that statement for a second. Really think about it for a moment.

"⁸ But if any provide not for his own, and specially for those of his own house, he hath denied the faith, and is worse than an infidel."

— 1 Timothy Chapter 5:8

(This book was written by the Apostle Paul.)

If you are a Dad you must provide for your kids. If you need to get three jobs, do it. If you need to work 65 hours per week do it. I know that in route to building (pre-Christ in my life) DJConnection.com into one of America's largest wedding entertainment companies I was working every day from 5 AM to 7 PM. In order to raise the money needed to fund the growth of DJConnection.com I was willing to work at Applebee's, Target and DirecTV at the same time and that was just because I was a highly motivated individual who knew where I was going.

How much more motivated should you and I be to provide for our families? If you are sleeping in late, watching Netflix and playing video games all day rather than providing for your significant other, you need to kick your own tail into gear, get out there and provide. Your kids are going to observe how hard you work and how hard you don't work. Be intentional about providing for your family or God considers you to be worse than an unbeliever.

Pictured from Left to Right: Annie Leuba, Scarlett Clark, Angelina Clark, Aubrey Clark, Havana Clark, Laya Clark and Vanessa Clark. Everyone in this photo is enjoying their time in Breckenridge, Colorado on a trip that I paid for. What? Yes! It is my job as a man to provide for my family. I am writing this section of the book at 3:47 AM in the morning while my family is sleeping. While my family is sleeping I am working. Last night my son went to a great Brandon Lake concert with his friend Hank driving a truck that I paid for using tickets that I probably paid for. This is how it is supposed to work. I am supposed to provide for my family because I am a father and I am a man. The Bible literally states in 1st Timothy Chapter 5, "If any provide not for his own, and specially for those of his own house, he hath denied the faith, and is worse than an infidel." What does that mean? That means that if any man chooses not to provide for his own family he is actually worse than an infidel (an unbeliever) in the eyes of God. Do I get tired? Yes. Is it stressful? Yes. Does that matter? No. It is my job and duty to provide.

Man Law #22
Create Positive
Family Traditions

> "⁶And these words, which I command thee this day, shall be in thine heart: ⁷And thou shalt teach them diligently unto thy children, and shalt talk of them when thou sittest in thine house, and when thou walkest by the way, and when thou liest down, and when thou risest up."

— Deuteronomy 6:6-7

(Moses is the author who wrote most of the book of Deuteronomy. However, it would have been hard for Moses to have finished writing the book of Deuteronomy by himself as the book does describe in detail the death and burial of Moses. Many experts, scholars and historians believe that Moses did not finish writing the book of Deuteronomy after his death and that Joshua, Ezra and a few scribes may have finished writing the book.)

It is our job as parents to diligently teach our children about God, the Bible, how to raise great families, how to be diligent and how to grow up to not be idiots. In that order! YES!

You and I must diligently teach our children to know God and to know the Bible!

You and I must diligently teach our children how to raise great families!

You and I must diligently teach our children how to be diligent!

You and I must diligently teach our children how to not be idiots!

So what is the best way to teach our children how to succeed in life? We must establish family traditions. As an example:

1. We strive to take our children to Sheridan Church and the home of Pastor Jackson Lahmeyer every Sunday at 10:00 AM.

2. I aim to celebrate family and to have family night every Tuesday night at 7:30 PM so that my children can learn from their grandparents and to prevent them from drifting out of fellowship, friendship and relationship with their grandparents and with each other.

3. I strive to bring my wife with me on every business trip. Throughout my entire career I can sincerely only remember a handful of speaking events where I was speaking out of time and I did not bring my wife with me.

4. I work hard to rearrange my schedule to take the children to the lake during each and every summer weekend possible.

5. I diligently push to move my schedule around to attend the events that my children are involved in.

6. I celebrate overcoming poverty every month by paying my bills.

7. I showcase diligence every day by being the first person to get to my workplace and the last person to leave every day.

8. My wife and I take our children with us when I have speaking events, or when I am hosting business conferences.

9. My son runs the audio and visual for our business conferences.

10. I celebrate my wife by taking my children with me to buy her Christmas gifts starting in August every year.

11. I create an annual family video to help remember all of the great things God has done for us each year that we all watch together during Christmas!

12. My wife and I take our children to Breckenridge, Colorado, for Thanksgiving each year.

13. When my kids were young I used to take them into major retail stores, the mall and other department stores and I would tell them they had 10 minutes to find the items on the list I gave them. Even though all five of them were under the age of 10 when I did this, they learned how to find items, how to ask questions and how to pay for things. I called this "operation self-sufficiency."

14. When my kids were young I used to take them out for "Man Lunch" which consisted of them all eating the same things and the same time because that is what men do when we are working. We find the fuel we need to keep our bodies energized, we buy it, and then we eat it. Mission accomplished.

15. When my kids were young I used to devote an entire weekend to gearing up for the New England Patriots Sunday games. I would pick a theme and I would take the kids with me to the store to gear up on food supplies and then we would decorate the house with a Patriots theme. Aubrey would set up sound systems and lights and then I would invite friends and family and then 50 guests later we would celebrate the New England Patriots, Tom Brady and Coach Bill Belichick's coaching mastery.

You get it! I know you get it! If it's going to be, it's up to me! However, in this case it's up to you! But will you do it? I know it requires a lot of work, but I know that you are up for it in your quest to become the world's second best father. Let's go and start those family traditions today!

Pictured from Left to Right: Havana Clark, Laya Clark, Angelina Clark, FBI Director (Kash Patel), myself (Clay Clark), Vanessa Clark, Scarlett Clark and Aubrey Clark. I don't go to Washington, D.C. to meet with my friend and FBI Director, Kash Patel. However, when I do go to Washington, D.C. to meet with my friend and FBI Director, Kash Patel I always want to involve my family. I try to involve my family in everything because that is an intentional tradition that my wife and I started. What is a tradition? According to Webster, a tradition is an inherited, established, or customary pattern of thought, action, or behavior (such as a religious practice or a social custom).

Man Law #23
Hug Your Kids & Tell Them That You Love Them More Often

As a father, I can tell you that I should hug my kids more and tell them that I love them more. As soon as our kids leave our homes they are immediately forced to interact with and engage with an increasingly perverse and wicked world where their teachers are pushing globalist and Godless ideologies, the music industry is pushing visions of sexual promiscuity, the movie industry is pushing Satanic ideals and dystopian narratives, the billboards are pushing marijuana use, social media is pushing Godless morals, jealousy and comparison. Thus, I believe that I should do a better job and we should all do a better job of telling our kids how much we love them and more importantly how much God loves them.

Pictured from Left to Right: Laya Clark, Havana Clark, Aubrey Clark, Scarlett Clark and Angelina Clark. I wish I would have hugged my kids one more time when they were this age, when they were every age and every day.

I believe that it is of paramount importance that your children know what the Bible has to say about God's infinite love for them:

"For God so loved the world, that he gave his only begotten Son, that whosoever believeth in him should not perish, but have everlasting life."

— John 3:16

(The book of John was written by John the Apostle. John was the son of Zebedee and Salome (a family of fishermen). The Apostle John was a beloved disciple of Jesus. In the New Testament, there are many references to the 12 disciples of Jesus, and John is one of them. Scripture often refers to John as the disciple "whom Jesus loved." John the Apostle wrote five books found in the Bible, all of which are found in the New Testament: the Gospel of John, the three epistles of John, and the book of Revelation.)

Pictured In This Photo: Grandpa Rick Moore snuggles and hugs his five grandchildren: Havana Clark, Aubrey Napoleon-Hill Clark, Angelina Clark, Laya Clark and Scarlett Clark.

"But God commendeth his love toward us, in that, while we were yet sinners, Christ died for us."

— Romans 5:8

(The Epistle to the Romans is the sixth book in the New Testament, and the longest of Paul's thirteen epistles. Before Paul became the Apostle Paul, he was known as Saul. Before God revealed himself to Paul, Saul was known as one of the leading persecutors of Christians. Paul's conversion to becoming a follower of Christ is also known as the "Road to Damascus" event. While traveling on the road to Damascus Saul was blinded by God and he heard the voice of God. While experiencing this blinding light and the voice of God, Paul was actually on the way to Damascus to arrest those that were choosing to follow Christ. After encountering the blind light and voice of God Saul was physically blinded. After being blinded, Saul was led to a nearby city where a follower of Christ by the name of Ananias prayed for Saul and Saul's sight was restored. Saul was then baptized and hence he was known as Paul. The Apostle Paul went on to write the majority of the new testament and was a big part of spreading the gospel all around the world.)

"We love him, because he first loved us."

— 1 John 4:19

(1st John was written by John the Apostle. John the Apostle wrote five books found in the Bible, all of which are found in the New Testament: the Gospel of John, the three epistles of John, and the book of Revelation.)

For I the LORD thy God will hold thy right hand, saying unto thee, Fear not; I will help thee."

— Isaiah 41:13

(Isaiah is known by many Bible scholars as the first and the greatest of the four major prophets found within the Bible ahead of Jeremiah, Ezekiel and Daniel. Isaiah started his journey as a prophet by having his lips burned by an angel. In the sixth Chapter of the Book of Isaiah, Isaiah details encountering God and a six-winged seraph (angelic being). The angel takes a piece of coal from a heavenly altar and sears Isaiah's lips to purify them.)

"Herein is love, not that we loved God, but that he loved us, and sent his Son to be the propitiation for our sins."

— 1 John 4:10

(1st John was written by the Apostle John.)

"³⁵ Who shall separate us from the love of Christ? shall tribulation, or distress, or persecution, or famine, or nakedness, or peril, or sword? ³⁶ As it is written, For thy sake we are killed all the day long; we are accounted as sheep for the slaughter. ³⁷ Nay, in all these things we are more than conquerors through him that loved us. ³⁸ For I am persuaded, that neither death, nor life, nor angels, nor principalities, nor powers, nor things present, nor things to come, ³⁹ Nor height, nor depth, nor any other creature, shall be able to separate us from the love of God, which is in Christ Jesus our Lord."

— Romans 8:35-39

(The book of Romans was written by the Apostle Paul. The book was written to the church in Rome which Paul had yet to visit. The book of Romans provides a detailed explanation of the gospel while also attempting the unify the church which had become filled with both Jewish and Gentile believers in Christ.)

"The LORD hath appeared of old unto me, saying, Yea, I have loved thee with an everlasting love: therefore with lovingkindness have I drawn thee."

— Jeremiah 31:3

(Jeremiah was a Hebrew prophet who served in the late 7th century before Christ. Jeremiah was known as the "weeping prophet" for his emotional pain over Israel's unfaithfulness and their coming judgment.)

He that loveth not knoweth not God; for God is love."

— 1 John 4:8

(1st John was written by the Apostle John.)

"I am crucified with Christ: nevertheless I live; yet not I, but Christ liveth in me: and the life which I now live in the flesh I live by the faith of the Son of God, who loved me, and gave himself for me."

— Galatians 2:20

(The Apostle Paul wrote the book of Galatians. This book argues that salvation and eternal life comes through having faith in Jesus Christ, not through works of the Law.)

"Behold, what manner of love the Father hath bestowed upon us, that we should be called the sons of God: therefore the world knoweth us not, because it knew him not."

— 1 John 3:1

(1st John was written by the Apostle John.)

"The LORD thy God in the midst of thee is mighty; he will save, he will rejoice over thee with joy; he will rest in his love, he will joy over thee with singing."

— Zephaniah 3:17

(The Book of Zephaniah was written by the prophet Zephaniah, who prophesied during the reign and time of King Josiah in Judah.)

"Greater love hath no man than this, that a man lay down his life for his friends."

— John 15:13

(The book of John is written by the Apostle John, one of Jesus's twelve disciples. John is often referred to as "the disciple whom Jesus loved.")

"And to know the love of Christ, which passeth knowledge, that ye might be filled with all the fulness of God."

— Ephesians 3:19

(The Apostle Paul wrote the book of Ephesians, while under arrest in Rome. The letter is considered one of the "Prison Epistles" and is addressed to the church in Ephesus.)

Man Law #24
Be Intentional About Living the F7 Life

"¹⁸ Where there is no vision, the people perish: but he that keepeth the law, happy is he."

— Proverbs 29:18

(King Solomon is the primary author of the book of Proverbs. The book of Proverbs is a book in factor of action, pro-verbs.)

In my shameless attempt to help us all to become the second best dads in the history of humanity, I want to hammer home the importance of being about viewing every day as a gift from God and what we do with it as a gift to God. Because I chose to become an entrepreneur, every morning of my life starts with burning fires of employees that can't come to work because they are sick, employees that can't stop fighting with each other about girlfriends, paying rent, working next to each other or some other conflict they have with each other. If my employees aren't fighting with each other then we are experiencing a key mechanical failure where the internet is out at one of our locations, or a key piece of software is not working or we have a water leak at one of our locations and amidst the daily jackassery and the plague of problems that gets shoved in my face every morning before 5 AM it is very easy to lose sight of the importance of viewing every day as a gift from God and what I do with it as a gift to God.

I would highly recommend that would start your day every by asking yourself what your daily goals are in the following 7 areas:

Faith - What are your goals for this area and when will you spend time focusing on this area this week?

_____

Family - What are your goals for this area and when will you spend time focusing on this area this week?

_____

Finances - What are your goals for this area and when will you spend time focusing on this area this week?

_____

Fitness - What are your goals for this area and when will you spend time focusing on this area this week?

_____

Friends - What are your goals for this area and when will you spend time focusing on this area this week?

_____

Fun - What are your goals for this area and when will you spend time focusing on this area this week?

_____

Focused Attention - Where will you direct your free time this week? I personally love writing songs, designing things, working on printing pieces, editing videos, recording podcasts and more...I am personally not a fan of napping, watching TVs, watching movies, engaging in chit-chat, etc. Ask yourself every day where you will choose to direct your free time each week?

_____

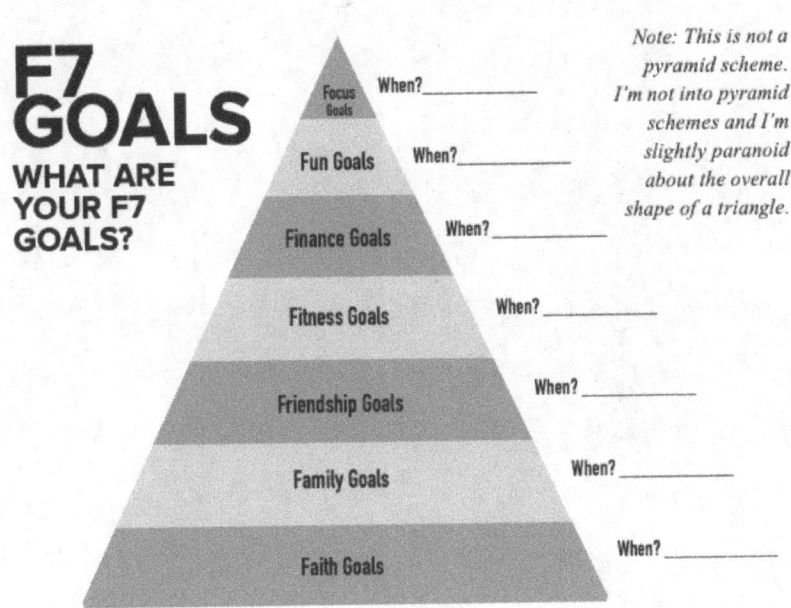

F7 GOALS

WHAT ARE YOUR F7 GOALS?

Focus Goals — When?_____

Fun Goals — When?_____

Finance Goals — When?_____

Fitness Goals — When?_____

Friendship Goals — When?_____

Family Goals — When?_____

Faith Goals — When?_____

Note: This is not a pyramid scheme. I'm not into pyramid schemes and I'm slightly paranoid about the overall shape of a triangle.

Man Law #25
Get Serious About Becoming a Responsible God-Fearing Human

"We must all suffer from one of two pains: the pain of discipline or the pain of regret. The difference is discipline weighs ounces while regret weighs tons."

— Jim Rohn

(Who was Jim Rohn? Jim Rohn (1930 – 2009) - Jim was an American entrepreneur, author, and motivational speaker. He wrote numerous books including How to obtain wealth and happiness. Rohn mentored Mark R. Hughes and life strategist Tony Robbins in the late 1970s. Others who credit Rohn for influencing their careers include authors/lecturers Mark Victor Hansen and Jack Canfield (Chicken Soup book series), Everton Edwards (Hallmark Innovators Conglomerate), Brian Tracy, Darren Hardy, and Harv Eker. Rohn coauthored the novel Twelve Pillars with Chris Widener. Find Jim's work on the Jim Rohn Motivation Youtube Channel.)

As a father, our entire focus should be on raising our kids to fear God and nothing else. If we teach our children to be good at reading, writing, arithmetic, speaking, sports and how to become a world-class entrepreneur and we have not taught them to fear God and nothing else, we have failed.

As a father, our entire focus should be on raising our kids to fear our Lord and Savior Jesus Christ and nothing else. If we teach our children to be good at fitness, constitutional law, public speaking and how to become productive citizens and we have not taught them to fear God and nothing else, we have failed.

"[1] Whoso loveth instruction loveth knowledge: but he that hateth reproof is brutish."

— Proverbs 12:1

(The word "proverb" is typically used to reference a clever or witty concept or piece of wisdom. However, the book of Proverbs is a collection of wisdom written down and recorded by King Solomon who was the world's wealthiest man and a man who prayed relentlessly for God to give him divine wisdom.)

"The fear of the LORD is the beginning of knowledge: but fools despise wisdom and instruction."

— Proverbs 1:7

(The book of Proverbs is found within the Bible and the book's central theme is the constant and relentless pursuit of wisdom.)

"He that spareth his rod hateth his son: but he that loveth him chasteneth him betimes."

— Proverbs 13:24

(The Biblical book of proverbs has been often referred to as the best self-help book of all-time.)

In today's world of moral relativity and perpetual perversion, we must get serious about teaching our children to become God-fearing humans! That is our entire mission as Fathers. Could I do better at teaching my children to fear God and nothing else? Yes!

You and I must lock in here! We must focus on achieving the goal and that goal must be for our children to spend eternity in heaven with our Lord and Saviour Jesus Christ as opposed to burning in hell by default.

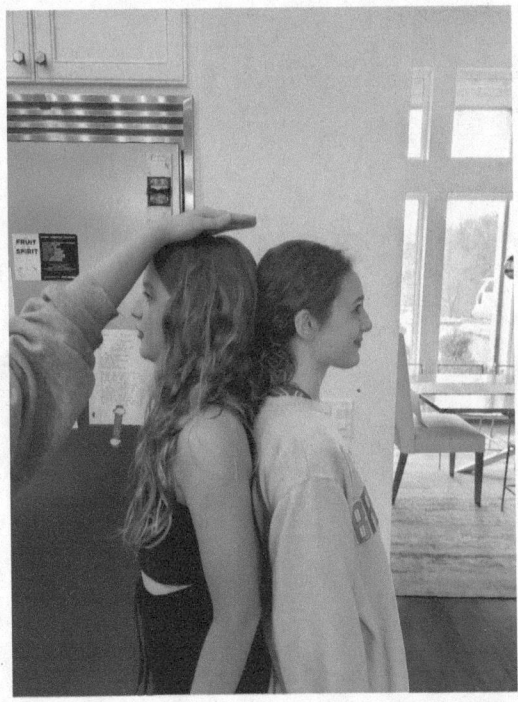

Pictured from Left to Right: Scarlett and Angelina compete to see who is taller. I'm not sure when it happens exactly, but at some point our children are no longer children.

Man Law #26
When You Blame You B-Lame

As fathers, you and I must teach our children to accept personal responsibility for their actions, both good and bad. We must teach our children to take personal responsibility. We must teach our children that they cannot change the circumstances that they are born into. We must teach our children that they cannot change the economy, the seasons, the geopolitical landscape or many of the variables that impact their lives. However, we must teach our children that they can change themselves, and that *is* something they have the power to change.

"Ninety-nine percent of the failures come from people who have the habit of making excuses."

— George Washington Carver

(George Washington Carver was an American agricultural scientist and inventor who promoted alternative crops to cotton and methods to prevent soil depletion. He was the most prominent black scientist of the early 20th century.)

In our culture today it is 100% socially acceptable to blame others for everything. However, if you want to teach your children how to grow up to be successful in the eyes of the Lord, we must teach our children to take responsibility for their actions. The Bible is very clear and consistent when it comes to the importance of taking responsibility for our actions. We must teach this concept of taking responsibility for our actions to our children with great enthusiasm.

"He that hath no rule over his own spirit is like a city that is broken down, and without walls."

— Proverbs 25:28

"He that refuseth instruction despiseth his own soul: but he that heareth reproof getteth understanding."

— Proverbs 15:32

"Poverty and shame shall be to him that refuseth instruction: but he that regardeth reproof shall be honoured."

— Proverbs 13:18

"The soul of the sluggard desireth, and hath nothing: but the soul of the diligent shall be made fat."

— Proverbs 13:4

"He becometh poor that dealeth with a slack hand: but the hand of the diligent maketh rich."

— Proverbs 10:4

As a far-fetched example that could and would never possibly ever happen we must teach our children to honor their agreements and to buy insurance when starting a business. No matter how exciting and urgent their new business venture is, we must teach our children to not mislead themselves and their partners by stating that they have insurance when they do not. And if for some odd reason (in this entirely hypothetical example) our children chose not to buy insurance when starting a new business we must teach our children that when something bad happened and they did not have the money to cover the damages they should act like adults and accept responsibility for not having insurance. We should teach our children to not hide behind lawyers, religious epiphanies and technicalities. We should teach our children to find a way to still honor their commitments by cutting their expenses and offering their core product and service themselves directly (while operating a lean business) for a few years until they can honor their agreements and pay back those they owe money to.

However, as a cautionary tale, I would advise you, your children and myself to avoid working with the kind of men and women who have shown a pattern of sleeping with people they just met, being deeply divisive, and having chosen to seek out and watch copious amounts of Andrew Tate videos while revering them as their long-time virtual mentor.

> "Beware of dogs, beware of evil workers, beware of the concision."
>
> **— Philippians 3:2**

NOTE: In the Bible, the concept of "concision" (Greek: katatome) is a term used by the apostle Paul. Paul used "concision" to criticize Christians who were focused on physical rituals and fleshly works rather than the spiritual circumcision of the heart through faith in Jesus Christ.

"Before success comes in any man's life, he is sure to meet with much temporary defeat, and, perhaps, some failure. When defeat overtakes a man, the easiest and most logical thing to do is to quit. That is exactly what the majority of men do. More than five hundred of the most successful men this country has ever known told the author their greatest success came just one step beyond the point at which defeat had overtaken them."

— Napoleon Hill

(The best-selling author of "Think & Grow Rich" which is the book that changed my life so much that I named my son Aubrey Napoleon-Hill Clark.)

Man Law #27
Teach Your Kids the Bible or They Will Do What Is Acceptable In the World Eyes And You Will Be Liable

This just in...BREAKING NEWS!!!!! As of 2025, the world's moral standards are rapidly declining. And I shall list the ways in case you have been living under a rock since 1971.

Language - Words now used in public that were never allowed in public before.

Clothing - Clothing that was once considered clothing reserved for the bedroom is now on display by the customers drifting around at your local mall, movie theatre or big box retail store.

Music - Today's music could be considered audio pornography. The lyrics found in today's music is without boundaries.

Movies - Today's movies showcase sexual perversion, witchcraft and an unrelenting barrage of Satanic concepts on display for the world to see.

Social Media - Concepts, images and premises that were once considered taboo are on display for the whole world to see whether they want to or not.

And the list goes on...

"Children, obey your parents in the Lord: for this is
right. Honour thy father and mother; which is the first
commandment with promise; that it may be well with thee, and
thou mayest live long on the earth. And, ye fathers, provoke not
your children to wrath: but bring them up in the nurture and
admonition of the Lord."

— Ephesians 6:1-4

*(This beautiful and ENCOURAGING book was written by the Apostle Paul
while he was in PRISON. Paul was in PRISON knowing that he was going
to be put to death soon while he wrote this ENCOURAGING book.)*

FUN FACTS:

1971 | What In the World Happened In 1971?

Why Did the Following Events All Take Place In 1971?

- 1971 - Why Was *Rules for Radicals* (Which Is
  Dedicated to Lucifer), Which Is Often Quoted by
  Barack Obama and Hillary Clinton, Written by Saul
  Alinsky Written In 1971? *(Learn More - https://thehill.
  com/blogs/ballot-box/presidential-races/288457-
  carson-explains-lucifer-comment-clinton-and-
  alinksy-on-a/)*
- 1971 - Why Did America Begin Legalizing Abortions
  (Sacrificing Babies to BAAL) In 1971?

    » Remembering an Era Before Roe, When New York Had the 'Most Liberal' Abortion Law *(Learn More - https://www.nytimes. com/2018/07/19/us/politics/new-york-abortion- roe-wade-nyt.html)*

    » When Abortion Was Only Legal In 6 States *(Learn More - https://fivethirtyeight.com/ features/when-abortion-was-only-legal-in-6- states/)*

- 1971 - Why Was America Taken Off of the Gold Standard by President Richard Nixon Per the Recommendation of Henry Kissinger In 1971? The United States under the leadership of President Richard Nixon in 1971, ended the dollar convertibility to gold and implemented wage and price controls, which soon brought an end to the Bretton Woods System. *(READ - https://www. federalreservehistory.org/essays/gold-convertibility- ends)*

    » Henry Alfred Kissinger served as the Secretary of State under President Richard M. Nixon.

- 1971 - Why Did Klaus Schwab Found the World Economic Forum In 1971 Per the Recommendation of Henry Kissinger? *(https://www.weforum.org/ agenda/2019/12/world-economic-forum-davos-at- 50-history-a-timeline-of-highlights/)*

- 1971 - Why Did the Pope Complete The Paul VI Audience Hall In the Shape of a Snake Head In 1971? (Italian: Aula Paolo VI) also known as the Hall of the Pontifical Audiences is a building in Rome named for Pope Paul VI with a seating capacity of 6,300, designed in reinforced concrete by the Italian architect Pier Luigi Nervi and completed in 1971.[1] It was constructed on land donated by the Knights of Columbus. *(https://hope-of-israel.org/popeshall. html)*

- 1971 - Why Was The Darkseid / New Gods Comic Book Series Which Prophesied the "The Fourth World" / The Fourth Industrial Revolution Written In 1971? *(READ - https://en.wikipedia.org/wiki/ Darkseid)*

- 1971 - Why Was Disney World Featuring the Experimental Prototype Community of Tomorrow (EPCOT Center) Opened to the Public On October 1st 1971? *(READ - https://en.wikipedia.org/wiki/ Epcot)*

- 1971 - Why Was the Musical Communist Manifesto-Pushing Song "Imagine" Released by John Lennon In 1971? *(READ - https://www.azlyrics.com/lyrics/ johnlennon/imagine.html)*

- 1971 - Why Did Yuval Noah Harari's Look Alike Daniel Emilfork Play the Part of the Devil In the 1971 Film, The Devil's Nightmare? *(READ - https:// en.wikipedia.org/wiki/The_Devil%27s_Nightmare)*

Pictured from Left to Right: My mom (Mary Clark) and my father (Thom Clark) getting married in 1974.

Pictured from Left to Right: Dale Tranberg, Thom Clark and Ed Guthmann. My father is pictured hanging out with his best friends.

Man Law #28
View Everything from a
Christ-Focused Perspective

If you and I want to become the second best fathers in the history of the planet Earth we need to raise our standards to God's standards and we need to start to view everything from a Christ-focused perspective, which is very different from the world's standards.

"I beseech you therefore, brethren, by the mercies of God, that ye present your bodies a living sacrifice, holy, acceptable unto God, which is your reasonable service. ² And be not conformed to this world: but be ye transformed by the renewing of your mind, that ye may prove what is that good, and acceptable, and perfect, will of God. ³ For I say, through the grace given unto me, to every man that is among you, not to think of himself more highly than he ought to think; but to think soberly, according as God hath dealt to every man the measure of faith. ⁴ For as we have many members in one body, and all members have not the same office: ⁵ So we, being many, are one body in Christ, and every one members one of another. ⁶ Having then gifts differing according to the grace that is given to us, whether prophecy, let us prophesy according to the proportion of faith; ⁷ Or ministry, let us wait on our ministering: or he that teacheth, on teaching; ⁸ Or he that exhorteth, on exhortation: he that giveth, let him do it with simplicity; he that ruleth, with diligence; he that sheweth mercy, with cheerfulness. ⁹ Let love be without dissimulation. Abhor that which is evil; cleave to that which is good. ¹⁰ Be kindly affectioned one to another with brotherly love; in honour preferring one another; [11] Not slothful in business; fervent in spirit; serving the Lord; [12] Rejoicing in hope; patient in tribulation; continuing instant in prayer; [13] Distributing to the necessity of saints; given to hospitality. [14] Bless them which persecute you: bless, and curse not. [15] Rejoice with them that do rejoice, and weep with them that weep. [16] Be of the same mind one toward another. Mind not high things, but condescend to men of low estate. Be not wise in your own conceits. [17] Recompense to no man evil for evil. Provide things honest in the sight of all men. [18] If it be possible, as much as lieth in you, live peaceably with all men. [19] Dearly beloved, avenge not yourselves, but rather give place unto wrath: for it is written, Vengeance is mine; I will repay, saith the Lord. [20] Therefore if thine enemy hunger, feed him; if he thirst, give him drink: for in so doing thou shalt heap coals of fire on his head. [21] Be not overcome of evil, but overcome evil with good."

— Romans Chapter 12

(This book of the Bible was written by the Apostle Paul. Yes! The Apostle Paul wrote a large portion of the New Testament. Paul wrote the book of Romans around 57 AD (after the death of Jesus Christ our Lord and Savior.)

Every day as fathers we must choose to renew our minds through the reading of the Bible and through meditating and thinking about God's word and how to apply it to our life. My friend, the Bible cautioned us that as we draw closer and closer to the return of Christ that the world around us would get further and further away from following God's laws.

"I charge thee therefore before God, and the Lord Jesus Christ, who shall judge the quick and the dead at his appearing and his kingdom; 2 Preach the word; be instant in season, out of season; reprove, rebuke, exhort with all long suffering and doctrine. 3 For the time will come when they will not endure sound doctrine; but after their own lusts shall they heap to themselves teachers, having itching ears; 4 And they shall turn away their ears from the truth, and shall be turned unto fables. 5 But watch thou in all things, endure afflictions, do the work of an evangelist, make full proof of thy ministry. 6 For I am now ready to be offered, and the time of my departure is at hand. 7 I have fought a good fight, I have finished my course, I have kept the faith: 8 Henceforth there is laid up for me a crown of righteousness, which the Lord, the righteous judge, shall give me at that day: and not to me only, but unto all them also that love his appearing. 9 Do thy diligence to come shortly unto me: 10 For Demas hath forsaken me, having loved this present world, and is departed unto Thessalonica; Crescens to Galatia,

Titus unto Dalmatia. [11] Only Luke is with me. Take Mark, and bring him with thee: for he is profitable to me for the ministry. [12] And Tychicus have I sent to Ephesus. [13] The cloke that I left at Troas with Carpus, when thou comest, bring with thee, and the books, but especially the parchments. [14] Alexander the coppersmith did me much evil: the Lord reward him according to his works: [15] Of whom be thou ware also; for he hath greatly withstood our words. [16] At my first answer no man stood with me, but all men forsook me: I pray God that it may not be laid to their charge. [17] Notwithstanding the Lord stood with me, and strengthened me; that by me the preaching might be fully known, and that all the Gentiles might hear: and I was delivered out of the mouth of the lion. [18] And the Lord shall deliver me from every evil work, and will preserve me unto his heavenly kingdom: to whom be glory for ever and ever. Amen. [19] Salute Prisca and Aquila, and the household of Onesiphorus.

[20] Erastus abode at Corinth: but Trophimus have I left at Miletum sick. [21] Do thy diligence to come before winter. Eubulus greeteth thee, and Pudens, and Linus, and Claudia, and all the brethren. [22] The Lord Jesus Christ be with thy spirit. Grace be with you. Amen."

— 2 Timothy Chapter 4

(Second Timothy was Paul's last letter and it was written to inspire and encourage Timothy. Throughout this letter Paul challenged Timothy to accept the calling to follow Christ despite the pain and suffering that was guaranteed to happen as a result of doing so.)

If we want to become the second best father in the history of our planet Earth, we must choose to be intentional about viewing every aspect of life from a Christ-focused perspective.

This just happened! But what does God have to say about it?

This might happen! But what does God have to say about it?

This politician just said this! But what does God have to say about it?

Pictured from Left to Right: Myself (Clay Clark), Aaron Antis, General Flynn, Eric Trump, Jim Breuer, John Rich and Kash Patel backstage at the Nashville ReAwaken America Tour. One of the things that has always kept me grounded is knowing that in the end even the world's most successful and elite will be confounded (deceived) if they don't know the contents of the Bible and Jesus Christ as their Lord and Savior.

Man Law #29
Putting the Smartphone, the iPad and the Digital Device Down Is Profound

When living in a world where people are perpetually allowing their smartphones to make them dumb. Instead of using smartphones as a tool, we are allowing smartphones to turn us into "tools." Instead of using our smartphones, our smartphones are using us to show us content, advertisements and to track our every movement. However, I sincerely believe that in order to become the second best father in the history of the planet Earth you and I need to do a better job of being present. Being present is a present and every day is a gift, and with this mindset, this is how we should live.

What?

Being present is a present and every day is a gift and with this mindset, this is how we should live.

FUN FACT: According to Nielsen, "American adults spend over 11 hours per day listening to, watching, reading or generally interacting with media." - July 2018 *(https://www.nielsen.com/insights/2018/time-flies-us-adults-now-spend-nearly-half-a-day-interacting-with-media/)*

Think about that statistic for a second. The average person is now spending 11 hours per day on their smartphone watching, reading or generally interacting with media! That is beyond a full-time job. Think about that? How is it even possible to get anything done if you are watching 11 hours per day of media on your smartphone? How is it possible to develop a solid relationship with our daughters and sons if we are on the smartphone 11 hours per day?

"We need to re-create boundaries. When you carry a digital gadget that creates a virtual link to the office, you need to create a virtual boundary that didn't exist before."

— Daniel Goleman

(Daniel Goleman has been a guest on the ThrivetimeShow.com podcast and he is an internationally recognized psychologist, and the New York Times best-selling author of Emotional Intelligence which has sold over 5 million copies world-wide and has been printed in 40 languages. The Harvard Business Review called emotional intelligence— which discounts IQ as the sole measure of one's abilities — "a revolutionary, paradigm-shattering idea" and chose his article "What Makes a Leader" as one of ten "must-read" articles from its pages. Emotional Intelligence was named one of the 25 "Most Influential Business Management Books" by TIME Magazine.)

It is very important that as fathers, that you and I become very intentional about being present with our children. I know in my world and I know in yours that there is always going to be another urgent text, email or phone call flowing in. As an entrepreneur I am bombarded with an endless barrage or urgent and emotional texts from employees, clients, podcast listeners, politicians and others that is the life that I signed up for as an entrepreneur, but we have to declare and be intentional about laying out clear boundaries for our lives or you and I are going to drift into a dystopian world of endless interruptions and no sincere conversations with our families, friends and people that we love. Hopefully I am communicating in a way that makes sense here.

"¹⁰ Be still, and know that I am God: I will be exalted among the heathen, I will be exalted in the earth. ¹¹ The Lord of hosts is with us; the God of Jacob is our refuge. Selah."

— Psalm 46:10-11

It's hard to hear God's voice, your wife's voice or your kid's voice if you and I are constantly and dumbly scrolling through our smartphones looking for likes, false-validations, viral cat videos, get-rich-quick related reels, and shorts related to "information that they don't want you to know." Trust me your conversations and relationships will get more profound if you will just put the phone down. You can do it! We must be able to get away from the perpetual distractions that your smartphone is constantly throwing at you. We must become intentional about making sure that your smartphone is not present if you want sincere conversations with your family, clear communication with God and solid long-time relationships to be present in your life. Remember, my friend, even Jesus had to get away to get with God!

"[36] Then cometh Jesus with them unto a place called Gethsemane, and saith unto the disciples, Sit ye here, while I go and pray yonder. [37] And he took with him Peter and the two sons of Zebedee, and began to be sorrowful and very heavy. [38] Then saith he unto them, My soul is exceeding sorrowful, even unto death: tarry ye here, and watch with me. [39] And he went a little farther, and fell on his face, and prayed, saying, O my Father, if it be possible, let this cup pass from me: nevertheless not as I will, but as thou wilt. [40] And he cometh unto the disciples, and findeth them asleep, and saith unto Peter, What, could ye not watch with me one hour? [41] Watch and pray, that ye enter not into temptation: the spirit indeed is willing, but the flesh is weak. [42] He went away again the second time, and prayed, saying, O my Father, if this cup may not pass away from me, except I drink it, thy will be done. [43] And he came and found them asleep again: for their eyes were heavy. [44] And he left them, and went away again, and prayed the third time, saying the same words. [45] Then cometh he to his disciples, and saith unto them, Sleep on now, and take your rest: behold, the hour is at hand, and the Son of man is betrayed into the hands of sinners. [46] Rise, let us be going: behold, he is at hand that doth betray me."

— Matthew 26:36-46

(The book of Matthew is written by Matthew, a man who was once a tax collector and a man who went on to become one of Jesus' direct twelve apostles. In this book of the Bible Matthew teaches that Jesus is the fulfillment of Old Testament prophecies. Matthew teaches and highlights the royal lineage of Jesus from David and Abraham to prove his claim to the throne. My friend, Jesus is King and Matthew proves it time and time again in the book of Matthew.)

PRO-TIPS for Making Sure That You Don't Allow Your Smartphone to Make You Dumb:

1. If possible, don't allow your smartphone to be physically present while you are having family time.

2. If possible, simply refuse to check your smartphone after you get home.

3. If possible, turn off notifications that are constantly dinging, pinging and causing you to turn your focus away from what matters.

4. If possible, be honest with yourself about how much time you are spending on your smartphone.

5. Set your phone on fire and move into a remote cabin located deep in the woods of Arkansas. Change your name to Enoch, dress like Adam Sandler and commit to never shaving again. This will ensure that you are never distracted by the world again.

As you and I are on this quest to truly become the best father we can possibly be I would sincerely encourage you AGAIN, being present is a present and every day is a gift and with this mindset, this is how we should live. Don't allow your smartphone to make you dumb.

The tall guy in the photo above was my father, Thomas Clayton Clark. My father and mother chose to name me Clayton Thomas Clark. My father's father was Thomas Clayton Clark. My dad was Thomas Clayton Clark Jr.

Man Law #30
Be a Mentor for Your Kids Every Day That They Live

As we join together to learn how to become the second best fathers in the history of the world, I found this book writing process to be incredibly convicting and even conflicting. Objectively and sincerely I believe that I am not in the bottom 5% of fathers. I did not leave my family, I am not in prison, I have not lived a secret double life as a double agent for a foreign adversary, but I could do better as a father. Why? Because I am not God and we all fall short of being our best. However, we should know what God has to say about fatherhood and we should strive and push to be the very best fathers that we can humanly be based upon the standards set by God. However, I hope that this book motivates you to become at least 2% better.

"12 Blessed is the man that endureth temptation: for when he is tried, he shall receive the crown of life, which the Lord hath promised to them that love him."

— James 1:12

(This book was written by Jesus' half-brother James around A.D. 45 (after the death of Jesus Christ). It is a book of practical wisdom for living out one's faith through actions, not just words, with strong parallels to Jesus' Sermon on the Mount. Some of the key themes found within this book include: watching what you say, mixing our faith with action, in this book, James famously wrote, 2:26: "faith without works is dead.")

We must teach our children how to resist temptation and we must do this on a daily basis. Talk to your children about the daily issues they are facing.

"Train up a child in the way he should go: and when he is old, he will not depart from it."

— Proverbs 22:6

Contrary to popular belief we are not supposed to raise our children up to "choose their own path" and to "follow their heart." We are supposed to teach our children to fear God and nothing else.

"The fear of the Lord is the beginning of wisdom: and the knowledge of the holy is understanding."

— Proverbs 9:10

We are supposed to teach our kids to have a healthy fear of God and nothing else. We must teach our children that God has the power to reward your children with an eternal heaven or hell. We must teach our children to fear God and nothing else.

"The father of the righteous shall greatly rejoice: and he that begetteth a wise child shall have joy of him."

— Proverbs 23:24

Raising your children is like growing a garden. Every day you must pull the weeds or your garden is going to turn into a weed-infested nightmare. By default the weed will choke out the growth of the fruits and vegetables that you are intentionally trying to harvest. You must pull the feeds every day so that you can enjoy the harvest of watching your children grow up to become great productive God-fearing adults!

"He who walks in his integrity is righteous; happy are his children who follow him."

— Proverbs 20:7

According to Webster's dictionary, Integrity means, "firm adherence to a code of especially moral or artistic values. The quality or state of being complete or undivided." You and I must commit completely to following what God has to say about becoming a great father and we must 100% tune out what the world and Andrew Tate has to say about being a great father and a man.

"Fathers, do not provoke your children to anger, but bring them up in the discipline and instruction of the Lord."

— Ephesians 6:4

(The book of Ephesians was written by the Apostle Paul. Paul wrote the book of Ephesians while in prison. Think about that? Paul was a former persecutor of Christians who converted to becoming a follower of Christ after God appeared to him in a vision which was so profound that it actually knocked Paul off of his horse and caused him to become blind. Paul became a massively influential missionary and profound writer of 13 books found within the New Testament. Because Paul was a Roman citizen at the time of his conversion, this gave Paul special privileges and legal protection. Paul's status of being a Roman citizen was very uncommon for Jews, and it allowed Paul to travel more freely and even appeal his case directly to Caesar when he was imprisoned (Acts 22:28).)

I have personally never understood the concept of parents that want to bring their children to tears over petty issues, but I do see this happening all of the time. If you find yourself wanting to constantly harass your children to the point of tears about petty issues, go and put your head in the nearest toilet and flush it over and over until this desire to pursue "jackassery" goes away.

"Teach the older men to exercise self-control, to be worthy of respect, and to live wisely. They must have sound faith and be filled with love and patience."

— Titus 2:2

(Titus was a travel companion of the Apostle Paul, and a Gentile who converted to Christianity. Titus was also a recipient of the biblical Book of Titus. The Apostle Paul wrote the Book of Titus. Paul referred to Titus as the "true son in our common faith.")

You and I must learn that our children watch what we do more than they listen to what we say. You and I must demonstrate self-control if we want our children to demonstrate self-control. Is this tough to do? Yes! Could I do it better? Yes! You and I must be very intentional about modeling the behaviours for our children that we want them to learn. If you are an avid streaker, who tends to sprint through golf courses while nude at 3 AM this is probably the best time to stop this illegal and risky habit.

Man Law #31
Do Your Best & Forget the Rest

In my shameless attempt to teach you and I how
to become the second best father on the planet,
I need to direct both you and I to read Ephesians
Chapter 5 again. Yes! You may have already read this
chapter before, but let's read it again because this
chapter deals with how to keep your family intact and
specifically how husbands and wives are supposed to
love each other from a Biblical perspective. Divorce is
terrible. Divorce rips families apart and often destroys
the confidence of children who feel as though they
no longer have a source of stability on a daily basis.
So with great enthusiasm I encourage you to read
Ephesians Chapter 5 again with a renewed enthusiasm!

Pictured above is our son, Aubrey Napoleon-
Hill Clark who is graduating from high
school in 2026 if we don't get raptured first.

"²¹ Submitting yourselves one to another in the fear of God. ²² Wives, submit yourselves unto your own husbands, as unto the Lord. ²³ For the husband is the head of the wife, even as Christ is the head of the church: and he is the saviour of the body. ²⁴ Therefore as the church is subject unto Christ, so let the wives be to their own husbands in every thing. ²⁵ Husbands, love your wives, even as Christ also loved the church, and gave himself for it; ²⁶ That he might sanctify and cleanse it with the washing of water by the word, ²⁷ That he might present it to himself a glorious church, not having spot, or wrinkle, or any such thing; but that it should be holy and without blemish. ²⁸ So ought men to love their wives as their own bodies. He that loveth his wife loveth himself. ²⁹ For no man ever yet hated his own flesh; but nourisheth and cherisheth it, even as the Lord the church: ³⁰ For we are members of his body, of his flesh, and of his bones. ³¹ For this cause shall a man leave his father and mother, and shall be joined unto his wife, and they two shall be one flesh. ³² This is a great mystery: but I speak concerning Christ and the church. ³³ Nevertheless let every one of you in particular so love his wife even as himself; and the wife see that she reverence her husband."

— Ephesians 5:21-33

(Ephesians is a book written by the Apostle Paul around 60 A.D. (After the death of Jesus Christ our Lord & Savior. This letter and book of the Bible is primarily divided into two parts. The first part of the Ephesians is focused on the wealth that God has stored up for believers in Christ and God's plan for them. Part two of Ephesians is focused on how believers in Jesus Christ should go about living out their faith on a daily basis.)

So what did you learn? Men, I discovered again that we are supposed to love our wife the way Christ loved the Church and not the way Karl loves the bowling alley. Think about that for a second. How does Christ love the Church? Christ gave his life for the Church.

Women! If there are any sneaky women out there that are reading this book written specifically for men. What did you learn? The Bible says that, "Wives, submit yourselves unto your own husbands, as unto the Lord."

What does that mean? What that means is that anything that has two heads is a monster. If we do not follow God's commandments and teachings on how to start, grow and raise families is it any wonder that today's parents are producing a divorce crisis while today's children are producing a moral crisis as a bi-product?

If you want to become the second best father in the history of the world you must commit yourself to follow the instruction provided to us in the irrefutable word of God known as "The Bible."

Man Law #32
Unexpectedly Show & Tell Your Kids How Much You Love Them

As we strive to become the second best father in the history of our glorious planet Earth we must make sure that our children know that we view them as a blessing and not a burden.

"Lo, children are an heritage of the Lord: and the fruit of the womb is his reward. As arrows are in the hand of a mighty man; so are children of the youth. Happy is the man that hath his quiver full of them: they shall not be ashamed, but they shall speak with their enemies in the gate."

— Psalm 127:3-5

(Psalm consists of a collection of 150 ancient Hebrew poems, songs, prayers and verses that were written by King David.)

I love my five children, and I sincerely believe that my wife and my five children are the best gift that God has ever given me. However, I don't know if I do the best job at telling them that and showing them that. What am I saying?

I am saying that as we attempt to become the world's second best father, we must let our children constantly know that we love them, that we cherish them and that we are excited to see them. As an entrepreneur most of my days start with a burning fire and then end with a slow burn followed by a series of unexpected fireworks and banging sounds that won't end. All night and all day I get text messages, emails, voicemails, direct messages, pieces of mail, deliveries, urgent interruptions and constant demands from the entrepreneurial world that I have created. However, despite the unrelenting nature of my career, your career and any career, our desire to let our children know that we view them as a blessing and not a burden must persevere.

Pictured from Left to Right: Vanessa Clark, Aubrey Napoleon-Hill Clark, Havana Clark, myself (Clay Clark), Laya Clark, Scarlett Clark and Angelina Clark. We must schedule time for what matters and what gets scheduled gets done. This photo was taken at the resort town of Rosemary Beach, Florida where I believe we did not stay for free. The businesses that I started, grew and managed allowed us to page for this vacation. However, what would be the point of having a business if we never scheduled the time needed to experience this trip and to take this photo?

"I go into my closet, I got a bunch of t-shirts and shorts, kinda they're all the same ... I usually go t-shirt first ... I just want to cover that quickly. I'm like what the hell, grab anything...Then I go with shorts and I throw them on. Sometimes they'll be slightly too tight. I go let me take those off and get the triple-X shorts on."

— Adam Sandler

(March 28th 2023 Interview with People Magazine. Adam Richard Sandler (born September 9, 1966) is an American actor and comedian. Adam Sander was the highest paid actor in the world in 2023 earning an estimated $73 million during that year alone. Happy Madison Productions is the film and television production company founded by Adam Sandler in 1999 after his hugely popular comedy films Happy Gilmore and Billy Madison. The company has produced numerous comedy films starring Sandler, often featuring his close friends and collaborators, and its iconic logo features an image of Sandler's late father, Stanley. Adam Sandler was a cast member on the NBC sketch comedy series Saturday Night Live from 1990 to 1995. He returned to Saturday Night Live as a host in 2019 earning a Primetime Emmy Award nomination. He has starred in Hollywood comedy films that cumulatively grossed over $2 billion worldwide. Sandler had an estimated net worth of $420 million in 2020, and signed a new four-movie deal with Netflix worth over $250 million.)

Man Law #33
Discipline Your Kids or They Will Be Disciplined By the Consequence of Being an Adult Who Perpetually Makes Poor Decisions

"⁶ Train up a child in the way he should go: and when he is old,
he will not depart from it."

— Proverbs 22:6

(Proverbs is a book found in the Bible filled with timeless wisdom relating to taking massive action and achieving success. This book was written by King Solomon and it is found in that controversial book known as The Bible.)

As a Dad, you don't want to be the bad guy. Over the years I have become friends with many police officers and they also typically don't want to be the bad guy. However, if you raise a child and your number one priority is to never discipline your child because you never want to be the "Bad Guy" you are going to raise up a "Bad Guy" who will ultimately get arrested by the "Good Guys" (the police). Unfortunately, growing up I personally witnessed parents desperately wanting to become friends with their children and to be liked by their children to the point that:

1. They would buy alcohol for their kids because they "figured that their child was going to drink alcohol anyway so they might as well do it at their home because it's safer."

2. They would buy condoms for their kids because they "figured that their child was going to have pre-marital sex anyway so they might as well buy condoms for them to make sure they were having safer sex."

This perverse and jackassery-inspired thinking causes poverty, pain, regret and the development of adults who need to be disciplined by the law enforcement community because they cannot self-discipline themselves. If you want to raise productive and God-fearing children who grow up to become productive and God-fearing adults you must hold your children accountable for following God's laws and you must discipline your children when needed.

Vanessa and I both could not be more proud of the man that our son Aubrey Napoleon-Hill Clark is choosing to become and is growing up to be. He is kind, diligent, driven, funny and most importantly he fears God and nothing else.

Pictured from Left to Right: Myself (Clay Clark), Phil Pressey and Vanessa Clark. Since we have known Phil Pressey he has gone from a successful, yet undrafted and undersized college point guard to an NBA player to now a professional basketball coach. As our children grow up, our clients and our friends have too. However, you and I will only grow in the right direction if we are intentional about achieving success on a daily basis. It's amazing to see our friends and clients turn their dreams into a reality as a result of daily diligence and embracing the tirelessly and daily grind needed to move up success mountain of success one step at a time. To encourage yourself that success is possible, I would highly recommend that you visit www.ThrivetimeShow.com and click on the testimonials tab to see thousands of clients that I have helped to turn their dreams into reality.

Man Law #34
Don't Allow Emotions to Drive Your Finances

If you and I are sincere in our quest to become the second best father in the history of mankind, you and I must teach our children to not allow their emotions to dictate their actions and to drive their finances.

So often over the years I have witnessed business coaching clients of mine punishing each other in a way that hurts both parties and that weaponizes the financial aspects of life.

I see husbands who get mad at their wife and they use this negative emotional energy to justify buying a boat, a car, or some massive stereotypical man purchase.

I see women getting copious amounts of cosmetic surgery done, buying designer clothing and jewelry they can't afford to get back at their husbands.

I see people within my office buying highly speculative stocks and investments as their way of gambling because they are not happy with the way their life is going.

You must teach your children to not allow emotions to drive their finances. Once someone goes down the road of making decisions based upon emotions, they often times become financially suicidal because of deep empathy for every homeless person they pass on the street. They become deeply in debt because of their lust and strong desire to look more successful than they are and they in up enslaving themselves to debt.

"⁷ The rich ruleth over the poor, and the borrower is servant to the lender."

— Proverbs 22:7

(The richest man in the history of the world, King Solomon asked God specifically for divine wisdom and God gave it to King Solomon. King Solomon wrote down God's wisdom into a book. That book is called Proverbs.)

"Emotions will either serve or master, depending on who is in charge."

— Jim Rohn

(Jim Rohn was a legendary self-help author who inspired the careers of Tony Robbins and countless self-help trainers, teachers and authors. Jim Rohn has great content and if you ever find anything that Jim Rohn has written that goes against the Bible, go with the Bible.)

"A fool uttereth all his mind: but a wise man keepeth it in till afterwards."

— Proverbs 29:11

(Have I mentioned that this is the book written by the richest man in the history of the world, King Solomon? King Solomon asked God specifically for divine wisdom and God gave it to King Solomon. King Solomon wrote down God's wisdom into a book. That book is called Proverbs.)

People allow their emotions to control their finances usually have regrettable tattoos, a lot of new shoes and they are one step away from accidentally hanging themself with a financial noose...and that is the TRUTH.

We must teach our children to not make financial decisions based upon their emotions. Financial decisions must be made after gathering all of the facts, looking at the pros and cons of each decision and then acting without emotion.

Man Law #35

You Become the Average of the Five People You Spend the Most Time With, Even If They Are Your In-Laws.

In our unending attempt to become the second best father of all time we must be intentional about making sure that our children are not spending their time developing relationships with nefarious children who often have nefarious parents. We must do our very best to make sure that our children are surrounded by God-fearing friends who often have God-fearing parents. Don't fool yourself, your children will be encouraged to become God-fearing Christians or they will be corrupted by their friends to a lifestyle that celebrates Satan.

"He that walketh with wise men shall be wise, but a companion of fools shall be destroyed."

— Proverbs 13:20

(The Book of Proverbs is the second book in the third section of the Hebrew Bible (Tanakh) and a book in the Christian Old Testament.)

"³³ Be not deceived: evil communications corrupt good manners. ³⁴ Awake to righteousness, and sin not; for some have not the knowledge of God: I speak this to your shame."

— 1 Corinthians 15:33-34

(1 Corinthians is a letter written by the Apostle Paul to the church in Corinth, around approximately 55–56 A.D. (After the death of our Lord & Saviour Jesus Christ). Paul wrote this letter to address big issues like division, sexual perversion, and disputes over spiritual gifts. The city of Corinth at the time was a major Roman trade center with a hard-earned reputation for immorality. Paul wrote this letter to provide God-inspired coaching and correction for the church's problems related to marriage, unity within the church, worship, and the importance of love and the resurrection of Jesus Christ. The Apostle Paul died by execution and decapitation in Rome somewhere between 64-67 AD (After the Death of Jesus Christ) under the rule of Emperor Nero.)

Remember, you and your children will become the average of the five people that you choose to spend time with. Be intentional. Choose to surround yourself with high quality people who are doing their very best to follow God.

Pictured Above: My wife (Vanessa Clark), myself (Clay Clark), my 3XL hoodie and my 3XL And1 shorts pose for a photo in front of our "hotel room" inside the light house found at Turnberry Golf Course in Scotland. This trip was an anniversary gift to us from President Trump's son and my friend, Eric Trump. Thank you Eric!

Man Law #36

Choose to Become Better & Not Bitter. When You Focus On the Past You Finish Last.

If we are going to attempt to be the second best father that the earth has ever seen, we must teach our kids about what the Bible says about standing up for your faith as we draw closer to the return of our Lord and Savior Jesus Christ. We must teach our children that bad things do happen to people and that we must choose each and every day to become better and to not become bitter. We must teach our children that when we focus on the past we will always finish last.

"¹⁰ Blessed are they which are persecuted for righteousness' sake: for theirs is the kingdom of heaven. ¹¹ Blessed are ye, when men shall revile you, and persecute you, and shall say all manner of evil against you falsely, for my sake. ¹² Rejoice, and be exceeding glad: for great is your reward in heaven: for so persecuted they the prophets which were before you."

— Matthew 5:10-12

(The Biblical book of Matthew is the first book of the New Testament and was traditionally written by Matthew, a tax collector and one of Jesus' twelve Apostles. Key aspects of the book of Matthew include explaining the genealogy and tracing of Jesus' lineage, the Sermon on the Mount, and The Great Commission.)

"If the world hate you, ye know that it hated me before it hated you."

— John 15:18

(The book of John was written by John who most theologians consider to be the Apostle Jesus loved the most? What? Did Jesus have favorites? John the Apostle was one of the original twelve disciples of Jesus, and he was the brother of James. John was known in the Bible as the "beloved disciple" and "Son of Thunder.")

"Having a good conscience; that, whereas they speak evil of you, as of evildoers, they may be ashamed that falsely accuse your good conversation in Christ."

— 1 Peter 3:16

(Peter, originally named Simon. Peter was a fisherman from Bethsaida who was actually known to have become one of Jesus's first and most prominent Apostles. Peter was known for his passionate, intense and sometimes impulsive nature. Jesus was renamed "Peter," meaning "rock," by Jesus, who declared he would build his church upon him. Although Peter did deny that he knew Jesus three times, Peter actually went on to become a leader in the early church, a key figure at Pentecost. Peter was believed to have been martyred in Rome.)

Bad things do happen to good people. Bad things will happen to me. Bad things will happen to you. Bad things have happened to me. Bad things have happened to you. However, we must choose to become better and not bitter.

In fact, according to Forbes.com it is statistically not likely that you will not be sued as a business owner. Think about that for a second. According to Forbes.com it is unlikely that you will not be sued. Take a moment and ponder that.

FUN FACT: "Statistics show that somewhere between 36%-53% of small businesses are involved in at least one litigation in any given year and 90% of all businesses are engaged in litigation at any given time." *(READ - https://www.forbes.com/sites/ basharubin/2014/07/14/youre-going-to-get-sued/)*

To get really uncomfortable about the harsh realities of my life. During my short 45 years on the planet the following terrible things have happened to me and every year the list of terrible horrible and bad things that have happened to me just gets more EPIC, worse and bigger.

1. I grew up without access to money. However, my father was willing to work multiple jobs to put food on the table. He worked the night shift when needed and I sincerely appreciate his efforts.

2. I have had hundreds of thousands of dollars stolen from me.

3. I used to stutter as a kid and kids would mercilessly pick on me.

4. I struggled with many aspects of traditional schooling (algebra and memorization).

5. My lifetime best-friend died and my roommate died in a car accident while we were attending college together.

6. I have been robbed countless times by employees.

7. My businesses have been broken into.

8. My wife and I have invested into the lives of many entrepreneurs that have chosen not to honor their agreements once the win-win payouts became large.

9. Most of the major competitors that I face in business today are former employees who decided to rise up against me and to pull a Darth Vader move on me where they decided to attack the very person that mentored them.

10. There is not a day that goes by where an employee is not stealing from me or lying to me (when you have hundreds of teammates that happens).

11. Many of the massively successful clients that I have helped over the years have lied to me about massive amounts of commission now totalling in the millions.

12. My father died of suffocation caused by Lou Gherig's disease after slowly shrivelling up into a shadow of his former self.

13. When I decided to keep my businesses open during the COVID-19 lockdowns, quarantines, curfews and mandates the vast majority of the people I had met up until that point in my life refused to associate with me ever again.

14. The vast majority of the guests that I invite onto my ThrivetimeShow.com podcast decline the offer.

15. I am related to men who cannot stop sticking their penises into the bodies of women they are not married to, which has caused for an interesting relationship with extended family.

However, every day I choose not to become bitter. I choose to become better. You must teach your kids that bad things will happen to good people and we must focus on choosing to become better and not bitter.

"You have enemies? Good. That means you've stood up for something, sometime in your life."

— Winston Churchill

(The only world leader willing to stand up against Adolf Hitler during World War II. Sir Winston Leonard Spencer Churchill (30 November 1874 – 24 January 1965) was a British statesman, military officer, and writer who was Prime Minister of the United Kingdom from 1940 to 1945 (during the Second World War) and again from 1951 to 1955. For some 62 of the years between 1900 and 1964, he was a Member of Parliament (MP) and represented a total of five constituencies over that time.)

The ReAwaken America Tour team takes a moment to take a photo at the Trump Doral (Florida) ReAwaken America Tour. Because I hold people to a high-standard many of the people in this photo love me and because I hold people to a high-standard many of the people in this photo hate me. But, I shall never become bitter. I shall only focus on becoming better.

The DJConnection.com team takes a moment to take a photo at the DJConnection.com annual Christmas Party and because I hold people to a high-standard many of the people in this photo love me and because I hold people to a high-standard many of the people in this photo hate me. But, I shall never become bitter. I shall only focus on becoming better.

"Blessed are they which are persecuted for righteousness' sake: for theirs is the kingdom of heaven."

— Matthew 5:10

(Matthew was a book written by one of Jesus' twelve Apostles. Most scholars believe that Matthew was martyred (murdered and killed) with a sword because he would not renounce his faith.)

Man Law #37
Agree On Your Goals &
Your Roles Or You Will Be a
Perpetually Conflicted Soul

"And if a house be divided against itself, that house cannot stand."

— Mark 3:25

(In that controversial book called, The Bible, Mark is also referred to as John Mark. Mark was the wing-man for both Barabas and Paul during their EPIC missionary journeys. During his first missionary journey he bailed out, but he later made it right with Paul and was intentional about reconciling with Paul. Mark is believed to be the man who founded the church in Alexandria as he was later martyred (killed). Mark was killed in the most gruesome way possible. Mark was dragged through the streets of Alexandria, Egypt with a rope tied around his neck until he died. The mob seized Mark during Easter services and they dragged his body horrifically and violently over stones and pavement.)

For anybody reading this that may want to call yourself a modern Apostle, or for anyone reading this that has aspirations of being a modern-day Apostle, I thought I would take a moment to share with you how the Apostles that followed Jesus and who went town to town and house to house sharing the Gospel died.

HOW THE APOSTLES DIED.

1. Matthew Suffered martyrdom in Ethiopia, Killed by a sword wound.

2. Mark Died in Alexandria, Egypt , after being dragged by horses through the streets until he was dead.

3. Luke was hanged in Greece as a result of his tremendous preaching to the lost.

4. John Faced martyrdom when he was boiled in a huge Basin of boiling oil during a wave of persecution In Rome. However, he was miraculously delivered from death. John was then sentenced to the mines on the prison Island of Patmos. He wrote his prophetic Book of Revelation on Patmos. The Apostle John was later freed and returned to serve as Bishop of Edessa in modern Turkey. He died as an old man, the only Apostle to die peacefully.

5. Peter was crucified upside down on an x-shaped cross. According to church tradition it was because he told his tormentors that he felt unworthy to die in the same way that Jesus Christ had died.

6. James, the leader of the church in Jerusalem, was thrown over a hundred feet down from the southeast pinnacle of the Temple when he refused to deny his faith in Christ. When they discovered that he survived the fall, his enemies beat James to death with a fuller's club. * This was the same pinnacle where Satan had taken Jesus during the Temptation.

7. James, the Son of Zebedee, was a fisherman by trade when Jesus Called him to a lifetime of ministry. As a strong leader of the church, James was beheaded at Jerusalem. The Roman officer who guarded James watched amazed as James defended his faith at his trial. Later, the officer walked beside James to the place of execution. Overcome by conviction, he declared his new faith to the judge and knelt beside James to accept beheading as a Christian.

8. Bartholomew, also known as Nathaniel, was a missionary to Asia. He witnessed for our Lord in present day Turkey. Bartholomew was martyred for his preaching in Armenia where he was flayed to death by a whip.

9. Andrew was crucified on an x-shaped cross in Patras, Greece. After being whipped severely by seven soldiers they tied his body to the cross with cords to prolong his agony. His followers reported that, when he was led toward the cross, Andrew saluted it in these words: 'I have long desired and expected this happy hour. The cross has been consecrated by the body of Christ hanging on it.' He continued to preach to his tormentors for two days until he expired.

10. Thomas was stabbed with a spear in India during one of his missionary trips to establish the church in the sub-continent.

11. Jude was killed with arrows when he refused to deny his faith in Christ.

12. Matthias, the Apostle chosen to replace the traitor Judas Iscariot, was stoned and then beheaded.

13. Paul was tortured and then beheaded by the evil Emperor Nero at Rome in A.D. 67. Paul endured a lengthy imprisonment, which allowed him to write his many epistles to the churches he had formed throughout the Roman Empire.

Reminder to us that our sufferings here are indeed minor compared to the intense persecution and cold cruelty faced by the Apostles and disciples during their times for the sake of the Faith.

Why do we feel sleepy in prayer, but stay awake through a 3 hour movie?

Why are we so bored when we look at the HOLY BOOK, but find it easy to read other books?

You might be thinking to yourself, "Hey, I thought this book was about parenting, marriage and how to become the world's second best dad?" Well that is true, but I want to make sure to teach you as much as I can about our real Father who art in heaven hallowed by His name while teaching you how to become the best dad that you can be.

Now, back to the main thing. If you are going to have a happy and successful marriage you must take the time to sit down with your spouse and agree on both your goals and roles. This is SO IMPORTANT! Unless you want to hate yourself and find yourself engaged in endless passive aggressive long-term never-ending fights with your spouse who lives in your house, you must take the time to define both your goals and your roles for the following F7 areas of your life.

1. What are your goals for your faith?

2. What are your goals for your family?

3. What are your goals for your finances?

4. What are your goals for your fitness?

5. What are your goals for your friendship?

6. What are your goals for your fun?

7. What are your goals for your focused attention?

Then after you have taken the time to discuss your goals, you now must invest the time to clarify your roles. Who is going to be doing what and when?

1. What are your roles for your faith?

2. What are your roles for your family?

3. What are your roles for your finances?

4. What are your roles for your fitness?

5. What are your roles for your friendship?

6. What are your roles for your fun?

7. What are your roles for your focused attention?

Personally, I am obsessed with writing songs, writing books and writing business plans for growing successful businesses. Personally, I am obsessed with learning, earning and burning. Personally, I have massive goals that I want to accomplish during my time here on this earth.

My wife has big goals for her life and for our children as well. And do you want to know why we rarely fight? It's because we clearly have taken the time to map out our goals and roles. I simply refuse to spend my day debating over every decision on a day to day basis. In our relationship, my wife and I have decided that I will manage the businesses and that she will manage the family during each day and once I return home from a busy day of running the businesses, I am ready to help her to raise our wonderful kids. That is how we do it. Stop fighting about every little decision and every petty issue. Take a moment to determine your goals and roles and remember that anything with two heads is a monster.

"²³ For the husband is the head of the wife, even as Christ is the head of the church: and he is the saviour of the body."

— Ephesians 5:23

(Ephesians was written by the prolific writer of a large part of the New Testament, the Apostle Paul. Before turning his life around and choosing to follow Jesus Christ, Paul used to go by the name Saul and he was THE WORST. Saul used to spend his day persecuting Christians, rounding up Christians and feeding Christians to lions. When in doubt. Don't feed your enemies to lions.)

Pictured from Left to Right: Laya Clark, Angelina Clark and Scarlett Clark. If all of my children do not grow up to be followers of Christ I have failed. Thus, you can be the judge as to whether I was a good father or not. Only time will tell.

"Train up a child in the way he should go: and when he is old, he will not depart from it."

— Proverbs 22:6

(King Solomon, the son of David is credited as having been the author of Proverbs. King Solomon also wrote Ecclesiastes and Song of Songs.)

"He that spareth his rod hateth his son: but he that loveth him chasteneth him betimes."

— Proverbs 13:24

(King Solomon, the son of David is credited as having been the author of Proverbs. The time of King Solomon's leadership and the time of King Solomon's reign was known as the peak of wealth and prosperity for the nation of Israel.)

Vanessa Clark holds Aubrey Napoleon-Hill Clark. I believe Aubrey is somewhere under the age of 18 in this photo. Aubrey was born blind and was healed of blindness as a result of a miracle. My wife's book, "Now I See," explains this story.

Man Law #38
Don't Get Bitter, Focus On Making Yourself Better

"13 A foolish son is the calamity of his father: and the

contentions of a wife are a continual dropping."

— Proverbs 19:13

Regardless of what the rest of your family is choosing to do with their lives, you must be intentional about being the head of the household and focus on becoming better and not bitter. You and I could spend hours and hours lamenting and complaining about all of the people that have screwed us in the past and all of the people that are screwing us over and taking advantage of us right now. However, you and I must simply choose to be the positive source of inspiration for our families on a daily basis whether we feel like it or not.

Pictured above is my wife's book, "Now I See," where she explains the miraculous healing of our son, Aubrey Napoleon-Hill Clark, who was born blind.

"People around you, constantly under the pull of their emotions, change their ideas by the day or by the hour, depending on their mood. You must never assume that what people say or do in a particular moment is a statement of their permanent desires."

— Robert Greene, Mastery

(A guest on the Thrive Time Show podcast, An iconic author on strategy and power. When reading Robert Greene's books it is important to know that people that do not read the Bible and who do not adhere to God's laws often use The 48 Laws of Power against you in a nefarious way. I believe that it's important to know the moves that nefarious people will use against you so that you can protect yourself against the evil moves and the problems they will cause you. He has written seven international bestsellers, including The 48 Laws of Power, The Art of Seduction, The 33 Strategies of War, The 50th Law (with rapper 50 Cent), Mastery, The Laws of Human Nature, and The Daily Laws.)

As General Flynn and I take a photo in front of this massive crowd of people at the Tampa Florida ReAwaken America Tour. I do not know if any one in that crowd will ever remember my name, but I know that my children remember what kind of father I was or wasn't.

Man Law #39
Create a Family Culture of Success or Jackassery Will Happen by Default

"Likewise, ye husbands, dwell with them according to knowledge, giving honour unto the wife, as unto the weaker vessel, and as being heirs together of the grace of life; that your prayers be not hindered."

— 1 Peter 3:7

(The book of 1st Peter was written by the Apostle Peter. Peter died via crucifixion in Rome under the tyrannical rule of the Roman Emperor Nero.)

You must choose to create a family culture that is not dysfunctional. If you are not intentional, your children will spend their youth staring into their smartphones and digital devices while you spend your prime parenting years scrolling through Instagram and Netflix. Be intentional!

What family traditions do you want to start?

What generational habits do you want to break?

What intentional habits do you want your family to develop?

Man Law #40
What Gets Scheduled Gets Done

"14 Whereas ye know not what shall be on the morrow. For what is your life? It is even a vapour, that appeareth for a little time, and then vanisheth away."

— James 4:14

(The Book of James was written by the brother of Jesus. This about that for a moment. The book of James a book filled with calls to action to true believers in Jesus Christ as our Lord and Savior.)

There is a statistically high probability that you and I will experience death on Earth. However, the Bible does teach us that both Enoch and Elijah were taken up directly to heaven without needing to experience death of the human body...so there might be a chance that you won't die. Why am I writing about the certainty of death? I am writing about the certainty of death because you and I must get serious about valuing the time we spend with our children and the incredible wife that God gave us. You and I must recognize that what gets scheduled gets done and that which does not get scheduled will not get done. Be intentional and schedule time for faith, family, finances, fitness, friendship and fun. Don't get caught up in the hypnotic rhythm of drifting around through life and missing out on the formative years of your children's lives. Remember, God only gave your children one biological father and that is YOU.

"No one wants to die. Even people who want to go to heaven don't want to die to get there. And yet, death is the destination we all share. No one has ever escaped it."

— Steve Jobs

(The man who revolutionized the personal computer, recorded audio, telecommunications and animated movie industries. Steve Jobs co-founded Apple, turned around PIXAR while serving as their CEO and founded a company called NeXT which created an operating system that was later acquired by Apple.)

In this photo I am taking Aubrey Napoleon-Hill Clark to Guitar Center for the 1,776th time. My goal was always to teach Aubrey to have a love for sound, lighting, music, recording and video so we could always have something to talk about as he creates a career path. Knock on wood, but so far it is working!

Fun Fact: Did You Know That the Average Person Now Spends 11.3 Hours Per Day Consuming Media According to Nielsen?

"American adults spend over 11 hours per day listening to, watching, reading or generally interacting with media." *(https://www.nielsen.com/insights/2018/ time-flies-us-adults-now-spend-nearly-half-a-day- interacting-with-media/)*

When is your weekly scheduled family time?

_____

When is your weekly time to take your wife on a date?

_____

When is your weekly time to mentor your children?

_____

When is your weekly time to have dinner with your kids?

_____

Man Law #41
Do Not Succumb to the
3-P Disease
(If You Decide to Become a
Business Owner)

What is the "3 P Disease?" The "3 P Disease" is what happens when you decide to embrace suicidal empathy in your attempt to make every one happy all of the time.

If you choose to become a business owner you must accept the fact that within the world of entrepreneurship you shall find a perpetual struggle, battle and fight between the "3 Ps." These "3 Ps" will always be fighting and we cannot do something to stop them from fighting each other all day every day? What are these "3 Ps?"

P #1 - **Prices** - All customers want to pay less and receive more.

P #2 - **Pay** - All employees want to get paid more for doing less.

P #3 - **Profit** - Nobody on the planet cares about whether you earn a profit or not.

Bottom line, if you choose to become a business owner you must pay yourself first and off the top, because in reality no one else cares whether you make a profit or not. Think about it.

"You don't get paid for the hour. You get paid for the value you bring to the hour."

— Jim Rohn

(Jim Rohn (1930 – 2009) - Jim was an American entrepreneur, author, and motivational speaker. He wrote numerous books including How to obtain wealth and happiness. Rohn mentored Mark R. Hughes and life strategist Tony Robbins in the late 1970s. Others who credit Rohn for influencing their careers include authors/lecturers Mark Victor Hansen and Jack Canfield (Chicken Soup book series), Everton Edwards (Hallmark Innovators Conglomerate), Brian Tracy, Darren Hardy, and Harv Eker. Rohn coauthored the novel Twelve Pillars with Chris Widener.)

In this photo Aubrey visits the "Man Cave" studio at our Broken Arrow house where I recorded the ThrivetimeShow.com Podcast, songs, and things that I believed to be profound or just audio recordings that involved me liking the sound. Although certain clients and employees came and went I was intentional about introducing Aubrey Napoleon-Hill to the world of audio, video, lighting, recording, production and more.

As long as you are managing a business on the planet Earth that involves working with humans, you are going to be dealing with A-Players, B-Players, C-Players and people who are 100% obsessed with being poor and staying poor.

- **A-Players:** A-Players show up to work early, they don't leave until the work is done and they are focused on exceeding your expectations.

- **B-Players:** B-Players show up right on time, they leave right on time and they are focused on doing the least acceptable amount to not get fired or to get in trouble.

- **C-Players:** C-Players show up late, they leave early and they are focused on doing the worst job possible at all times. These people are shocked when they get fired and they are always chasing new things hoping to get inspired.

- **D-Players:** D-Players act like A-Players while making nefarious plans to divide your team, destroy your reputation and to cause you financial harm. These people often watch Andrew Tate videos when not perpetually thinking about ways to destroy you and that which you have built.

"⁹ And when ye reap the harvest of your land, thou shalt not wholly reap the corners of thy field, neither shalt thou gather the gleanings of thy harvest. ¹⁰ And thou shalt not glean thy vineyard, neither shalt thou gather every grape of thy vineyard; thou shalt leave them for the poor and stranger: I am the LORD your God."

— Leviticus 19:9-10

(This book was written by Moses after receiving the text directly from God.)

Aubrey Napoleon-Hill was always on the receiving end of intense rhythm therapy when I was around because I love music and I love R&B. Pictured above Aubrey practices playing the drums while keeping on his orange jacket that he loved so much. I love Aubrey!

Picture Left to Right: Doctor Robert Zoellner, James DeCristofaro and myself (Clay Clark) take a moment to take a photo amidst the craziness caused by COVID-19 and the year of 2020. From my perspective the year 2020 gave me perfect vision and perfect look into who was a true believer in Jesus Christ as our Lord and Savior and who was not. I believe that the year 2020 exposed who had the real eyes to realize the real lies. In this picture the attorney James DeCristofaro is holding up a copy of the lawsuit that we filed against the city of Tulsa for forcing unconstitutional lockdowns and mask mandates upon the people of Tulsa, Oklahoma.

Man Law #42
When Your Father Dies of Lou Gherig's Disease Don't Allow His Unpublished Manuscript to Die With Him

My father and I took a moment to pose for a quick photo. In this photo my father is wearing the signed NBA draft jacket that Paul Pressey was given when he was drafted by the Milwaukee Bucks as the 20th overall pick in the 1st round of 1982. When Paul Pressey discovered that my Dad was dying from Lou Gherig's disease he sent his prized NBA draft jacket to my father to encourage him. While working as an assistant coach for the Los Angeles Lakers during Kobe Bryant's final season in the NBA, Paul would routinely call my father to check on him and to pray with him. Paul Pressey is a great husband, father and friend.

My father (Thomas Clayton Clark) attempts to introduce me to the hamburger and to his authentic and 100% genuine love of food.

My mother (Mary Clark) and my father (Thom Clark) posed for a photo while Dad was fighting for his life, attempting to beat Lou Gherig's disease.

My father (Thomas Clayton Clark) takes a photo with his grandchildren, Aubrey Napoleon-Hill Clark and Havana Clark.

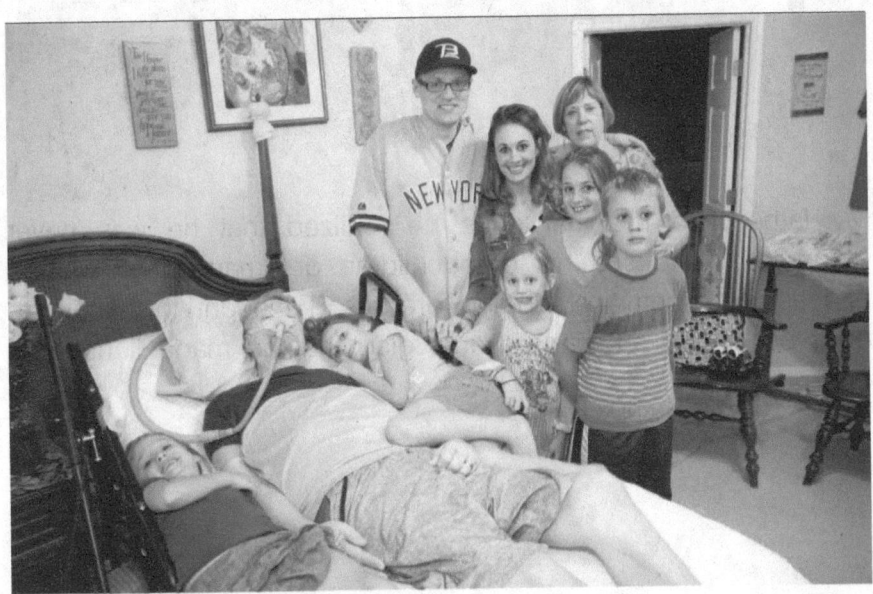

Our family gathers around my Dad to encourage him and pray for him as he struggled to breathe while battling Lou Gherig's Disease.

My father told me that once he realized that he was never going to live to see his grandchildren get married he wanted at least see them in wedding dresses. I thought this sounded odd, but now I am unbelievably glad that he made it happen.

Pictured from Left to Right: Aubrey Napoleon-Hill Clark, Havana Clark, Scarlett Clark, Angelina Clark and Laya Clark posed for a photo with their dying grandfather and my dad, Thomas Clayton Clark. At the time of this photo we had all traveled to Waco, Texas so that my father could attend his final high school reunion. My father was a high school all star baseball and basketball player and a man who was respected, so a massive number of his high school graduating class showed up to the high school reunion to say goodbye to their friend, their classmate and my father one more time. As I type this, I feel a need for a trip to Atwoods coming up in my near future. Dad, I miss you! D$#ammit, I wish I didn't miss you so much.

Despite being an NBA assistant coach for the Los Angeles Lakers during Kobe Bryant's final season and despite being an NBA basketball player with an impossibly busy schedule Paul and Phil Pressey traveled to Tulsa, Oklahoma to say goodbye to my father one last night. I wish I could say goodbye to my father one last time. He was a great father who was willing to work the tireless night shift at the QuikTrip gas stations year after year to provide for us and I will never forget that. Thank you Dad!

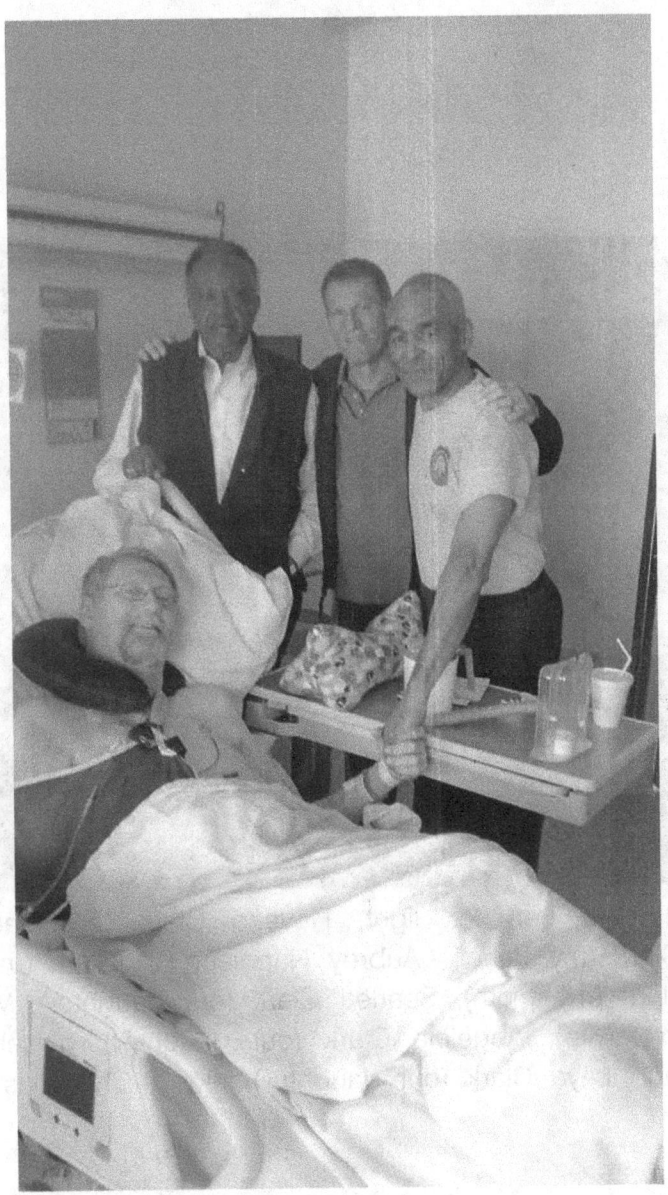

Pictured from Left to Right: My father's great friends, Clifton Taulbert, Ed Guthmann and Virgil White chose to never leave my father's side as he slowly died. WOW! These men were so loyal and faithful. Thank you Clifton, Ed and Virgil.

Pictured from Left to Right: Havana Clark (our daughter), Thom Clark (my father), Aubrey Napoleon-Hill Clark (my son), Mary Clark (my mom), Scarlett Clark (our daughter), Vanessa Clark (my wife), Angelina Clark (our daughter), myself (Clay Clark) and Laya Clark (our daughter) take a Christmas photo.

Pictured from Left to Right: Myself (Clayton Thomas Clark), my father (Thomas Clayton Clark) and my mother (Mary Clark).

What is the purpose of this portion of the book? After my Dad (Thom Clark) died, I discovered that he had left us a fantastic collection of musings, stories and deep thoughts and I thought it was the right thing to do to share them with you. My goal in publishing this content is to help my father to posthumously publish his first book and for the legend of Thom Clark to live on. My father was an allstar high school athlete and an allstar father who did his very best to teach me about the following 10 things:

1. Believe in Jesus Christ as my Lord and Savior.

2. Believe In Capitalism and the wealth it can produce.

3. Believe in Steve Martin, Airplane, Naked Gun and the power of humor.

4. Believe in writing legibly so that other humans can read what you wrote.

5. Believe in the uniting power of basketball, baseball and football.

6. Believe in doing unto others as they would have them do unto you.

7. Believe in QuikTrip gas stations and the high quality customer service they provide.

8. Believe in the importance of great food, and barbecue.

9. Believe in consistently going to church and reading the Bible.

10. Believe in the power of stories.

In order to be true to both my Dad and his writing, I have decided to make virtually no edits to the content he created. I hope you enjoy reading this book as much as I know he enjoyed writing it. Mom, I hope you enjoy reading it.

Thom Clark 101
(January 27th 1953 - September 5th 2016)

Anyone who had the privilege of knowing my 6 foot
5 inch tall Dad knew that he loved fellowship with
friends, lending a helping hand to those in need, talking
baseball, seeking out local food, unique food, fast
food, slow food, seafood and any kind of food when not
discovering a new barbecue restaurant, eating chicken
fried steak, and telling short (10-minute) real-life stories
that always ended with a comical twist and a moral
lesson or a good laugh.

My dad's stories were legendary to his friends and
family and he seemed to know just enough about
everything to have DOMINATED Jeopardy if he had
ever aspired to appear on the game show. In youth
sports my Dad was the legendary star pitcher on
his Little League team that made it all the way to the
1965 Little League World Series. In high school my
Dad excelled academically and athletically while
playing basketball and baseball at a high level. My
dad excelled as a college student at Oral Roberts
University. As a Father through his actions my Dad
showed me what it meant to be willing to do whatever it
took to provide for our family. As a Grandfather he was
a wise man and mentor who taught my children (his

grandchildren) what it meant to schedule time for what matters most and how to not lose your faith when your death from a degenerative disease is guaranteed and quickly approaching.

Who Was Thom Clark?

My Dad (Thom Clark), was the only child of Dorothy and Thomas Clayton Clark Sr. He was born and raised in Waco, Texas, which is famously known as the birthplace of the "Dr. Pepper" and "Big Red" beverages, the home of Chip and Joanna Gaines and the home of David Koresh and the Branch Davidian "Cult" that burned alive on national TV while America watched.

My Dad graduated from Waco High School as the Valedictorian (and I believe this to be true) because he was always much smarter than I am. My father graduated from Oral Roberts University where he met my Mom (Mary Jane Meinhardt). Dad graduated from Oral Roberts University with a Bachelor of Arts degree in Communications and later in life he completed a second degree in Applied Measurement Science. After my Dad graduated from Oral Roberts University, both my Mom and Dad decided to make Broken Arrow, Oklahoma, their home.

My Mom and Dad got married on May 17, 1974, and they set an example for my wife and I by staying married for 42 years before his passing. These two "love birds" co-produced, my brother Carson and myself.

Moving to Minnesota

When I was twelve my parents decided to move to Cokato, Minnesota, (which is located within 15 minutes of the often missed tourist attraction known as the "World's Largest Ball of Twine") to be near Mom's large family. The town we lived in (Cokato) had a population of 2,038 people according to the green sign that everyone passed when driving into town.

My Dad Was a Provider

Throughout my Dad's career he did what he believed he had to do to put food on our table and a roof over our heads and for that I am unbelievably grateful. I remember my Dad working the night shift at QuikTrip store #66, I remember my Dad delivering pizzas in his 30s, and I remember my Dad working at Rich's Furniture which would become Ethan Allen Furniture. I remember Dad attempting to launch an insurance business career and I remember my Dad designing a small 9-hole golf course concept and I remember my Dad ultimately pivoting to become a Calibration Specialist before I was able to hire him to come and help me to dominate the wedding industry galaxy as father and son at www.DJConnection.com before I sold it. After I sold www.DJConnection.com, my Dad chose to stay at the company that I sold and to help the new owner Jason Bailey to expand the company.

My Dad Was Committed to the Cause of Christ

My Dad was a long-time member of Christian Chapel and he served in various roles at all of the churches he attended. My Dad knew how to play the drums and was always the church's plan C in the event that the plan A drummer and the plan B drummer were unavailable to play. My Dad always helped those in need by volunteering his time to help others, including investing his time into the Big Brothers/Big Sisters program, serving as the Co-Director of Awana, serving on various ministry boards, volunteering at Royal Family Kids which was a summer camp for foster children and he helped many troubled youth. Dad also served as an assistant coach on my baseball teams when his work schedule would allow it. My mom and dad always opened their home to people in need including unwed mothers who were choosing to put their babies up for adoption.

The King of Kindness and Compassion

My Dad had a strong faith and love for Jesus that could be seen in the way he strived to handle every situation with kindness and compassion. I only ever saw him really freak out when I threw a baseball bat in disgust during a baseball game, threw a basketball at a member of my own team who refused to hustle on the basketball court and would curse people out who worked for me when they failed to meet their deadlines. If I am the Bob Knight of business, my Dad was the soft-spoken Super Bowl winning head coach Tony Dungy of the game-of-life. If you don't know about Tony Dungy, let's just say that I am one of the most aggressive, and intense people you will ever meet, and my Dad was one of the calmest, nicest and most tactful people on the planet.

Fascinated With Fishing and the Game of Golf

My Dad was always very interested in fishing and the game of golf. He loved to travel, he loved writing plays and writing short stories. As a kid I remember my Dad always putting on magic shows, playing the drums and loving dogs.

I truly believe that my Dad's greatest joy was spending time with my brother, his grandchildren, my Mom and I. I was with my Mom, Ed and Marilyn Guthmann as my dad, Thomas Clayton Clark Jr. died and went on to be with Jesus on Sept. 5, 2016, at his house.

Discovering That My Dad Was Going to Die

I'll never forget where I was when my Dad called me to tell me that he had been diagnosed with amyotrophic lateral sclerosis (ALS). I was driving in my H2 Hummer headed back from some "important meeting" when my phone rang and I saw it was my Dad. My Dad knew that I am a horse-with-blinders type of person that does not like distractions and therefore when he called I knew that something had to be up.

I said, "Dad's what up boss?!"

Dad said, "Son, I wanted to let you know that I have ALS."

I said, "................."

Dad said, "Son, are you there?"

I said, ".....I'm sorry Dad....I'm sorry...Dad...I need a Dad...I'm sorry..."

Dad said, "Son I have Lou Gherig's disease and...(I don't remember what he said...)

I said, "Dad, I love you. I love you. I love you. I'm so sorry...."

I don't remember the rest of the conversation, but I do remember immediately experiencing the EXACT SAME FEELINGS that I had when I returned to my Oral Roberts University dorm room to learn from Adam Guthmann and the guys living on the dormitory floor that my best friend Mark DePetris had just died in a car accident. When I discovered that my Dad was going to die I felt emotions that were heavy, dark and terrible like when I watched Dr. Deborah Birx and Dr. Anthony Fauci exaggerate and lie to every American about the dangers of COVID-19 everyday to justify ushering in the "Great Reset" and to destroy of our freedom-loving American way of life. I felt terrible knowing that my Dad was going to die, yet there was nothing that

I could do to stop it. As an internal optimist my mind was scrambling for solutions and for a reason to have hope and then it occurred to me! ALS is terrible and knowing that my Dad has ALS is worse, however, at least my Dad and I could say the things to each other that most people normally don't get a chance to say to each other. In a way my, Dad and I were actually blessed because we knew of the approximate time that he was going to cease living on this Earth and of the approximate day that he would join Jesus in heaven to experience eternal life and endless fellowship with God our father. Knowing that my Dad had accepted Christ as his Lord and savior and was thus going to spend eternity with Jesus really helped me to stay positive. Everybody hates death, but death is the only way we can pass on to heaven so what do you do? My Dad and I chose to not leave anything unsaid to each other and I sincerely believe that my Dad felt loved and appreciated. However, Dad I know you are watching me write this, so if you didn't feel loved and appreciated, please forgive me.

Surviving Cancer and Living On Bonus Time

In the 18 months before the time of my Dad's diagnosis of having ALS he had just beat stage 4 colon cancer and was already a statistical anomaly and a miracle man. In a way, after he beat cancer it felt like my Dad was living on bonus time, yet whenever anyone dies it always feels too soon.

Fighting for Life Until September 5th

Let me tell you how great my Dad was. It has always been a life-long dream of mine to host a live / daily radio show and I was told by the producer of AM Talk Radio 1170 that my radio show, The Thrivetime Show, which was currently being aired at 5 PM central was going to be moved to AM's primetime slot (noon to 2 PM) to compete with 740 AM Talk Radio's Rush Limbaugh on September 5th of 2016. I told my Dad about this good news and he promised me that he would live until September 5th of 2016 and that is exactly what he did. My Dad literally fought death off until the day he promised. My Dad, Thomas Clayton Clark refused to die until the day that my daily AM Talk Radio Show was aired live during talk radio's primetime hours.

As Lou Gherig's Disease Ravaged His Body, My Dad Remained Positive.

As my Dad suffered through Lou Gherig's Disease, over time his physical body stopped working and he needed someone to feed him, to clothe him, to wash him and to do everything for him, yet his mind remained sound. In my opinion, my Dad, who was one of the kindest men on the face of the planet, died one of the cruelest deaths possible and for that I am still MAD. However, I am not sure who I am MAD at, but that is the emotion I experience every time I think about my Dad losing his battle with Lou Gherig's disease. Dad, YOU won the war when it came to the game of life and I am proud of you!!! You showed me what it meant to push through adversity while never losing your faith in our Lord and Savior Jesus Christ and you are inspiring me to become a better father.

"Blessed is the one who perseveres under trial because, having stood the test, that person will receive the crown of life that the Lord has promised to those who love him."

— James 1:12

Chapter 1
5TH CHEMO SESSION

I just finished my 5th chemotherapy session with 3 more to go. My appreciation for all the people who have held me up in prayer is beyond my ability to express in words. So many of you have complimented me for my attitude, bravery, etc., that I thought I should take a few minutes to explain some 'inside information.' I have to admit to being scared out of my mind regarding cancer, but I'm not afraid of dying. My oncologist, Dr. Muhammed Janjua, was clear, direct and compassionate when he told me that I had stage 4 colon cancer. There was a tumor on my adrenal gland and another in an area near the bottom of my right lung. So, I knew what I was facing.

My first response was numbness. Then I realized my greatest fear, the loss of time with my wife / angel, Mary, and the possibility of not seeing my grandchildren grow up. My 'bravery and attitude' is not an act. It is solely from God. Peace that passes all understanding has been a gift from God. It makes no sense unless you are in a tough situation because, for all intents and purposes, things are out of your control in this natural world. The doctor makes the decisions about treatment protocols. I can only follow the plan and make every effort to live a healthy lifestyle. The healing power from God and your prayers that have brought my body before God is the key dynamic for healing.

For me, dealing with cancer has been a decision. Do I believe in Jesus Christ as my Savior? Yes! Once that decision is made, it is a matter of living out what I believe. It is a decision to choose the attitude that I am going to have. Granted, it was a little hard to stay perky and happy during the 11th day of non-stop migraine headaches.

I have stolen a line from Dr. Randy Pausch, the professor at Carnegie Mellon University, who died leaving behind a wife and 3 children under the age of 8, "If I don't seem as depressed or morose as I should be, sorry to disappoint you." (Look up Randy Pausch, the Last Lecture, on Google. Well worth the time to watch the YouTube video).

Curtis Neimeister was a friend whom I have written about earlier. We learned at about the same time that each of us had cancer. Curtis' had metastasized leaving him with 4-6 months to live if he were to take aggressive chemotherapy, but that would only prolong his suffering. I spent as much time as I could with Curtis. He was being my mentor in a number of areas, but the issue of cancer is tough to talk about unless you are talking with someone that shares your condition. He said, "I have a bumpy road ahead of me, but no matter what, I win. I get to visit with friends every day. I have a loving wife who gives me love and every comfort I need. And, I know when I have passed across this bumpy road, I step directly into the loving arms of Jesus. I've got everything to gain."

I asked Curtis what he thought about my condition and medical options. He said if it were him, he would fight with every ounce of strength because there were grown children, young grandchildren and a lovely wife to live for. But as he reminded me, "Keep a good attitude because everything works out for the good when you know Jesus."

Curtis had the most wonderful attitude imaginable all the way to the end of his life. He encouraged me to do all I can to help others whether it is helping the kids camp for foster children, helping with projects at church or helping my grandchildren. I told Curtis I was concerned that I might not live long enough to attend each grandchild's weddings, which is my deepest wish. The average age on both sides of my family is 75, even with good health. I would have to live another 20+ years to attend their weddings and that would be age 81 or so. Curtis helped me hatch an idea for my grandchildren.

Mary and I celebrated our 40th anniversary on Saturday, May 17th. We got all the granddaughters dressed in mini-wedding gowns and I danced with each one—Havana, Angelina, Laya and Scarlett. I'm going into a studio to record some ideas for a successful marriage and a prayer of blessing for each girl and her future husband. I will also take the time to let them know about my faith and what that type of relationship will mean for them. I will record one video for each of the girls. If I live to be at their weddings, the video is not needed. If I don't, I'll still be there and I'll get to be a part of their wedding. By the way, the video of me dancing with a 9-year-old, a 6-year-old and 3-year-old twins is, if I won't lose my 'Man Card' for using the word, will be "PRECIOUS."

Pictured from Left to Right: Laya Clark, my mom (Mary Clark), our daughter (Angelina Clark), our daughter (Scarlett Clark), our daughter (Havana Clark), my father (Thom Clark) and my son (Aubrey Napoleon-Hill Clark) at my mom and dad's 40th anniversary.

Finally, the odds of me being at these weddings went up this past Wednesday. This is not my opinion, this is from Dr. Muhammed Janjua, I am in REMISSION. No cancer can be found.

Pictured above: My father (Thom Clark) and my mother (Mary Clark) hold their twin granddaughters Scarlett and Laya Clark.

Chapter 2

BACK IN THE SADDLE

"Hi, Guys," as Ted Knight (alias Ted Baxter) used to say on the Mary Tyler Moore Show. I'm back writing some stories after an absence. It seems that following chemotherapy and the implant of a pacemaker, I was more than a little foggy. I have come to the conclusion that the lack of blood to the brain creates much the same symptoms as a concussion. It felt like a long time ago when I tried to play basketball in pick games with the team members of the ORU basketball team. They were FAST and I was SSSSSLLLLLLOOOOOOOWWWWW. Same with my head. Gee, am I ever slow in keeping up.

Months later, I'm functioning quite well. I have been given a clean bill of health. No signs of cancer. Nine months in remission. The heart doesn't go below 62 beats per minute. No more permanent haze.

I stated before that colors are more vivid to me and I wonder why. Is there an actual neurological difference that affects my vision? Maybe. I know that reading was almost impossible for about 3 months. Was my schedule upside down resulting in me sleeping during the day (with shades drawn) and being awake during the night? This resulted in only being exposed to dark lighting situations. Or, was I simply so happy to be alive that I appreciated the colors of everyday life even more than before? There is probably a lot of truth to that. Perhaps it is a function of all three factors. The bottom line is: I feel good. And, I'm back.

Chapter 3

BE VERY, VERY CAREFUL WHAT YOU SAY...............

This is the 'old folks' medical report. I have come to the conclusion that if everyone over the age of 50 were not permitted to talk about their maladies, conversation would come to a grinding halt. As I have explained in the past, it is better for me to explain as best I can what is happening to me physically (with this Facebook post) than to have people wonder 'how long I have to live.' It was simply putting too much pressure on friends as they tried to figure out how they would get the time off to attend my funeral. FYI: the pressure is off. I'm going to live...for a while longer.

On August 8th, I had a pithy little post saying that I was going to die on August 14th…almost. The story behind that was that I was going to have a Cardioversion performed. That is where they take the paddles and shock the heart back into rhythm. I have known about my irregular heartbeat since I was 12 years old. There was some question about holding me out of the Little League World Series due to the irregular heart rhythm. Since I did not then or do I now have lightheadedness, fainting or other signs of a lack of oxygen to my brain, doctors have passed on imposing any restrictions. It was surmised that my irregular rhythm might be a contributor to atrial fibrillation (commonly called A-fib) that was discovered in January prior to surgery for colon cancer. And if you haven't heard, I am considered in remission. There are no signs of cancer as of the current time.

Prior to the Cardioversion, a device similar to the one used to examine babies in the womb was put down my throat to check out my heart. A-fib is known to be the cause of blood clots. Well, that is exactly what happened to me. I have a blood clot in my heart. Blood thinners will keep other clots from forming. Eventually, the current blood clot will be absorbed back into my body without any part of it breaking off in the meantime. The timetable for that is unknown. A few months, a year...who knows.

Isn't this spellbinding reading? I'm feeling older every moment that I recount the story. Obviously, I'm over 50 years of age. Since there was nothing to be done, Mary and I proceeded to Minnesota for our niece's wedding. I was going to sleep and Mary was going to drive. We had our granddaughter, Angelina (aka, Bay) with us. We picked up Carole Liston in Joplin. Carole was invited to the same wedding since her college roommate at ORU was the bride's mother, Bonnie is my wife's sister, Mary. We spent the night in Lamar, Missouri, rather than to make the hard drive all the way to Minnesota.

My father dances with his granddaughter Angelina (also known as "Bay"). Angelina, "Papa Thom" loved you very much! I am going to need to go to Atwoods after looking at this photo.

Friday, August 15th, was to be a crazy day. After breakfast and Mary driving for a couple of hours, I began to get sick. We stopped twice for me to throw up. A series of other symptoms began to appear. By the time we had driven through Des Moines, I was on my cell phone looking up symptoms of a heart attack. I had 8 out of the 10 listed. By the time we were 20 minutes from Ames, Iowa, I had 9 out of 10. So, this pig-headed fool finally asked Mary to find a hospital. We were able to get to the Mary Greeley Medical Center in Ames, Iowa, very quickly.

The short version of the story is that enzyme tests showed there was no heart attack. My heart rate, which was normally around 45-50 beats per minute, was in the 30 beats per minute range. The staff and doctors were wonderful. This is not said lightly. Dr. Cai at the hospital reviewed my history and pointed out that the medication that I was taking for heart rhythm was depressing my pulse rate. In essence, I was not getting enough blood. They held me overnight in the new wing of their hospital. There were only 3 patients on the floor. Gee whiz, talk about excellent personal care! It doesn't get any better.

During the night at about 3:30 am, my heart rate fell to a low of 24. I'm told that a really bad thing happens when the heart falls below 20 beats per minute. In other words, my prediction about the 14th almost came true on the 15th. The nursing staff piled into the room with what I believe is called a 'crash cart.' They were shaking me and charging up the paddles. The nurse asked, "Are you okay, Mr. Clark?"

"I was until you woke me up so enthusiastically...and you can call me Thom!"

My heart rate returned to the mid 30s. They discharged me on Saturday and we continued on to Minnesota, arriving an hour and fifteen minutes before the wedding.

Now that I am back in Tulsa, my heart beats at 30-32 beats per minute in the morning. As best as I can tell, I don't get over 40 beats per minute when I check during the day.

Can you spell F-A-T-I-G-U-E?

I'm drinking a lot of water trying to flush out the medication that I was taking.

Most importantly of all for those that pray for me, I need the following:

1. I need the Blood Clot dissolved.

2. I need the wrong medication out of my system ASAP.

3. I need energy to do my work.

4. I need a proper intervention for A-fib issue.

The kids attempt to pull my fathers hair as we attempt to take a family photo of our kids with their "Papa Thom."

I still have confidence in the Lord to handle everything. My somewhat odd sense of humor is intact, which I use in ways that might offend some people. When I'm at the point of danger, I find it better for me to laugh than cry. But, the issue of lack of energy is difficult for me. Please don't think I'm rude if I appear to dismiss a person and walk on by. I hate being rude. The truth is that I am out of energy for engaging in conversation. I am drained for which I need your prayers. Thanks everybody. Your support has been tremendous. I love you all (I realize that the second person plural for a Texan is Y'all. I must have become an Oklahoman now).

Pictured above: My father (Thom Clark) and my father-in-law (Rick Moore) take a photo together at Tarp Chapel in Broken Arrow Oklahoma during our wedding celebration.

Pictured above: My father (Thom Clark) holds his grandson (Aubrey Napoleon-Hill Clark) and his granddaughter (Havana Clark).

Chapter 4
CAMP RAMADA

This is a combination of true stories mixed into one. The names of the characters have been changed to protect the guilty. If anyone from Tulsa, Oklahoma State, or Oklahoma city reads this, they will know in an instant who Geoff Conner is. So, let's just keep this story to ourselves.

Geoff Conner enthusiastically served his Uncle Sam for two weeks every summer. It was either that or lose his student deferment. Given that the Vietnam War was at its peak, Geoff considered it a fair trade. Two weeks in scenic southern Louisiana with plenty of exercise, sunshine, and meals provided a nice diversion from his summer lawn care job. The screaming of Drill Instructors was just a tad annoying, but manageable.

A couple of weeks away from his girlfriend was a downer. But then it also meant that Geoff didn't have to deal with her overly protective brother. Just to show Geoff what sort of fellow he was dealing with, his girlfriend's brother would flex his muscles and strike poses like a bodybuilder when Geoff came to pick her up for a date. Geoff thought that was just a bit weird.

Then, one day as Geoff was walking up the driveway, he was using his sister as a barbell and doing overhead presses. Maybe Geoff should curb his thought life just a bit. Getting out of line with the 5'8" very athletic girlfriend wasn't such a good idea seeing as how her brother was both crazy and strong as a gorilla. Geoff could barely pick her up much less press her overhead.

What would he do with a skinny basketball player like Geoff if he really got riled? Again, why bother thinking about it? Two weeks in Summer Camp would be a nice vacation; or so Geoff thought.

Life at boot camp didn't appear to be all that bad. Getting up early didn't faze Geoff. He did that every day working for the lawn care company. Getting yelled at with a bullhorn was another matter. Starting the day with a headache, that was bothersome.

The first order of the day was to get into formation for the special introductory session with Master Sergeants Schwartzweiler and Gallego.

Master Sergeant Gallego informed the troops that he had just returned from Vietnam where it was his job to pick up dead bodies and put them in bags for shipping back home. He purposely gave gory details just to make some of the soldiers retch. Then Master Sergeant Gallego said he was going to train this group of pathetic excuses for soldiers how to survive. "Some day when you are lying on your belly in a rice patty, you will thank the heavens that I taught you how to stay alive." Geoff thought that the training may help him stay alive, but the student deferment that he kept by virtue of being here would be even more effective than Master Sergeant Gallego's special training.

Then, it was Master Sergeant Schwartzweiler's turn to enlighten the troops. Geoff learned quickly that Master Sergeant Schwartzweiler was from an area of the country that he had never had the privilege of visiting.

In a language vaguely reminiscent of English, the assembled troops were told that, "All you'll mens need buns. Causin' mens without buns aren't thinkin' ahead."

Seems logical Geoff thought.

"Mens, Uncle Sugar loves you. He gives you brand spanking new uniforms. He gives you guns with bullets. He points you to which way to go. He tells you who to shoot at. And all Uncle Sugar asks is that you buy his buns."

Geoff asked out of the corner of his mouth, "Who is Uncle Sugar?"

The soldier to his right said, "I think he's talking about Uncle Sam."

"What about the buns?"

"Beats me. I ain't got a clue."

Then the epiphany happened. "If you buy US Savin's Buns, you'll make Uncle Sugar really happy. These buns will give you the highest yield allowed by law. That'll make you happy, too. And if you don't come back alive from Vietnam, your family will be happy, too..............after they bury you, of course."

Geoff muttered, "I came here for financial counseling?"

"Wait until tomorrow," said the recruit to the left of Geoff. "Schwartzweiler will enlighten us about the hazards of VD."

"You're kidding."

"Nope. I've been to this camp twice. Same stories every time."

"Any way to get out of this?"

"Yep, Vodka."

"What?"

"We bought Schwartzweiler a quart of Vodka at the end of the last camp. Then he would get up an hour later and wouldn't leave enough time for his early morning story telling."

"Did it work?"

"Yep. Just find someone old enough to buy booze at the liquor store and he will be a pussycat for the rest of camp."

Then Master Sergeant Schwartzweiler finished his financial seminar with the order to "report to your barracks, find your assignment listed there on the duty roster and report back here in 5 minutes with your gear. Dismissed!"

Geoff went to his barracks. There he learned a very important fact about 'Uncle Sugar's' army. The army was great at marching, shooting, and blowing things up; but paperwork, that was another issue. Try as he might to find it, Geoff Connor's name was nowhere to be found.

Each soldier's daily schedule was listed hour by hour for the next 14 days with the exception of Saturday and Sunday afternoons. That was free time. A 9-hole golf tournament and a bowling tournament were available during the free time. Available, provided the soldiers had the stamina to participate.

Geoff had quick decisions to make. "Do I inform the Master Sergeant of the oversight? What happens if I don't inform him? Who cares?" So Geoff thought to himself, "Why not see how long it takes them to find out that I'm missing?"

Geoff took a minute to be sure that his bunk was properly made up so as not to draw attention. He grabbed a duffle bag full of civilian clothes. While everyone filed out of the barracks and turned left, Geoff turned right. He walked to the front gate. The guard was checking everyone coming onto the base and ignored everyone leaving. Geoff hailed a cab.

"Where to?" asked the cabbie.

"Any good hotels on the other side of town?"

"How about the Ramada Inn?"

"Sound's good to me." And with that, Geoff was on his way to check in at the Ramada Inn, using his military discount of course.

Louisiana can be miserably hot during the summer. Geoff appreciated the ice-cold air conditioning after reading a book at poolside for a couple of hours. A swim in the morning was good for the appetite. It was just the thing to prepare Geoff for the buffet in the hotel restaurant.

An afternoon dip in the pool, read a few chapters from his book, and a little gawking at the poolside scenery made for a pleasant day. The cable television offered a selection of games; Chicago Cubs on WGN in the afternoon and Atlanta Braves on WTBN in the evening.

By Saturday, Geoff was a bit bored. So, he decided to try his luck at golf. It was a bit daring to go back on base, but Geoff felt like he was riding a hot streak. Why stop now? But first, he stopped at the liquor store for a quart of Vodka. Geoff entered the base, flashing his ID, saluting, and saying, "Returning with supplies for the Master Sergeant."

Geoff went to the barracks. He set the bottle on the bed of the soldier that knew about Master Sergeant Schwartzweiler's taste for vodka. He looked at the duty roster for the week's schedule. It told where and when the golf tournament was to be held. So, it was off to the golf course. Geoff had a 5 handicap, which was far better than anyone he faced that afternoon.

And, his arms and legs hadn't turned to rubber from hard labor. Geoff won by 12 strokes. And he was off to the hotel for a grueling night of watching movies.

Master Sergeant Schwartzweiler was lying on his bed, knocking back another shot of vodka, thinking 'this is the best bunch of young men that I've had in a long time.' Six quarts of vodka were on the dresser. Two empties were in the trash can.

Geoff repeated the same trip to the base on Sunday. This time he brought a bottle of aspirin.

Geoff carried a 195 average in his summer bowling league. Without his own personal ball, he managed to average 176, which was good enough to win by 45 pins. But then again, Geoff was the only one whose arms and legs weren't quivering like jello from climbing ropes. Now it was time to return to the hotel for another grueling week of swimming, sunning, reading and watching TV.

Master Sergeant Schwartzweiler didn't know where the bottle of aspirin came from, but he was happy to have it after having a nightlong romance with shot glasses full of vodka. Five quarts of vodka were on the dresser. Three empties were in the trash can.

For Geoff, it was a matter of repeating the same verse. The only variation from the previous week was having to stay up later for the Cub games since they were on a West Coast road trip to play the Giants and Dodgers. Oh yeah, there was that cute blonde by the pool that helped apply sunscreen to Geoff's back on Monday, Tuesday and Wednesday. Then the concierge informed Geoff that the blonde was sixteen and her father was a Colonel at the base.

Discretion was the better part of valor as Geoff avoided the Colonel's daughter.

The week flew by all too quickly as Geoff's tan was nearing the level just short of perfection.

Geoff paid his bill with the credit card that his Father gave him for emergencies, making sure that he received his military discount. Everyone would be packing up on Saturday morning for a noon departure on the bus. Geoff planned to get back to the barracks as early as possible. He thought he would be able to change into his fatigues before anyone noticed, then sort of hide out until it was time to board the bus for the trip back to Oklahoma City.

Geoff glanced at the duty roster on the way out the door. "Oh, NO!" Geoff's heart sank. His name was on the duty roster for getting his pay from the Quartermaster. Someone was bound to notice that Geoff hadn't been there for two weeks, except for the golf and bowling tournaments. If he didn't show to get paid, they would ask questions. If he did show up, someone would ask where he had been. It appeared that Geoff had no choice but to appear at the appointed time for payroll disbursement. He just hoped he would go unrecognized.

It was 10:45 a.m. Geoff's squad met at the barracks. They were ordered to march in formation to the Quartermaster's office where payroll would be disbursed. The soldiers were called in alphabetical order to get their check and sign for it. Following about 10 soldiers in front of him, the Quartermaster bellowed, "Conner, Geoffrey. Front and center." Geoff walked forward to the table where the Quartermaster sat with his stack of paperwork and checks.

"Private Conner, sign here."

"Sir, yes, sir."

"Conner, you have the darkest tan I've ever seen. How did you get that?"

"Sir, I work outside for a lawn service when not serving my country, Sir."

"So, you were tanned before you got here?"

"Sir, yes, sir."

"That's smart thinking, Connor. Most of the pansies I see here get burnt to a crisp after 2 weeks. Did the Army work you hard?"

"Sir, yes, sir. My tan is much darker now thanks to the United States Army, sir."

"I'm glad to hear that, Connor. Good, job."

"Thank you, sir."

Geoff darted out the door and jumped onto the bus. It didn't matter that it didn't leave for an hour. Hunkering down and hiding from the Master Sergeants was the plan. Perhaps, the other soldiers were following Geoff's lead. They boarded early, also. The bus was now full making it easier for Geoff to blend into the crowd.

At 11:55, Master Sergeant Schwartzweiler entered the bus. He looked up and down the seats. Geoff sank a bit lower in his seat so that only the top of his head showed.

"Listen up," bellowed Master Sergeant Schwartzweiler. "Mens, I'm disappointed with all of y'all. Not one of you bought any buns. Uncle Sugar does and he does for you and this is the thanks he gets. I've got half a mind to take all of y'all off this here bus and take you for another trip through the obstacle course. But, I ain't gonna, cause I got another bunch of pansies comin' in right after you leave. Get outta here."

He started to leave the bus. Then, he turned around.

"Oh, no," thought Geoff. "He's spotted me. I'm a dead man."

"I forgot to mention. Thanks to some of you boys, I never got thirsty this week. Just wanted to say thanks." Master Sergeant Schwartzweiler stepped off the bus.

He slapped the door and said, "Get goin'. If anyone's late, let 'em walk."

The bus pulled out. Summer camp was done and he didn't get caught. Geoff finally began to breathe again. He pulled out his check and looked at it. It was only $5 short of paying the hotel bill. Another stroke of good luck! It wasn't going to be so hard to explain the bill to his Father if he had the money to pay the bill.

The soldier next to Geoff asked, "Weren't we in the same squad? I saw you the first day, but never after that. Did you get transferred?"

"Yea, something like that."

"You've got a sweet swing," said a voice behind Geoff. "I saw you at the golf tournament. You won didn't you?"

"Yep."

"And the bowling tournament, too?"

"Yep, again."

"Come to think of it, I never saw you all week except for the tournaments. What did you do for 2 weeks?"

"Oh, a little of this and a little of that."

Geoff walked up the driveway to his girlfriend's house. There was her brother doing bench presses on his exercise equipment that was set up on the front porch.

No sign of his girlfriend anywhere.

"You missed her," said her brother, which was about as much of a conversation as he had ever initiated.

"Where did she go?"

"Don't know."

"Do you know when she'll get back?"

"Nope."

"Will you tell her I'll call her?"

"Nope, ain't my job."

"I see. I'll tell you what; just forget about it."

"Hey, you looked real tanned. They must have worked you hard."

"You could say that."

"Did they make a man out of you?"

"Guess you'll have to wait and see."

"By the way, what was the name of the place the Army sent you to?"

"Camp Ramada."

Pictured above: As my father battled cancer his grandkids never missed an opportunity to battle for him by giving him copious amounts of hugs.

Chapter 5

COLLEGIATE BASKETBALL CAREER ENDED

Okay folks, I want you to remember that the statutes of limitations have passed. And...there will be no stories regarding punch and cookies during a Christmas party in high school.

~

I attended Oral Roberts University (ORU) in Tulsa, Oklahoma. It was there that I made a big discovery regarding basketball. I wasn't any good.

Flash back to Waco High School: I played basketball against Arlington Heights, in Fort Worth. Their center was Cedric Joseph. He was around 6'8" with a backside wide enough to screen out 3 players. Going around Cedric took a $5 cab ride. And, if that was not enough, he could JUMP. He crushed me. I had maybe 4 points that came while Cedric was sitting on the bench. I blamed my poor performance that evening on a party from earlier that day. Coach Schrader said, "Thom, I just don't know what got into you tonight." I muttered under my breath, "you don't want to know."

Now flash forward to ORU, 1973: Texas A&M was coming to Tulsa to play against our Oral Roberts University Titans. Their starting center is none other than 'THE' Cedric Joseph. The very same Cedric Joseph that destroyed me 2 years earlier. He was matched up against our 6'11" McDonald's High School All-American, David Vaughn. And how did Cedric perform against big David Vaughn, you ask? Cedric was shut out. Zero points. Must have had 4 of his shots blocked and slammed back into his face by Big David. I'm sure Cedric had a few rebounds from balls that bounced out far away from the basket. But underneath the bucket, he got nothing. In short, David treated Cedric like he was a boy playing against men.

I'll try to create a mathematical formula to establish my basketball ability. If David crushed Cedric, and Cedric crushed me. The result equals 'I am not any good.'

I was asked to 'walk on' at ORU to fill out the freshman team. In a pick up game, Big David Vaughn got a tuft of his afro caught on the prong that holds the net to the rim. I could barely dunk the ball and David was almost hitting his head on the rim. It was at that moment that I said, "If you will excuse me gentlemen, I think I am going to retire from competitive basketball."

I'm sure that Wayland Baptist University never knew how fortunate they were that I turned down their basketball scholarship to attend ORU.

Pictured above: My father (#44), Thom Clark playing basketball at Waco High School.

Pictured above: My father (#44), Thom Clark drives to the basket while playing basketball in high school.

Chapter 6

CONFESSION IS GOOD FOR THE SOUL.........MAYBE

The late baseball pitcher and television announcer Dizzy Dean said, "It ain't braggin' if you do it." Well in my case, I could 'sort of do it,' but the truth is that I was 6'2" when I was 12 years old and I could throw rather hard. But that is exactly what I was, a thrower. I could hit a fastball. A curveball, forget about it.

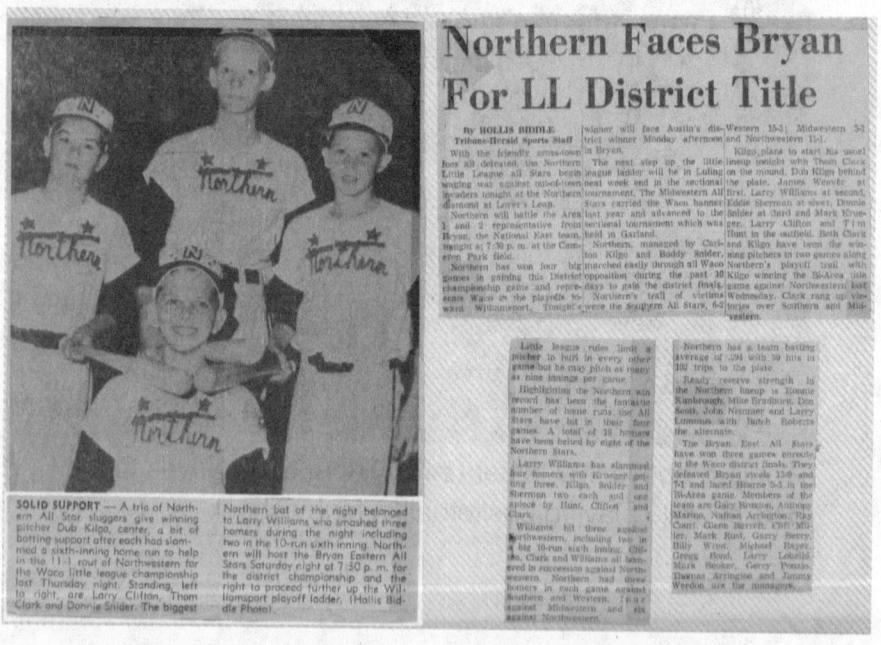

My father (Thom Clark) was the tall guy in this picture.

When I was chosen to be on the Waco Northern League All-Star team, I had the good fortune to be surrounded by some of the best Little League talent you would ever find. This is the never before told story of the State Championship game against Woodlawn Little League from San Antonio, Texas. Are you bored yet?

Let me tell you about my 'Moment in the Sun' and the secret that I have kept for 49 years. This time the story is about hitting a home run, not pitching.

Our team played in the 1965 Texas Little League State Championship game. We were tied in the bottom of the last inning. Dub Kilgo, my catcher, was on first base. The next two batters after Dub struck out. I was next up to bat. Their pitcher Dave Dollnig thought I was big enough that I could hit the ball a mile, so he pitched carefully and fell behind in the count. As for me, I was scared to death. Dub's dad, Carlton Kilgo, was our coach. He stared at me when I stepped out of the batter's box and repeated his mantra, "the pitcher has to throw a strike on a 3-1 count. Look for the fastball."

Coach Kilgo was right about the pitcher having to throw a strike. He was wrong about what the pitcher threw. It wasn't a fastball. It was a slow hanging curveball that came in 6 inches outside and waist high. I decided to step into the ball and hit it. The result: a walk off home run that won the 1965 Texas Little League Championship.

It's funny what goes through your mind when something big happens like that. First, I laughed at the guy in left center who had backed his truck up to the outfield fence. He was sitting in a chair in the back of his pick up truck. The ball I hit was hit on a line drive directly over the guy in the truck. The ball cleared his truck as it sat behind the 185 foot marker in left center. So, the guy tried to jump up and catch the ball. Bad idea. He fell back over the cab of his truck and rolled down across the hood. The last I saw of him was his two legs sticking up in the air as he tumbled.

Thought number two was 'be sure to touch each base.'

Thought number 2.5 was to 'be sure not to pass Dub in the base path.' That was no problem. He was way ahead of me.

Thought number three was not to let anyone touch me until I had touched home plate. The umpires were strict and could call me out for interference if I touched anybody. Everyone on the team stood back away from home plate until I had touched it. Then, the celebration began.

I had a lot of relatives who had driven from Dallas to Houston for the championship game. The high 5 had not yet been invented, so there were a lot of handshakes instead. By the letter of the law, I lost my amateur status that night. My uncle, Eugene Williams, included a $20 bill with his handshake. That was the equivalent of 200 bottles of Dr. Pepper in 1965. I darned sure wasn't going to tell Mom and Dad about the $20 bill. It was almost certain that $10 would have gone into savings if I had said anything.

Coach Carlton Kilgo congratulated me for hitting the walk off home run. He said something to the effect of 'I'm sure glad that you remembered to look for a 3-1 fastball.' There were several things I didn't tell Coach Kilgo, not that night or ever. First of all, that wasn't a fastball that I hit. It was a waist high hanging curve. But who cares? It went over the fence, didn't it? The second part would have been a little tougher to swallow. Golfers call penalties on themselves. It is a point of honor. In baseball, the umpires make the call. Sometimes an umpire misses a call that goes in our favor, which happens from time to time. Then, that's just the way it goes sometimes.

I was a dead-red left-handed pull hitter who could only hit fastballs. Throw me a curve. Lights out. I'm done for. Throw me a fastball and I had a pretty good chance of ripping the ball to right field. Perhaps some people thought it strange that I hit a home run to left field. In the excitement of the moment, probably nobody noticed. I stepped across home plate to hit that hanging curveball. The ruling should have been that I was out for stepping out of the batter's box and onto home plate. We would have remained tied 1-1 and gone on to the 7th inning. I knew I had stepped on home plate because my foot slipped and I almost fell as I started towards first base.

Our team went on to win the Little League Regional Tournament in Norfolk, Virginia, and then to Williamsport, Pennsylvania, for the 1965 Little League World Series where we took third place.

The old expression is that confession is good for the soul. So okay, I feel a little better now that I have told the truth 49 years after the fact. But, I can't say it bothered me that much to keep my silence which allowed us to have played in the Little League World Series. Come to think of it, nope, I was wrong. I never touched home plate until after I rounded third base. Yeah, that's the ticket.

Pictured above: My father celebrating life!

Chapter 7

THE CONFLICT RESOLUTION AREA (LIFE BEFORE POLITICAL CORRECTNESS)

In the days before PC (Political Correctness), conflict resolution at North Junior High was generally left up to the individuals to resolve using their own methods. Seldom did these 'methods' involve conversation. Perhaps it is more accurate to say that what conversation there was only served to escalate the conflict. Fisticuffs and kicks were the usual order of the day. But where would be the best location for this 'conflict resolution?'

It was determined to be the north side of the gym, near the exit from where the boy's locker room was located. The sidewalk was elevated above the open area just outside the locker room. This made a sort of amphitheater for watching the 'conflict resolutions.' A couple of guys would be posted at the eastern edge of the building while a couple of more would be posted at the western edge of the building. If the principal or vice principle heard about an impending resolution, he would have to run all the way around the gym to approach from the east or all the way around the cafeteria to approach from the west. There was never a chance for him to stop a 'conflict resolution' without the lookouts alerting everyone that the principle was on the way. Oh sure, they could have come through the gym, but the doors into the boys locker room were always locked in advance.

The coaches were sometimes in the locker room, but I don't recall them ever coming out unless there was a lot of blood. Then, the guys stationed in front of the door would go inside and ask to borrow a first aid kit. Only once did the amount of blood require calling a coach for help.

The coach who came out said, "Dang, I would like to have watched this."

"It wasn't that big a deal Coach," said one of the door guards. He tripped when he was backing away and hit his head on the handrail. Not one punch, but a lot of blood."

The biggest 'Conflict Resolution' was too large for the usual 'Conflict Resolution Area.' So, it was taken offsite to the 'Holy Land.' The conflict began early in the day with a lot of murmuring about the 'big Conflict Resolution' to be held after school. There was not enough space for everyone that wanted to watch so the individuals moved their resolution across the street into the open area between Reicher High School and St. Louis Catholic Church, aka....'The Holy Land.' Bad Idea! When the Parish Priest, Mark Deering, and the Reicher High School administrators got involved, that was the end of trips to 'The Holy Land' for Conflict Resolution. It seems that the Parish Priest had a 'Come to Jesus Meeting' with the Waco Independent School District Administration. There was probably little likelihood of an altar call. I'm sure North Waco Jr. High's principal had (in the words of Ricky Ricardo) some 'splainin' to do.' Thus ended the Conflict Resolution behind the boy's gym.

When I was in the 7th grade, the first method for reducing the occurrence of Conflict Resolution was to put the Vice Principal near the back of the gym. He made a few holes in the ground to make a "washer" game. He would play washers often with the likely losers of a Conflict Resolution. They figured the big time winners of Conflict Resolutions would leave them alone if they played "washers" with the Vice Principal. I suspect that the Vice Principal didn't like that job. He was gone the next year. He may have retired, but I suspect he took a job elsewhere because he didn't have the physical tools to handle the big boys in a fight. The look on his face showed he was scared of these bullies.

QUICK NOTE — I have no idea what the "washer" game is or is all about.

When I was in the 8th grade, Conflict Resolutions by and large stopped. One of the area basketball coaches was apparently demoted from coach to North Waco Jr. High's Vice principal. The probable demotion was possibly for disciplinary reasons for the former coach, and was definitely related to the lack of discipline to the bullies at North Waco Jr. High. The vice principal wore a crew cut and looked like a 5'10" Marine (aka, jarhead). It was clear from day one that you didn't mess with the vice principal. If someone were caught smoking, he would give a spanking (aka, licks) with a baseball bat filed to a ½" thickness and drilled with holes. He drilled holes in the bat that made it whistle when he swung the bat. If a bully tried to turn around and challenge the vice principal, he would take them down like a wrestler, then take them to the office using an arm bar. So let's just say, when the vice principal asked you to do something, he only asked once. I don't think his style would be allowed today. But as we found out, a little knowledge is dangerous.

Someone found out about the vice principal's indiscretion while he was coaching at the high school. When he was going to give licks to one student, he informed the Vice Principle that he knew about what he had done. "You hit me and your story will be in the newspaper tomorrow" (Guess it helps to have a father who worked at the hometown newspaper). The vice principal backed down. The word got out regarding his indiscretion and that was the end of spankings. He was gone at the end of the 2nd semester and moved out of Waco, not to be heard from again.

When I was in the 9th grade, the vice principle was a future politician. He went out of his way to dress like and wear his hair like President John F. Kennedy. He was constantly walking among the bullies of the school and talking about their futures. The bullies considered him a pest, but they couldn't shake him. He was ubiquitous. His method worked. There were fewer Conflict Resolutions. Parents were called in to meet with the student and vice principal if there were disciplinary issues. I guess it is hard to argue with results. The only time we heard about how he was handling discipline was if the object of the discipline said anything to his classmates. The vice principal left North Waco Jr. High to work his way into politics. 3 years later, he was the commencement speaker at my High School Graduation. His entire speech was about the benefits offered by the Democratic Party to the people of the great state of Texas. My girlfriend's parents got up and walked out, only to return when his speech was over.

Pictured above: My father battles Lou Gherig's disease while surrounded by his grandkids, my father-in-law Rick Moore and my Uncle Neil.

Chapter 8
THE COUNTER CLOCKWISE CLOCK

This story is about people with whom our paths crossed. In this instance, it started on a basketball court at Midway High School.

Coach Schrader put me on the varsity roster for a while during my sophomore year. Guess he wanted to see what I could do. I succeeded in getting the seniors mad at me. They didn't want sophomores taking their places. And frankly, they were right. I was too skinny and too weak to play with upperclassmen...at that time.

I was thrown into the fray against Midway High School in a game just before Christmas. Their senior center, "WW," took me to school. In other words, he beat me very badly. No hard feelings. It was a good lesson learned.

I heard a few years later that Midway High School's famous "WW" had gone to Brigham Young University. Or at least that is what he told me when I met up with him at Oral Roberts University. I tried to introduce myself and talk about being from the Waco area. He wanted as little to do with a sophomore punk as possible since he was a 'big, bad junior' that was going to take a starting job from one of the players on the Sports Illustrated's preseason #4 ranked team. I got the impression he was thinking about senior Richard Fuqua.

Ask me if I thought he was a bit 'stuck up' and I would reply, "Is the Pope Catholic?" I tried being friendly several times, but Mr. Midway would just walk off in a huff, making it very clear that he didn't want to talk to me....ever.

So I pulled an ace from up my sleeve to get his attention. I cornered "WW" on the escalator at the Mabee Center Arena and asked him a question. "Tell me something, "WW." Have you ever seen a clock that runs counter clockwise?"

"Yea. I knew a girl who had a clock like that. If you've got a point to your question, get to it?"

"Just wondering. I knew a girl who had one, too."

"So why ask me if you know all about weird clocks?"

"Just thought you might remember that particular clock."

"And why should I know something about THAT particular clock."

"Oh, I don't know. Guess it had something to do with having your picture on the wall next to the clock."

"What are you talking about?"

"Guess when you went to BYU, I started dating your ex-girlfriend."

Then, "WW" was interested in talking to me but I was busy. Couldn't talk right now. In fact, I was so busy that I blew him off that day and every day for the remainder of the year that he attended ORU.

WW was a pretty good basketball player, other than the fact that Eddie Woods, our center and only 2 inches taller than "WW," blocked every one of his shots. "WW" couldn't shoot very well from the outside. "WW" was slow. I don't know how good a passer WW was. He was always trailing the play when they ran off and left him behind on a fast break. "WW" couldn't jump high enough to dunk. "WW" couldn't dribble to his left side. And, his style of play indicated that "WW" thought that DEFENSE was what you put around 'de' house to keep 'de' dog from running away.

Maybe "WW" should have taken the scholarship at Wayland Baptist.

Pictured above is "Thom" the Turkey whom we named after my father Thom Clark.

Chapter 9

CHIEF PETTY OFFICER PURDUE

NOTE: I do not know why a "Chief Petty Officer" was assigned to watch a bunch of boys competing in The Little League World Series.

Years lend some perspective. The host/chaperone for the Waco Northern Little League team on the Naval in Norfolk, Virginia, was Chief Petty Officer (CPO) Purdue. One can only guess whom CPO Purdue pissed off to get the assignment of 'babysitting' for 15 boys ages 11-12. We seemed less like brats when Chief Petty Officer Purdue met us. And he got along well with Coach Carlton Kilgo and Assistant Coach Buddy Snider. I suspect that Coach Kilgo told Purdue that he would run us until we dropped if we got out of line.

Chief Petty Officer Purdue had to go with us everywhere. He found out at our practices that we were a pretty good team. I didn't know how good a team he thought we were until after we had won the Southern Regional, beating Decatur, Georgia, 4-2 in the championship game. More on that later.

The four teams in the tournament were from Monticello, Arkansas; Decatur, Georgia; Vienna, Virginia; and of course, our team from Waco, Texas. CPO Purdue must have decided that he was the chaperone for the 'winning horse.' He seemed to have a lot of meetings with his fellow Chief Petty Officers. It turned out they were talking about more than how to keep us busy during the days that the games were rained out.

Decatur was a loud bunch of guys. Pity the Chief Petty Officer in charge of them. Vienna was practically a home game. They had a whole rooting section that traveled from Vienna to Norfolk. It was a 3-hour drive to Norfolk. A good number of their fans stayed despite the rain delays.

Monticello, Arkansas, was simply the worst All-Star ever to reach the Southern Regionals. Decatur won 19-2. If Monticello were horses, they would have been euthanized. Decatur, Georgia, would have played every one including the sisters of their ball players if they could. The game could have been 50-0 if the Decatur coach had not 'called off the dogs.' But, it was still a free trip to Virginia, so they didn't care.

Yours truly threw the opening game against Vienna. It started ok......13 up and 13 down according to the newspaper article. But, Vienna was a good team. We were only up by 2 runs thanks to a home run by my

catcher, Dub Kilgo and super defense up the middle
by shortstop, Eddie Sherman, and second baseman,
Larry Williams. They kept a lot of batted balls from
being base hits. Then, I got wild and loaded the bases.
Vienna's pitcher, Ronnie McDonald, hit a long drive
over the fence, but foul by 2-3 feet. Chief Petty Officer
Purdue almost swallowed his gum, or whatever else he
was chewing. I got nervous and ran the count to 3-1.
The newspaper said that Coach Kilgo came out to the
mound to give me some words of wisdom. The words
of wisdom were "quit fooling around and throw the
damn ball over the plate." To which I said, 'Yes, sir." Two
fastballs later, end of the inning.

The 6th inning had been our lucky charm all season.
Donnie Snider singled off the top of the fence.
Sherman doubled off the fence. McDonald tried to
show me up by blowing a fastball past me. Should have
thrown a curve. I hit a homer around 300 feet or so. The
fence was 190 feet. The ball cleared the light towers
and landed on the mound of a regulation field backed
up to the little league field. The next 3 batters, Mark
Kruger, Tim Hunt and Larry Clifton, smashed the ball
for solid hits that loaded the bases. Chief Petty Officer
Purdue was feeling a little more comfortable now.
The next 2 hitters, James Weaver and Larry Williams

smashed the ball. Then up came Kilgo, who tripled to right clearing the bases. That's how the game ended. Waco 8 - Vienna 0. In all fairness to Vienna, they hit a number of shots, but they were right at someone.

Chief Petty Officer Purdue asked me after the game if I was trying to give him a heart attack in the 5th inning when McDonald hit that long foul ball. Later, I learned why he was so concerned.

We played Decatur, Georgia for the championship. The score was 2-0 in our favor when I made a bonehead play in right field, putting men in scoring position. Then, there was a soft blooper to leftfield that left fielder Mark Krueger and shortstop Eddie Sherman were chasing when they collided. Now, the score was tied. Chief Petty Officer Purdue was twisting in his seat.

Dub Kilgo was pitching. FYI: Dub pitched and I threw. He knew how to pitch effectively. I just did what Coach Carleton Kilgo told me to do. My style was: Here is the ball. Hit it if you can. Dub on the other hand tied batters in knots. He pitched up and in, down and away, and threw the most unhittable curve I have ever seen.

After almost giving away the game, who would lead off the 6th inning but me? I could feel Coach Kilgo's eyes boring a hole in me. I got part of the way out of his doghouse when I singled to right field. Eddie Sherman came up after me. His hand hurt from the collision with Mark Krueger. We thought it was a bruise. Eddie proceeded to hit a monstrous drive to leftfield that hit, appropriately enough, the Georgia flag. That was the end of the game for all practical purposes because no one on earth was going to hit Dub's curveball. A quote in the newspaper was that the Decatur coach admitted that Sherman had marched through Georgia, again.

The bad news was that Sherman had hit a home run with one hand because his right hand had a broken bone.

My validation for the effectiveness of Dub's curve came from none other that THE MAJOR LEAGUE BASEBALL LEGEND, Jackie Robinson, at the Little League World Series. He told Dub, "Son, I would never want to hit against you. Best curve I've ever seen."

For what it's worth, Vernon 'Lefty' Gomez was quoted in the Williamsport newspaper as saying that I reminded him of my hero, Don Drysdale. I think it wasn't my sidearm delivery as much as it was that I threw at so many people. Dub set up almost behind the dreaded clean up hitter, Dale Misek, from eventual World Series winner, Windsor Locks, Connecticut. I hit the target and Dale hit the dirt. I heard Coach Kilgo between innings tell Coach Snider, "that big boy can't hit anything when he is sitting on his butt."

Chief Petty Officer Purdue was seen after the game collecting a few hands full of money. I was so naïve that I didn't realize until years later that Chief Petty Officer Purdue had bet on us. And he really liked us after that. In fact, he got us out of some bad trouble.

Chief Petty Officer Purdue earned his money. We had multiple rainouts that week in Norfolk, Virginia. How do 4 Chief Petty Officers keep 60 boys out of trouble? Well, we toured an aircraft carrier. It was unbelievable that there were multiple decks full of aircraft. One deck was used for a full-length basketball court. At 6'2", I was the only one on the team that had to watch out for the low openings between hatches.

They took us to a couple of movies. One movie was a war movie starring Richard Widmark. I only remember that because his daughter was married to Los Angeles Dodger pitcher, Sandy Koufax. If I was a fan of Koufax, I guess I had to be a fan of Widmark. There were a lot of double meanings in the script that the sailors went wild laughing at. Guess our guys missed most of the sexual double meanings. The next movie was 'Ferry Across the Mersey' starring Gerry and the Pacemakers. It was a bad attempt to copy the Beatles movie, 'A Hard Day's Night.' But, I still liked their song Ferry Across the Mersey from which the movie got its name. 'It's Gonna Be Alright' was a pretty good song, also. I still give the movie a thumbs-down. Most of the sailors left the theater with five minutes of the movie starting. Guess there wasn't enough sex. Ok, I know. All sailors say that.

One night the guys got pretty restless. We slept on spring wired bunk beds that made awful squeaks when any one rolled over. This seemed to inspire the Georgia guys to start jumping on the bed, which was followed shortly by yelling like an Indian attack. Of course, it didn't take long before everyone was doing the same thing. Chief Petty Officer Purdue started walking down the isles. Then he yelled for quiet. When everyone piped down for a moment, Chief Petty Officer Purdue asked the dumbest question I ever heard, "is that all the blank-blank noise you guys can make?"

The answer was a unified, 'NO!'

"Okay," said Chief Petty Officer Purdue. "Just checking."

The noise died down shortly afterward. It just wasn't any fun if Chief Petty Officer Purdue didn't care. I don't know if he told Coach Kilgo. All I know is that we didn't run any extra laps or sprints. Besides, the Georgia boys did it. Right?

The last escapade of our visit to the Naval Base at Norfolk, Virginia, was the pulling of the fire alarm. Everyone got kicked out of the barracks, including sailors who were in the middle of their showers. A few unsuspecting souls ended up outside by the street with only a towel wrapped around them. One sailor had his towel snatched from him. It was passed from sailor to sailor until it was lost while everyone waited for the fire department to give the all clear. The sailor who had his towel stolen stood there covered by nothing but some tattoos. And wouldn't you know it, a group of WAVES walked by about that time. The victim of the stolen towel just folded his arms and waited like the rest of us.

NOTE: I do not know what "WAVES" are.

The Chief Petty Officers in charge of the Little Leaguers were bound and determined to find out who pulled the fire alarm Chief Petty Officer Purdue swore it was none of his charges. "Just look at them. All of them are perfect little gentlemen. But, I think you should check out the boys from Georgia."

All I can say about the fire alarm is that if I am ever a defendant in a trial, I would be scared to death by a jury that would come to sudden and rash conclusions. After all, it's very, very, very, very possible that they got the wrong person. VERY POSSIBLE.

We bid good-bye to Chief Petty Officer Purdue, who was now a much richer Chief Petty Officer Purdue. The next step to Williamsport was a flight to Washington DC, for a connecting flight to Williamsport, Pennsylvania. While we waited for the connecting flight, and since we were 'such well behaved' young men, we were given a guided tour of the control tower to watch the air traffic controllers at work. One of the controllers even asked if we would like to have a job like his some day. Times have changed. It is impossible to imagine 15 boys, ages 11-12, getting a tour of the Control Tower at National Airport. But it is possible to imagine one of the guys saying, "Hey, Mister. What happens if I flip this switch?"

Pictured above, Havana Clark, Aubrey Clark & Angelina Clark hang out with their grandpa as he attends his high school reunion.

Pictured above, Havana Clark is holding her bear while being held by her grandpa, Thom Clark.

Chapter 10

CURTIS NEIMEISTER DIED

Report on my last Chemo session and the report about my dear friend, Curtis Neimeister who passed away from cancer on April 16, 2014.

On a personal level, my chemotherapy could not have gone much worse. My session began on Wednesday April 16th. I began having a migraine headache that lasted until Saturday April 25th. I was nauseous each day and fell down multiple times because I couldn't maintain my balance. I have a throat infection and will be taking antibiotics. Then my friend, Curtis died on April 16th. A blessing and miracle occurred this Saturday when I woke up with no symptoms of illness that allowed me to participate in part of the eulogy for Curtis.

Personally, I'm taking 2 weeks off from chemotherapy plus changing the potency of the drugs that I'm taking. I need some time to recover from this last session of chemotherapy. The plus side is that the therapy is working. The test for the presence of cancer cells is even lower than the last test. It is just the side effects of chemo that are beating me like an old mule.

My friend, Curtis Neimeister, has finished his race and is now in Heaven. His humor and encouragement for leaving a Christian legacy is 'must share' information for me. This is long, but worth the time and the telling of Curtis' relationship to me.

Comedian John Byner once said that there are 3 stages in life:

- Youth
- Middle age
- "Gee, You look good"

I told my friend, Curtis Neimeister, that at least you still looked good. He told me he appreciated my dubious honesty. Curtis had a sense of humor all the way to when he passed away. He also taught me something interesting about being ill. "You know what it's like to be sick. So don't ask me how I feel. Ask me what I'm thinking about today. It's still important to feel useful in some way."

I got to know Curtis at the Royal Family Kids Camp for foster kids. One of our workers in the wood shop was injured and I was drafted to fill in. Curtis wanted to know if I had any experience working with wood.

"No, Sir. I don't."

"Do you know how to use a drill?"

"I'm afraid that's debatable."

Curtis said to no one in particular..."Well, at least they send us only the most qualified. I'll tell you what, just don't drill a hole in anybody's hand and you'll do fine. Stay close to me and I'll keep you out of trouble."

We swapped stories and listened to comedy albums that he had on his iPad between building all manner of boats and toys. Andy Griffith had passed away the day that I got to Royal Family Kids Camps and wouldn't you know it, Curtis had Griffith's first comedy album entitled, "What It Was, Was Football." So from that time on, I was always trying to top Curtis with a joke. And Curtis worked overtime trying to convince the kids that I knew what I was doing in the woodworking shop.

I was a facilitator for a Wednesday night class entitled 'Back to Mayberry.' We looked at the life lessons taught with humor from the Andy Griffith Show. Curtis would get me to laugh by rolling his eyes at the crazy over reactions in the programs. Then, he would point out some true-life lessons as told in the program. The truth be known, Curtis bailed me out when the lesson was not getting much reaction.

On or about January 15, 2014, Curtis and I discovered that we had something in common. Both of us had cancer. Curtis' condition was far more advanced than mine. Curtis told me that his cancer had metastasized and that intense chemotherapy would only give him a few painful months. He said, "this is where you live out your faith. I know this is an awful bump in the road, but when this is over I'm going to step into the loving arms of Jesus. You know what that means?"

"I'm sure I know, Curtis, but I want to know what it means to you."

"It means I win: Perfect peace and a perfect relationship with God for all eternity. What could be better than that?"

"Now, Thom, what are you going to do?"

"What do you mean?"

"It sounds like you have a very high chance of full recovery. Although, if it doesn't work out that way, what are you going to do about sharing your faith in Jesus? Your grandchildren may be too young to understand now, but they need to hear about your faith from you. So I'll ask you again, what are you going to do?"

"Curtis, I'll have to get back to you on that."

"Well get busy. I don't have that long to hear what you are going to do."

A week or so passed and I got a phone call from the beautiful—and feisty—Karol Neimeister, Curtis' wife and definitely his better half. A series of events came up and she didn't have anyone to stay with Curtis while she took care of a series of important errands. I had volunteered to help if she needed anything so I told the guys at work their paychecks would be on time, so don't worry if I wasn't there for most of the day on Monday.

Mark that day as a RED LETTER day for me. Karol said the medication that she was giving Curtis would probably knock him out. While there, I told Curtis about a type of jig that could preset holes in the woodshop. This would make drilling wood safer, not to mention protecting the kids from my rather inept wood shop abilities. Curtis asked if I could show it to him. The screen on my iPhone was too small to see the device. So, Curtis told me to haul him into his office so that he could see it on the computer. It wasn't long before he pulled out plans for items to be built in the woodshop. I told Curtis it seemed a bit presumptuous, but I would like to have his blessing to take his place in the wood working shop. He said, "Okay, how's this." At which point he made the sight of the cross over me. "I'm not Catholic, but that should be sufficient to have you take my place. But if you put a drill bit through someone's hand, don't blame me. That's your fault."

While he was looking up the woodworking plans on the computer, he said, "Here, read these. That ought to keep you busy." What he had given me to read were letters and poems that his children had written about Curtis as a father to them. The letters were enough to bring tears to your eyes. They did for me.

After working on the woodshop ideas for over an hour, we moved back to his chair in the living room. Curtis should not have had enough energy, but never underestimate the power of an engineer's mind when there is an idea upon which to work.

I helped Curtis back to his chair. He asked me if I had figured out what I was going to do.

"About the tool for the wood shop?"

"No. What are you going to do about leaving a legacy for your children? Especially for those grandchildren of yours."

"Yes, Curtis. I think I have the perfect idea. I just need to work out some details."

"I wish you would hurry up and figure it out. I don't have forever to wait for you to make up your mind."

"Okay, I need to verify something first and then I'll let you know immediately."

I went to see Curtis a couple of days later and told him my plan.

"Mary and I are having our 40th Anniversary on May 17th and we are having a reception. We'll dress up our grand daughters in miniature wedding dresses and then make a video of me dancing with them. If I don't live another 15-20 years, I'll still be there at their weddings. I'm going to share some words of wisdom about being married for 40+ years and pray a blessing over them."

Curtis said, "It sounds like a good plan to me. Wish I could be there for the video recording and the weddings."

"You will Curtis. This is just another example of a legacy that you have helped to pass on for generations to come. Thank you for pushing me, my very special friend."

My dear friend Curtis Neimeister was working to teach me the value of leaving a legacy to future generations even while he was suffering.

I dropped by to visit Curtis on the Saturday before he passed away. It was not the best day he ever had. The drugs had put him in a foggy state of mind. Having had chemotherapy, I could identify what he was going through. Karol and I helped him to his chair. He turned and recognized me, then said, "Hey, look. Thom Clark is here." I could tell Curtis was fighting through the drug-induced haze.

Curtis needed water, medication, a back rub where he appeared to have had a cramp or some other problem. Karol took care of everything. He said, "Karol, I want you to stop for a minute. Now, Thom, I want you to see something. Do you know what you are seeing right now."

Dummy that I am, I had no answer. "No, Curtis. What am I seeing?"

"You are seeing LOVE. Karol doesn't have to do all this. She could ship me off to some place to keep me drugged up and let me die there. But, she chose to care for me for one reason. LOVE. So just remember, this is what LOVE looks like."

Chapter 11
DEFPOTEC | ASK THE BLIND MAN, HE SAW IT TOO

This story is about a young man pulling a joke over on the Physical Education / Health Class. I don't know what it's like to have lost a body part in an accident. This story is in no way meant to embarrass this young man. In fact, he became our hero that day for pulling off one of the best tricks ever on a Junior High School teacher who never knew what happened because of his extreme boredom. Great job my friend. You took lemons and made lemonade.

~

Line 8 of the Snelle eye chart reads "D E F P O T E C." The ability to read this line from a distance of 20 feet indicates 'perfect 20/20 vision.'

Coach Kenneth Clark was required to administer the annual eye test to all students in his 8th grade health and physical education class at North Junior High. Coach's instructions were blurted out so quickly that the entire sentence sounded like one very long word.

"Put your right hand over your right eye and read the third line from the bottom of the chart. If you are unable to read that line, move to the next line above it until you reach a line in which you are able to read all the letters. Then place your left hand over your left eye and repeat the process."

The coach repeated the same instructions for each student.

He called each guy up one at a time in alphabetical order. There were about 40-50 students in his class. By the time we had gone through the As, Bs, and Cs, the 20/20 line had been memorized. The coach never looked up as the class went through the process. The coach was not a drinker, so he wasn't hung over. I suspect he was just anxious to retire and was thoroughly disgusted with having to teach a health class to a bunch of (in his words) laughing hyenas. So Coach Clark just sat there leaning back in his chair, marked check marks by the 20/20, 20/30, etc., boxes, then called the name of the next guy to get his eyes tested. Coach never looked up from his huge grade book ledger.

When we reached the Ms, the 'fix was in.' A guy named Murphy 'read' the eye chart with his hand over both eyes. "D E F P O T E C." The coach never looked up and said, "Shut up you bunch of hyenas."

Don Moses read the chart with his back to the chart. "D E F P O T E C." Again, Coach said, "D E F P O T E C." Another of the Ms was led to the 20-foot line marked on the floor by another guy who looked like he was helping a blind man across he street. He turned him so that he was pointed towards the eye chart. "D E F P O T E C."

One student was actually blind in one eye. As Coach Clark blurted out his instructions, he tried to explain that there was no need to cover one eye because...Coach Clark finally looked up from his book for the only time that morning to say, "I don't want to hear any excuses. Just follow the instructions."

"Okay, Coach," he said. Putting his hand over his blind eye, he read, "D E F P O T E C." He then put his hand over his 'good eye' and read, "D E F P O T E C."

Let's just say that Coach, at that moment, lost whatever control he had over a class of almost 50 14-year-old boys. He looked up to find the instigator of the near riot of laughter. But, he couldn't figure out who started the ruckus. Everyone was convulsing with laughter. The guy with vision in only one eye had pulled one over on the coach and he was the star of the day. This again was pre high-five days thankfully, or our hero would have had his hand worn out.

Everyone was still laughing by the time Glen Zgabay read for the last time, "D E F P O T E C."

Fortunately for Coach Clark, the bell rang. Everyone dashed for the door as Coach Clark yelled, "Get out of here you bunch of laughing hyenas!"

Pictured above: I visited my father at the hospital. I wish I had visited my father at the hospital one more time. I need to go to Atwoods again.

Chapter 12
DAD'S LEGACY

If this is too much about T. Clayton Clark Sr., feel free to move on. I'm just trying to recall things from my Dad that I wish to pass on. It may be odd for my cousins hearing the accounts from the viewpoint of a little cousin that is 5 to almost 20 years younger.

~

Trying to carry on a legacy from my Dad:

My Dad did not have a legal name until he was 6 years old.

NOTE: This is unbelievable to me. My grandfather did not have a name until he was 6 years old. How is that possible?

It was a minor civil war amongst the Coon and Clark families. One side wanted to name him James Ferguson Clark after an extended family member named James Ferguson who was formerly the Governor of Texas. According to some family members, naming a child Jim Ferguson in 1913 Texas was akin to naming a child in 1972 Richard Nixon (fill in the blank). James Ferguson was perceived by many to be a scoundrel. Dad's first name was Thomas...a win for the Coon family. His grandfather's name was Thomas Coon, but still no resolution for a middle name.

At a high school football game between Mart, Texas, and Moody, Texas, the starting quarterback for the Moody Bearcats was Clayton Sebastian. My Dad mentioned to me casually that night that he was named after the grandfather of the Bearcats' starting quarterback. No further explanation.

Once while visiting my Aunt Viola in Dallas, she decided that I should know the origin of my Dad's name, especially since I am Thomas Clayton Clark Jr. It seems that Clayton Sebastian Sr. was Aunt Viola's boyfriend when the family lived in Moody, Texas. A job shift in the Post Office moved my Grandfather Clark and the entire family to Mart, Texas, when my Dad was 6 years old. So, until the age of six, my Dad was only known as 'Sonny' or 'Sonny Boy.' All my Clark cousins referred to my Dad as Uncle Sonny. Grandma Clark decided that 'enough was enough' according to Aunt Viola.

Grandma, Eula Mae Clark, said to Grandfather Clark, 'Joe Willie, Sonny has to have a legal name before he starts school.' Well, it seems that Aunt Viola still carried a flame for Clayton Sebastian back in Moody, Texas. Enough so that she lobbied hard for my Dad's middle name to be Clayton. Call that a win for Aunt Viola. Just think, if Aunt Viola had an affinity for using the middle name like all the other Clark siblings, I could possibly be called Sebastian instead of Thom.

You could tell the time frame and where a person knew my Dad by the manner in which he was referred. If they knew Dad from Moody, he was called Sonny. If they knew him from Mart, he was called T. Clayton. And if a person knew Dad from the 50 years that he lived in Waco, Texas, he was called Clayton.

So what does this have to do with a legacy regarding my Dad? It has to do with long-term affection for family and friends. When Dad arrived in Mart, Texas, at age six, a boy who was Dad's age rode up to him on his pony, got off, and asked 'What's your name?' How many boys at the age of six would be stumped by answering with their name? After answering with various combinations of Sonny, Thomas, Clayton and Clark, Dad settled on T. Clayton Clark. The boy, Jack Drinkard, said something to the effect of, "Whoo Whee, you either got a lot of names or you're not very smart." From that moment, Jack and Dad were best friends for 71 years until the time that Dad passed away. After Dad and Mom had both passed away, Jack's wife, Joan, told me that she had dated my Dad before she dated Jack. And it was Joan that introduced my mother, Dorothy Pearl (aka, Dot) Wallace, to my Dad. Dad's legacy—he loved his friends unconditionally for 71 years. I couldn't go to Waco without seeing Jack and Joan.

My Dad tried to be a 'Special Uncle' to his nieces and nephews when he could. Some of the older ones were teenagers when I was born, so I didn't get to hear as many stories about them, but the younger niece and nephew were within 5-10 years of my age.

Dad told bits and pieces about his nephew, Bob Roddy, the son of Dad's Sister, Mildred (aka, Aunt Millie). Most of the stories that Dad told about Bob revolved around playing catch and having Bob ask endless questions about what Dad was doing while working on an automobile. Dad called Bob the fastest kid he had ever seen at whatever age Bob happened to be at that time. "Good thing that he paid attention. I'd never have caught him if he wanted to run off."

Dad told one story about Bob that would almost bring him to tears. Bob was asleep in the front room of our 2-bedroom house in Waco. Dad went in to check on Bob before he went to bed. Bob at that time had the habit of sleeping very soundly with virtually no movement. Dad thought that Bob had died in his sleep. I'm sure that Bob was scared half to death when my 6'4", 245-pound Dad picked him up and started shaking him in order to revive him. Bob was okay. Just sleeping.

One of the great regrets in my life is losing the letter that Bob wrote to Mom and I when Dad passed away. Bob can be a craftsman with words. He was able to express a deep affection for my Dad. Again, Dad had an enduring love and affection for his nephew.

I didn't get many stories about Aunt Viola's son, Rev. F. Clark Williams. But, there were times that Clark would somehow limp his broken down car from wherever he was going to school to Waco. Dad would tune up the car, replace plugs, replace belts, replace gaskets to stop the dripping oil, replace headlights and brake lights, put in new brake shoes, fix the radiator and even get the radio to work. Then Dad would say, "That ought to keep you on the road for a while, Clarkie."

Clarkie would always try to pay Dad, but the answer was always the same, "Your money's no good around here. Catch me some other time." The other time never came.

As long as my Dad was able, he actually loved fixing Clarkie's broken down old cars. He was another cousin with whom Dad had a long enduring affection. And F. Clark Williams felt the same way as I saw their interaction.

Dad's oldest brother, Willie Hoyt Clark (aka, Bill Clark), had a son, Billy. When Billy was 16 and Uncle Bill was 56, their wife/mother, Ann Clark died. Uncle Bill appeared to be what I would call being shell-shocked. Today, they would say that Uncle Bill had a version of post-traumatic stress disorder (PTSD).

Aunt Ann's brother, Hank, called Dad about Uncle Bill's condition. Dad hopped a train from Waco to Chicago to get Bill and bring him back home. One problem, there was no how and no way that Billy was coming to Texas. Hank agreed to watch out for Billy while Dad brought Uncle Bill home. It worked out okay. Billy was a fanatic about keeping the lawn mowed and trimmed. Dishes were always washed and put away. Clothes were also always washed, ironed and put away. We knew about this because Uncle Hank called and wrote telling Dad about Billy's progress. It appeared that the only negative was that Billy took up smoking just like his father, Uncle Bill.

In subsequent years, the apparent aloofness of Billy would lead one to believe that Billy didn't care much for my Dad. It seemed that Billy would send an occasional letter or Christmas card. Dad credited Billy's response to not handling it very well that my Dad had taken his Dad away shortly after the death of Aunt Ann.

In 1991, on a whim, I called Billy to check in on him using some pretense about asking about family history. The call led to monthly communication. Billy opened up a bit. Seems he felt cut-off from the family because he knew so little about the Clark family. The next year, our family met with Billy's family for a short vacation in Schaumburg, just outside of Chicago. I pointed out to Billy that he had an unusual way of positioning himself at the table after eating. He held a coffee cup in an unusual manner. These were mannerisms of my father. My Dad had huge and distinctively shaped hands. Mary pointed to Billy's hands and said, 'Look, look. His hands are just like your Dad's.' Billy almost knocked me over when he told me how much he admired my Dad. He even used Dad's name, 'Clayton' as his younger son's middle name. Come to find out, Billy held my Dad in high esteem. A year later, Billy died from a blood clot. At the meal following the funeral, who should I be sitting next to but Uncle Hank. My Dad had told me many times how much he admired Hank and I informed him of that. Hank said that was interesting, Billy had said the same thing many times about my Dad.

The abiding affection of my Dad for his nephew was lost in poor communication. The phrase applies here appropriately...........it goes without saying.

Bob Roddy's sister, and Aunt Millie's daughter, Fredene was one of the older of my cousins. She was married to Don Hays and moved into their own home when I was just a little tyke, so I have limited access to stories about Fredene. I do remember Mom saying many times that Fredene was such a beautiful child. Aunt Dot had a deep affection for her. I know that Dad loved Fredene dearly, but as the Grandfather of four granddaughters and one grandson, I understand it is a bit different with boys and girls. I think I missed out on some good stories with Fredene and Dad. I would give $100 dollars to see my Dad playing and having tea with a child's tea set with his niece.

I was the youngest of nieces and nephews. Just ahead of me was Nancy Riley, daughter of Dad's sister, Mabel, and brother-in-law, Leslie. Dad's repeating story about Nancy was to watch out, because she was a fan of Moe Howard of the Three Stooges. While riding with the Clarks and Rileys in the car, Nancy said, "Jook, Unkel Tunkey" (translation: Look Uncle Sonny). Dad turned his head and Nancy poked him in the eyes with two fingers. Fortunately, Dad wasn't driving. After he recovered his eyesight, he thought it was the funniest story in the world that he fell for the old poke in the eye trick. I suspect there may have been a little more wrestling between those two than some other cousins. Nancy always kept Dad grinning and on guard.

Mom, aka Aunt Dot, was a real piece of work when it came to Nancy. It was always 'Nancy is so pretty.' 'Nancy is so well behaved' (I suspect some, if not most, of the 'misbehaving' had to do with Dad's antics).

'It would be so wonderful if Nancy could stay with us for a while.' It was confusing at times. I didn't know if Mom wanted another child or just wanted to negotiate a trade.

Dad and Mom had a special affection for their nieces and nephews that was obvious to most. And even after the passing of Billy Clark, we learned how much he cared for my Mom and Dad.

Okay, what is the point of telling about all these special relationships relating to my Dad? I'm trying to consciously work on building a legacy in which they knew without a doubt that their Uncle Thom loved them just as his Dad, T. Clayton had loved his friends, nieces and nephews.

I've been able to have a special relationship with my younger nieces and nephews. I made a date to take them to the restaurant of their choosing for their birthdays. I found that my nieces love the Olive Garden. One niece agreed to try out the Mongolian Grill, the next year we were back at the Olive Garden. One nephew seems to appreciate breakfast at a pancake house. At age 5-6, one nephew changed his mind about going to McDonalds. He wanted to know if Uncle Thom would take him to a nicer place. When his Mom asked what he considered being a nicer place, he said, "Burger King" (Think McDonalds has some marketing work to do).

It's not that I don't have room in my life for other people, but I am trying to cultivate deep relationships with my dearest friends dating back to elementary school.

Eddie and Debbie Sherman from Waco. Eddie was the shortstop on our Little League World Series. Have known Eddie since the first grade. When I discovered I had cancer, Eddie and Debbie drove far out of their way to visit us in Broken Arrow, Oklahoma.

Reverend James Weaver and his wife, Susan from Urbandale, Iowa. James is Senior Pastor at New Hope Assembly of God. I first met James playing Pee Wee Baseball at age 9. He was also the first baseman on our Little League World Series Team. He has driven miles out of his way to visit us in our home.

Randy Willis and I were in Miss Dudley's first grade class together and we stood side by side for the class picture. Randy also drove up from the Dallas / Fort Worth area to visit us when I was going in for follow up after cancer surgery. Randy and his wife, Irene, are also cancer survivors. Randy was there when the Oncologist told Mary and me that I had Stage 4 colon cancer that had spread to my kidney area. Randy kept me from losing my mind that day.

The two other guys and their families upon whom I focus are part of the Three Amigos—Dale Tranberg, Ed Guthmann and me. I told Dale that he was the second best man at my wedding only because I was the one getting married. But technically, he was the Best Man. Ed is my brother from another mother. We were roommates in college and next-door neighbors for 17 years. Our boys were almost like brothers.

Virgil White is the friendship that both puzzles me and enriches me. One Black - One White, both from Texas and tastes so similar that it drives me crazy. We enjoy so many things in common that it's as if he is in my head, or vice versa. I can set him off into a laughing spasm almost at will because we laugh at the same triggers. He does the same to me.

There are so many other people as well that I want to maintain and build relationships with in the years that I have left. And I will. But the names I have listed are the ones that we have known the longest, lived next door to, lived together, gone to church together, worked together and shared each other's burdens.

The ones with whom I am running out of time for are my grandchildren. If I live to be 80-85, I will probably get to see the weddings of each grandchild. My family generally lives to be 75 (+/- 2 years). I'm counting on prayer to get me to 85. In case I don't make it to the granddaughters weddings, on this coming Sunday

March 18th, the day after our 40th Anniversary, I'm going to dance with each granddaughter who will be dressed in wedding gowns. Then, I'm going to give some personal insights about our marriage.

NOTE: I have saved and archived the videos that my Dad recorded for our kids and I am beyond frustrated that the video footage of my Dad dancing with his grand-daughters is forever lost by a careless videographer. I've forgiven his carelessness, but my mind is still blown every time that I think about the fact that he forgot to save the footage from "just another event" before deleting it to make room for "just another event."

Share my faith with my granddaughter and grandson-in-law. All of this will be captured on video so that no matter what happens, I will dance with my granddaughters at their wedding.

Like my Dad did, I want to build relationships that will last forever. Dad's legacy to me was his long held friendships.

Chapter 13

DOES ANYONE KNOW WHAT'S WRONG WITH OUR TEAM?

I sent this story to several of the basketball players. I wanted to check that they remember the day in question the same as I did. And they did.

Let's just say that our basketball team was just a few field goals short of successful. Or as James 'Lou Hudson' Bush liked to say, a few free throws short of victory. I remarked to 'Lou Hud' that I wasn't good at shooting free throws under pressure. To which he reminded me, "When was the score ever close enough that your free throws made a difference?"

Our fighting Tigers had given up over 100 points to Crozier Tech. Not once, but twice. How could that be? The high school game was only 32 minutes long (4 - 8 minute quarters). And this was basically the same team that had not lost even a handful of games all through junior high. It was an enigma.

Coach S. would have team meetings (also known as "skull sessions") before every practice. He wanted to impart motivation and strategy to the team. As our losses increased, it was obvious that we weren't getting the job done. And the coach was getting a bit depressed. One day he said, "I just don't understand. Why aren't we winning? Does anybody know what's wrong with our team?"

Anslum Hudlin immediately held up his hand and said, "I am Coach."

The coach looked surprised and said, "Well, Hud. Tell us. What's wrong with our team."

Hud said, "It's simple. We ain't worth a shit."

Several members of the team almost suffered internal injuries from stifling laughter. Coach got as mad as the proverbial 'wet hen' and kicked Hud out of the gym, then sent us out to shoot around while he lit up another Lucky Strike.

Several of the guys said it wasn't fair. "Hud gets to leave and we have to stay here. It's just not right."

Post Script:

The coach was quoted in the Waco newspaper as saying, "We just don't seem to be able to break a full-court press." So, guess what every team that played us for the entire year was to play? A full court press.

Chapter 14
DON'T TEST BEFORE SLEEP

A Pastor we knew was driving from Guymon, Oklahoma (a small town in the far northwest corner of Oklahoma), to Tulsa, Oklahoma, to celebrate an early Christmas with his son and daughter-in-law. The roads between Tulsa and Guymon were icy. The pastor hit a patch of black ice, losing control of the car, and driving into the ditch. Both the pastor and his wife were unhurt. Miraculously, the car had minimal damage also. The pastor and a passerby were able to push the car back on the road. So, they were back on their way to Tulsa, although they were in a much more guarded pace.

When they arrived in Tulsa, the pastor and his wife had quite a story to tell about the dangerous roads. The pastor seemed to be okay. He said, "I'm just not as young as I used to be. I think I pulled something in my left arm. It's really sore."

His son's next-door neighbor was a doctor, a friend from college who was doing his internship at Saint Francis Hospital. Despite the pastor's protest, Doc checked out pastor after which Doc called the hospital and told them he was bringing in someone for tests. The pastor protested strongly that he was all right. However, the doctor just said that he wanted to be sure.

It was Friday night. Most hospitals have limited if any staff available for cardiac testing, especially on a holiday weekend. The doctor then called in some favors from his associates. They did the tests and found that Bill was on the verge of a major heart attack. pastor was admitted to the hospital and placed in the Intensive Care Unit. They were able to locate a surgeon at his vacation home in northeast Oklahoma. A life flight helicopter was sent to pick him up. A multiple bypass operation was performed early Sunday morning. The surgery was successful, but it was a close call. If all the coincidences had not happened as they had, pastor would've died from a heart attack.

Everyone was in shock and relieved all at the same time. When the pastor awoke after surgery, he had tubes in his throat and was unable to talk, which was just as well since he was still heavily medicated. Being the strong-willed person that he is, the pastor persisted in trying to write notes to his family. The notes were all but incomprehensible. But one caught his son's attention. The note said, "don't test before sleep."

A couple days later, as the pastor's son was trying to keep the atmosphere light and positive, he asked his dad if knew what he had written on the notes because they were incomprehensible to the family. The pastor looked at the note that said, "don't test before sleep" and said emphatically, "I know exactly what I meant to say."

"What was that, dad?" asked the pastor's son.

"I know exactly what I meant to say. I thought the doctors were trying to cause a heart attack instead of preventing one."

"I don't get it. What do you mean?"

"The note meant don't test the saws before you have put me to sleep. The last thing I heard before I went under was ZZZZZZZZZZZZZZZZZZZZZZZZZ!"

Pictured above: My father smiles as he catches a fish. My father loved fishing.

Chapter 15

BET I CAN MAKE YOU FLINCH WITH JUST ONE WORD: DUMONT

If you don't react to the name Dumont, you never took chemistry at Waco High. Helen Dumont was a really tough teacher and, very good as well. She expected every student to complete their work properly (Gee, what a novel thought! High Expectations!?).

I had no siblings who had Miss Dumont for chemistry, but I had older cousins who did. It is almost 50 years later and I still flinch when I mention her name. I suspect many classmates found the same to be true when they told their parents that they were taking chemistry from Miss Dumont. She was a fixture at Waco High for many decades.

She expected everyone to live up to 'Her' standards, if you didn't (barring mental handicap), you were (and I quote her exactly), 'in a mel of a hess.' She tolerated no excuses. "I've got no time to listen to your tripe"........... whatever that meant. If she thought you were really off your rocker, Miss Dumont would respond to what you said with, "Oh, horse feathers and eagle fuzz." Still, I don't have a clue what that meant.

Her speech on the first day of the semester was masterful. She talked about a myriad of topics. Seemed almost to wander. I wish I were smart enough to say I discovered on my own what she was doing, but my cousin had already let me in on her secret. She was answering the age-old question before it was asked. Why do I have to take chemistry if I'm never going to use it after I leave high school? She was telling the students that a successful life is a never-ending journey of learning and chemistry was one of the tools needed for understanding the journey. That was just a bit too philosophical for me at age 17. Now in my 60s, it makes a bit more sense. Heck, I even went back to school at age 48 to get a degree in Metrology (aka, Measurement Science).

Okay, enough of the philosophical crap. She was tough.........almost mean. My source told me if I wanted to survive, or at least get her off my back, take a side regarding something she said and be prepared to defend it. "But whatever you do, let her win any arguments, or at least get the last word." And above all, pay attention or you would find that the chalkboard eraser that hit you in the middle of your back was thrown by none other than Miss Dumont herself. And incidentally, there were many examples of Miss Dumont going out of her way to help students that had unseen disabilities such as deafness or students that just couldn't grasp the content of the chemistry classes. She was a sweetheart down deep, but darned if she was ever going to let anyone know that.

One day she was discussing the relative value of alcohol powered machines vs petroleum powered. Which is better, she asked? I put up my hand immediately and chose the petroleum-powered machines.

'Okay, Mr. Clark. Tell me why.'

(Oh, @#$%, what have I done.) I said something to the effect of, "Well, Miss Dumont, gasoline powered machines have moved horsepower due to the greater amount of expansion from gas as opposed to the smaller expansion of ignited alcohol. Alcohol driven engines can make some adjustments to compensate, but all things being equal, gasoline gives more power. Also, alcohol has a corrosive effect on internal combustion parts. Alcohol tends to produce water as a by-product. This lowers the useful life span of the engine."

She replied, 'I see. So what makes you such an expert on the internal combustion engine?'

I said, 'I'm not ma'am. My father has been an auto mechanic for almost 40 years and I listen to what he says.'

She then said, 'Well, Mr. Clark, there may be some hope for you yet' (She did talk to me in a bit nicer tone for the remainder of my time in her class).

The highlight of the year was her discussion of the proper (proper meaning 'safe') method for the distillation of alcohol. In other words, she taught us how to make moonshine. She even had an idea or two about feeding the left over mash to cattle. I knew that she owned and operated a hobby farm. Could she have been fattening her cattle with mash from a still? Nah! She wouldn't do that.......would she?

She summarized telling us two things: 1) only use good quality copper for the tubing in the still so that you won't go blind from bad moonshine, and 2) as she pantomimed the reaction of taking a sip of moonshine, she said 'sip it real slooooooooooooooooooooow, because that stuff is going to light you up.'

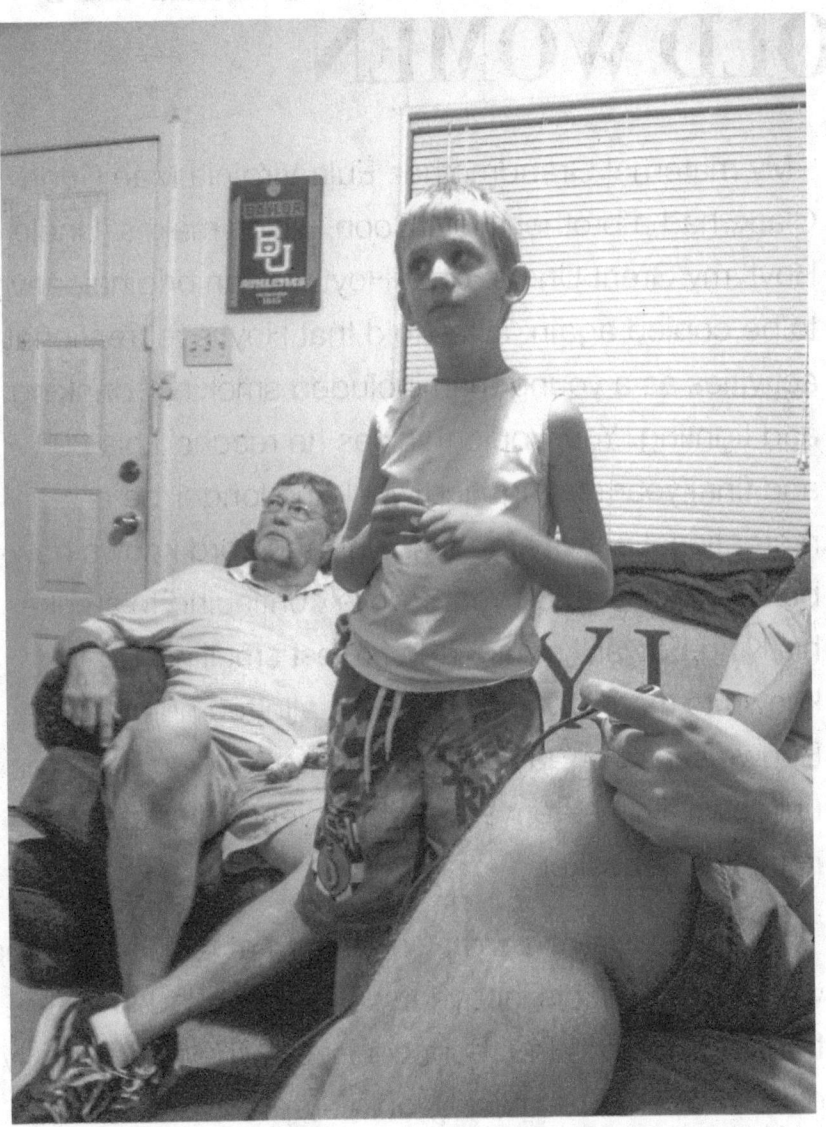

Pictured above: Aubrey Clark watches television with his grandfather, Thom Clark.

Chapter 16
EIGHTY-NINE YEAR OLD WOMEN

My maternal Grandmother, Eula Virginia Mae Coon Clark, had a brother, Hoyt Coon, which makes 'Uncle Hoyt' my Great Uncle. And, Hoyt was an original, never to be copied again. I was told that Hoyt's recreational activities as a young man included smoking, drinking, and fighting. You would think as he reached his 89th and final year that fighting would no longer be a recreational activity for him. Only the Lord knows how, but he made it to 89 years while continuing to smoke his King Edward cigars (the foulest smelling cigar known to mankind) and drink his allotted number of Budweiser's per day. The quantity of Budweisers was unknown, but there were always plenty of empty cans in the wastebasket.

My parents went to visit Uncle Hoyt at the 'Rest Home' where he spent his last years. They checked in at the front desk, telling the receptionist that they were family of Hoyt Coon. She quickly looked up and said, "I'm sure he will have a lot to tell you. But rest assured, he is doing okay, now."

"What do you mean, 'he is doing okay, now'?"

"Well, what I meant to say is that his hand is healing quite well."

"What happened to his hand?"

"He broke it," said the receptionist, "But, I'm sure he will tell you all about it."

"The man is almost stone deaf," said my Dad. "I doubt he'll even hear me when I ask him about his hand. How did he break it?"

"In a fight. He seemed rather proud about it."

"We're talking about the same person........Hoyt Coon. Age 89. Right?"

"One and the same."

"How does an 89 year old man break his hand in a fight?"

"You'll have to ask him, but I would say that there are some tough 94-year-olds in this world." Then, she directed my parents to the recreation area where he was trying to watch professional wrestling with the other 'kids' his age.

Sure enough, Uncle Hoyt had a cast on his hand. Mom and Dad tried to ask him about what happened to his hand. Between diatribes about Hans Schmidt being the dirtiest wrestler in the world, Uncle Hoyt told fragments of the story of his fight.

Mom and Dad almost 'busted a gut' laughing at Uncle Hoyt's explanation of what happened.

It seems that after breakfast in the dining room, all the wheelchair bound men would line up in the hallway to watch the 'women' pass by. On one particular day, there were some spacing problems and Uncle Hoyt was unable to park his wheelchair in his usual spot.

Think people get upset when you sit in someone's regular pew at church? Try taking an 89 year old's place when it is time to girl watch.

Uncle Hoyt told a 94-year-old man to get out of the way. He was parked in Uncle Hoyt's place. The 94-year-old, also almost stone deaf, took offense to whatever he thought Uncle Hoyt had said and told him to 'buzz off,' or something to that effect, only saltier.

Old habits die hard, so Uncle Hoyt leaned over to take a punch at his older nemesis. Sitting in a wheelchair restricted Uncle Hoyt's reach so that his punch fell far short of its mark. The other guy had the same results when he tried to punch back. So the only recourse for the older guy and Uncle Hoyt was to wheel their chairs into a clear spot for a primitive form of jousting.

It probably looked more like kids riding in bumper cars. They backed up, and then lurched forward making contact with their footrests. No damage done. Now each combatant tried another method. They attempted to side swipe each other. This allowed a jolting contact and put Uncle Hoyt within range to throw a punch. The 94-year-old tried to punch back.

Let's face it; punches from men/boys near the age of 90 don't have much force. It looked like Monday Night Football in slow motion. But, ramming each other did increase the g-factor as applied to contact.

NOTE: Dad, this is hilarious. Good job, you are cracking me up!

So, Uncle Hoyt and his 94-year-old opponent began to hit each other with their wheelchairs like a couple of bighorn sheep butting heads. That is when Uncle Hoyt miss-timed his thrust resulting in his hand getting caught between the chairs. The result; broken hand. Did that stop Uncle Hoyt? 'Oh, heck no,' (or something somewhat saltier) said Uncle Hoyt. The Rest Home personal had to grab their chairs and pull them apart. Each combatant was shouting at the other as they were wheeled away. The shouting was useless because they couldn't hear a word of what the other was saying.

This was funny enough for Mom and Dad to visualize what happened, but Hoyt's explanations were even better. The girl watching by the old man was not for the young girls (40-50 years old), rather it was for the 80-90-year-old women who went for their daily walk down the long hallway. The guys knew the 'young girls' were out of their league, but the 80-90-year-old women................well, that's another matter entirely.

Uncle Hoyt told how the 'lovely ladies' would walk down the hallway, smiling and waving at the 'boys' lined up in their wheelchairs. One thing that really impressed Uncle Hoyt was that some of the 'lovely ladies' didn't even need a walker or a cane. The guys would nudge each other and point, saying 'Look at her walk! Look at her walk!' All these guys lacked was background music of Sergio Mendes and Brazil '66 playing 'The Girl from Ipanema.'

I just can't get my mind wrapped around the idea of being attracted to an 89-year-old woman.

Now, for all those guys fighting for their place in the hallway at the rest home in Belton, Texas, this song is for you.

Cue Card: Take #1

Okay, roll the music:

The Girl from Ipanema

Tall and tan and young and lovely

The girl from Ipanema goes walking

And when she passes

Each one she passes goes "ah!"

When she walks she's like a samba that

Swings so cool and sways so gently

That when she passes,

Each one she passes goes "ah!"

Oh, but he watches her so sadly

How can he tell her he loves her?

Yes, he would give his heart gladly

But each day when she walks to the sea

She looks straight ahead not at him

Tall and tan and young and lovely

The girl from Ipanema goes walking

And when she passes he smiles

but she doesn't see.

Chapter 17

END OF ONE CHALLENGE AND THE BEGINNING OF ANOTHER

Today marks the last chemo treatment. I am attached to the "bag of poisons" (as my oncologist calls them) until Thursday morning. Then, I have a month off before I get my blood checked. So far my CEA (carcinoembryonic antigen) test that measures blood serum from cancer cells is below the level of anyone who does not have cancer. My PET (Positron emission tomography) scan in which a radioactive substance is injected makes cancer cells light up like a Christmas tree. And take it from this untrained layman; I could see cancer cells all up and down the right side of my body. They looked like plumes of water from a fountain on my first PET (positron emission tomography) scan. It's only $8,000 per PET scan, so run down to your local imaging center if you want to know what your insides look like. Now, there is NOTHING to be seen. The cancer is gone. My oncologist says I am in remission.

Okay, a round of applause is in order for God, our healer. And, let's have another round of applause for everyone who prayed for me. I want to say thank you to each and everyone who prayed for us and provided meals in the days following my surgery. Thank You,.........

Well, you get the idea.

Now round two begins. We (oncologist, Dr. Muhammad Janjua and I) were trying to find the source of my migraines. We pinpointed that they occurred following exercise/activity. He looked at my records and noted several things: my heart rate is getting lower; my previously irregular heartbeat is even more irregular now, and my atrial-flutter (less intense than atrial-fibrillation, but it is moving from flutter towards fibrillation). The probability of a stroke, embolism, or heart attack has been multiplied significantly. Even the medical techs in the chemo infusion lab noticed the change in my pulse and irregularity of the heart rhythm in the last 2 months.

Time out. Can you imagine a more 'old folks' blog than this? If people my age were not allowed to talk about their infirmities, there would be virtual silence.

Mary and I went on a tour of Hawaii for our 50th Birthday and we were the youngest people with the tour. After that tour, I knew then more about heart bypasses, cancer treatments, and polka than any other 50-year-old on the Mainland.

Back to the narrative which old geezers like me find so fascinating: I have an appointment with my cardiologist next week. Before talking with her, I already know that there are blood thinners that will lower the risk of stroke, but there are side effects that I would just as soon miss. Some of the blood thinners are simply rat poison in lower doses (As Rodney Dangerfield said, 'I don't get no respect.' I walked into a store and asked for rat poison. The clerk asked if I wanted it wrapped up or did I want to eat it here). Another possibility is a pacemaker. That is ironic in that I was calibration tech for Medtronic before I moved back to Broken Arrow, Oklahoma. I know the standards that they apply to their products. They are great. Medtronic is the largest manufacturer of pacemakers in the world. If I do require a pacemaker, I hope to get it while they are an American company (they are moving to Ireland and taking their $48 billion dollars with them. Just a side note that has no bearing on my Atrial fibrillation).

Okay, I was vain about losing my hair to chemotherapy (Didn't happen and I got a supply of great hats). Just as cell phones are getting thinner, I hope they have done the same with their pacemakers. No big deal. Guess Billy Stubblefied is going to be wrong now. He told me in the 7th grade that I was so skinny that my chest looked like the inside of a spoon. Not with a pacemaker it won't!

So, those are my best guesses I have regarding my heart. It is amazing what you can learn on a tour of Hawaii. Now I'll get to hear what a real live cardiac specialist has to say.

Finishing one race and beginning another race back to back is a little dis-hearting. I'm still in good spirits because I know God's Promise for me. According to the Bible,

"And we know that all things work together for good to them that love God, to them who are the called according to his purpose."

— Romans 8:28

I ask for your prayers again. Thank you for all who have prayed intensely for me since the cancer issue began in early January. As long as my sense of humor is intact, you will know that I am living out what God has called me to do. Am I worried? A bit, which indicates that I'm not entirely stupid or oblivious to my circumstances. The one thing that I want to do is accompany my wife to our grandchildren's weddings and dance with the brides (or do wheelies with my wheelchair, as the case maybe). This will require another 25+ years. So if you want something specific for which to pray, that is it.

Is my sense of humor and references to bizarre ironies still intact? I ask you, who could quote Romans 8:28 and Rodney Dangerfield in the same blog?

Pictured above: My father always worked to keep a smile on his face as he battled cancer then Lou Gherig's Disease. I really need to go to Atwoods and look at their inventory of sheds right about now.

Chapter 18
FAREWELL ADDRESS

I vaguely remember from History class stories about 'farewell addresses.' George Washington had a farewell address to his troops. Winston Churchill had a farewell address to Great Britain as he stepped down as Prime Minister. General MacArthur made a farewell address to the U.S. Congress as he retired from the military.

But the 'farewell address' that I remember was from Coach Robert C. Cloud as he spoke to his 7th grade football team at the end of the season. I have mentioned this 'address' to several of our Waco High School classmates as we talked about memories of North Junior High. The response is generally a blank stare. It is quite likely that I would have forgotten the essence of what Coach Cloud said had it not been for the reaction of several people. The responses were VERY different which is what burned the image into my mind.

Please note: I am going to be more 'vague' than usual out of respect to the personal feelings of several of our teammates. There are some deep emotional connections and reactions to what Coach Cloud said.

Pardon me as I paraphrase what Coach said. The words are not exact, but the message is on point.

"You are winners. Not just because you won all but one game, but because of the character you displayed. I worked hard for you hard, pushing you beyond what you believed you were capable of doing. Many young men quit the team. But, all of you sitting here didn't. You persevered. And, you won all but one game you played this year because you were dedicated and wouldn't quit. I am proud of your success, and I am proud of each one of you. If I didn't care, I wouldn't have pushed you so hard. I want you to know that I love you. I believe in you. And, I want you to continue making the right choices that will make you successful in your lives."

NOTE: After much deep thought, I have no idea how my Dad remembered a farewell address from a middle school basketball coach. I do not remember anything that my coach said to me at all during 7th grade and I can't remember my 7th grade coach's name.

There were 3 responses to Coach Cloud's address:

1. Wow! That was great! Let's go conquer the world!

2. Hey, what time does the bus get here?

3. Who are you kidding? There isn't anyone who cares about me.

I sat at the back of the bleachers, watching the reactions. The 'indifference' reaction was somewhat bothersome, while being a bit funny at the same time. I guess I was in the group with the 'enthusiastic' reaction. But the look of pain in the eyes of the group on the second row to my right was almost heartbreaking. There were several teammates that I specifically noted their reaction to. Sorry, I can't (and won't) say who they were. They appeared to have given up on life already at the age of 13.

"Some people die at 25 and aren't buried until 75."

— **Benjamin Franklin**

(One of the Founding Fathers of the United States, a printer, a leading writer, an inventor, a scientist, a postmaster, and a legendary polymath.)

I'll fast forward to today. I know that a couple of those former teammates chose to make bad decisions that have in turn ruined their lives. As for some of the others, frankly, I have no idea. But, there are a few that decided to make good decisions in their lives. They have achieved successes that we would have never dreamed for them, much less that they would have dreamed for themselves. You will have to work extra hard at our high school reunion to get these guys to tell you what they have done in their lives, because the pain in their early childhood has made them reclusive even with the great successes in their careers and their families.

Was Coach Cloud's address the turning point? I don't know. Probably not. It is more likely a series of people, like Coach Cloud, that influenced lives and contributed to helping change lives. And I know a couple of those teammates have made mentoring/coaching/teaching (whatever you want to call it) the focus of their lives. One of these teammates has spent millions of dollars to help friends whose lives have been shattered for a multitude of reasons.

I hope you asked around at the reunion to see what our fellow classmates have done to help others. You were sure to be surprised.

FYI (For Your Information)**:** Dr. Robert C. Cloud attended our informal get together on Friday night at Crickets restaurant. I suspect that he didn't have any memory of our team's farewell address. If you read his bio (you can find it via Google or via the Baylor University website), it refers to the 'encouragement' of his students while remaining supportive. The translation is: "Robert C. Cloud works you half to death because he believes in you and is committed to your success." It would appear that Dr. Cloud made a habit of encouraging right decisions. His farewell address is not likely to stand out as a specific event to him because this has been his modus operandi for over 40 years.

Thanks, Dr./Coach Cloud. (Even if you #%$@ near ran me to death).

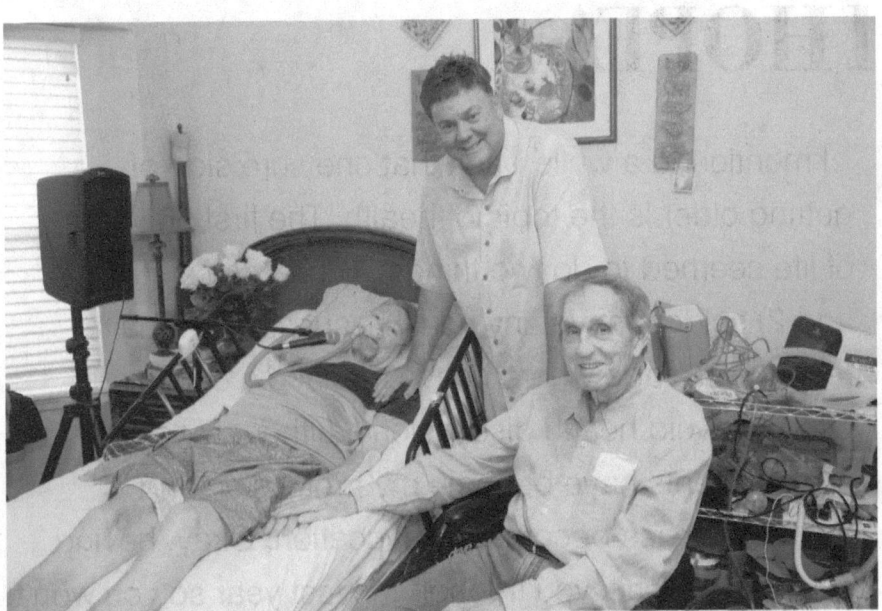

Pictured above: Legendary college basketball coach, Eddie Sutton and his son Steve Sutton stopped by to visit my father as he battled Lou Gehrig's disease. At the end I hooked up a microphone and speaker system so that people could hear my dad when he attempted to talk. I never thought my vast knowledge of microphones and sound equipment would be used to help people hear my father as he was dying and desperately wanting to be heard. Coach Sutton, I know you are also in heaven now. Thank you for holding my father's hand near the end. You were a great coach for my father sir.

Chapter 19

FINAL UPDATE FOR A WHILE............ I HOPE!

I mentioned a while back that one sure sign of getting older is the topic of health. The first 50 years of life seemed to do two things: 1) go by in a flash, and 2) seldom have any health issues. Well, I have reached the age where I have to make a conscious effort to avoid health discussions, although doctor appointments have become my profession and accounting has become my avocation. Okay, having said this, I'll walk you through the last year so you won't have to hear the details second hand. I also would like to filter the 'state of my health' address through the lenses of God's grace to me.

Starting in September 2013 and ranging over a number of months I had some weird intestinal problems. Watching cramps move across my abdomen like a snake crawling inside me was disconcerting. And yes, that hurt. My team of doctors went one step at a time trying to rule out simple issues. Finally, I had a colonoscopy ('many years overdue' per my wife, Mary...does it bother any of you guys out there that our wives seem to always be right? Well, get over it).

On January 15, 2014, I finally had that long overdue colonoscopy. A tumor the size of my fist was discovered (and remember, my hand can palm a basketball). They immediately had me take another test to verify that nothing had metastasized to the surrounding organs.

- Good news: the tumor had not spread.
- Bad news: A biopsy was done. The tumor was malignant.

Dr. Conkling explained several options for treatment, of which I heard "blah, blah, blah, blah, blah, blah, blah, blah, blah, blah, blah, blah, blah, blah, blah, blah." I was so stoned that I couldn't understand a word he said. The walk from my wheelchair to my car, which was about 6 feet, felt like climbing Mount Everest. Wow, talk about being stoned!

The immediate feedback indicated that most if not all of the cancer was removed with the tumor and apparently no cancer cells had metastasized to surrounding organs. Multiple people recommended Dr. Marc Rocklin as the surgeon that I should see.

Interestingly enough, I already had an appointment set up with Doc Rock before receiving the recommendations. It is already starting to happen. God is showing that he is in control.

This is the point at which God led me to a decision. How was I going to handle this situation? The answer is that I am going to have a positive attitude, no matter what. Easier said than done, but the simple issue for me was this: 'What good is it going to do by being chronically depressed and morose?' So, I stole a line from the late Dr. Randy Pausch from Carnegie Mellon University who said the following while delivering his last lecture, "If you are expecting me to be sad and morose, I'm sorry to disappoint you" (Do yourself a favor and Google 'Randy Pausch, last lecture').

I had the pre-op done in advance of my surgery, which was scheduled for January 27th. Sort of a bummer, since I would rather eat birthday cake on January 27th instead of having a tumor removed. God answered my wish. Surgery was postponed when they discovered I had atrial fibrillation, an abnormally slow heartbeat, and an irregular heartbeat (So, I got to eat my cake).

The nurse who performed the pre-op exam was a bit befuddled that Mary and I were acting like we were just there to pick up tickets for a movie. No big deal! The nurse said, "most people were more 'concerned' than you are." Mary gently explained that we had a supernatural peace that only comes from God. We talked for a while and learned that the nurse was a preacher's kid from Minnesota. Of course, I had to be a wise guy and steal Randy Pausch's line, 'If I'm not as sad or morose as I should be, I'm sorry to disappoint you. The end result of this is going to be good no matter what happens. If my condition goes down hill, my only regret will be missing the weddings of my granddaughters." She left the room crying. I really didn't mean to upset her, but I was a man on a mission to trust in God no matter what.

I had known about my irregular heartbeat since I was 12 years old when they almost did not allow me to play in the Little League World Series because of it. As fat as I am, I still considered a pulse of 45-50 as a badge of honor to show that there was still some 'athlete' left in me, yet. The A-Fib…that was a surprise. I visited a cardiologist who asked if I ever felt faint? 'No.' Can I walk a block? 'Several miles if I have to.' Can I climb stairs? 'I climb a 16 step stairway usually 20 or more times per day.' So, my cardiologist said I was fully able to undergo surgery. "BUT, I want to see you a month after you finish chemo."

Okay, so let's get this show on the road. Then: 'God to Thom. God to Thom. I have a message for you.'

'Yes, Lord. What is it?'

'You need to learn to be more adaptable to change.'

'Okay, Lord. Let's get this surgery out of the way and we can work on that adaptability thing.'

Granted a terrible joke, but I got put on hold. Patience was not my middle name when it came to waiting for surgery. My Cobra Insurance Policy ended the last day of February. It was, of course, a weekend day. Therefore, a delay of several days could be expected before my new insurance company could approve the surgery. Then, surgery could be rescheduled. There was nothing to do except say, 'Okay, Lord. You want this surgery delayed for some reason. And, I choose not to fight you about it.'

Then, the snake started crawling across my belly and I couldn't keep any food down beginning on Friday night, January 31. The pain was more than a little rough. Mary drove me to the emergency room making sure that she hit every pothole and bump in the road all the way from Broken Arrow to Saint Francis Hospital. Dr. Rocklin made a visit to the hospital. He determined that I was going to have surgery on Monday, February 3rd. And he also put me on the greatest weight loss diet known to mankind: nothing but ice chips for three days. They tell me that I was taken down for surgery at 9:00 p.m. on Monday night. I came out of surgery sometime around midnight. Doc Rock told my wife and sons that it looked like he was able to get most of the tumor, but the biopsy on the lymph nodes would tell me if it had spread.

Chapter 20

HOYT AND WILLIE, BORROWING HORSES AND THEIR FUTURE

My grandmother, Eula Mae Coon Clark, had a much younger brother, Hoyt Coon. He would pay me a quarter to fetch something for him; like his box of cigars, lighter, and a couple of cans of Budweiser.

Grandma's oldest son was Willie Hoyt Clark, who was just a few years younger than her hesitate to call Hoyt a 'never do well,' perhaps a hustler was a better description. He always had enough money for food, a little liquor, and some smokes. His lifelong preference was King Edward cigars that were undoubtedly the foulest smelling tobacco product ever produced. Hoyt could always hustle up a dollar. 'How' was none of our business. Some cousins told me that they thought Hoyt was a mean man and scared them to death. Being the youngest of the cousins, I only knew Great Uncle Hoyt as a stooped over old man who used a pair of canes to walk. He and his brother, Hoyt, were always bribing me. It is unclear from my Uncle Bill (he changed his name from Willie to William when he began his career as a commercial artist) whether he instigated some of Hoyt and Willie's shenanigans. Uncle Bill told some great stories about himself and Hoyt, especially since the statute of limitations had run out. It seems they were prone to 'borrow' horses from time to time. They were careful to put the horses where they could be easily found; sort of like borrowing a car for the evening and returning it a block away from where it was 'borrowed.'

Hoyt had no particular vision regarding his future. His qualifications for any specific career were unclear. He was a fast runner, brutal fighter, and an excellent shot with a firearm. He was about 5'7" tall and was an excellent baseball player. I was told that he was a shortstop. Whether he was good enough to advance to some level beyond town ball would never be known because of his temper. Though an excellent athlete, he was a better fighter. He liked to tell me that 'the bigger they are, the harder they fall.' His participation in games was limited due to being thrown out of games for fighting. Hoyt was also an excellent shot with a rifle or shotgun. I had a hard time believing his stories about shooting snakes until I saw him shoot the head off a 5+ foot long diamondback rattlesnake. He made a believer out of me.

Willie (known to me as Uncle Bill) was, as mentioned, just a few years younger than Hoyt. As Willie told the family, "Me and Hoyt were good at raising hell, but not so good as to get thrown in jail." Hoyt seemed to be the ideal guy. There was no shortage of liquor and tobacco. The inference that I got from Willie was that they would go down to Stampede Creek, just south of Moody, Texas, to just sit around and get liquored up. Since cars weren't widely owned in the late 1910s, there wasn't much chance of running over someone and killing them. The biggest problem was not getting killed when trying to mount a horse when in an intoxicated condition. Since Hoyt was the heavy drinker, Willie's job was to somehow push Hoyt onto his horse. Then, Willie would lead him home.

I deduced from Willie's stories that he and Hoyt enjoyed 'bathroom' humor. More specifically, out-houses. Hoyt and Will were experts at moving the outhouses back a couple of feet and scuffing up the ground in front so as to make everything look undisturbed. This was particularly effective in the dark. The first step into the outhouse was a doozy...... or should I say nasty. Another favorite was to get a beehive and put it in the outhouse. That was a rough task for Hoyt and Willie, but the plan would work to perfection whether day or night.

Incidentally, the outhouse on the Coon's farm was a '3-holer.' Somehow I never thought of going to the bathroom as a communal event. I was told that there was a high stack of Sears and Roebuck catalogs in the corner. As for their purpose, let your imagination run wild and you will probably be correct. How Hoyt managed to obtain the stacks of catalogs was something that Great Grandpa Coon apparently didn't bother asking Hoyt about.

Willie told the story about when he and Hoyt were sitting around a fire, drinking and smoking. It came to Willie that perhaps they could be more constructive with their lives. Surprisingly, Hoyt listened. The inspiration for this conversation was a poster they saw telling about a traveling evangelist who was having a tent meeting in Moody, which was about 5 miles away.

Willie said, "Hoyt, so you think that tent meeting would do us some good?"

Hoyt took another hit from his bottle and said, "Nephew, you might just have a good idea. I know it would make your Momma and Daddy happy."

So it was off to Moody for the tent revival. Five miles was a long way to walk, so Hoyt decided to 'borrow' some horses from the farm a couple of miles down the road. They quietly took the horses and headed towards Moody. Hoyt made sure he had his bottle, tobacco, rolling papers, and some matches with him. Willie thought it was a good idea to get rid of all their sinful items by the time they arrived. Hoyt agreed. They pledged to consume all the liquor and tobacco before arriving at the tent meeting so that they wouldn't have any 'contraband' with them.

NOTE: This is hilarious. I love that my Dad remembered these things and actually took the time to write them down.

Besides, Hoyt said he didn't want to tempt anyone by leaving a partially filled bottle of liquor where someone might find it. Upon arrival, the borrowed horses were skittish and making some noise. No problem. Hoyt and Willie 'borrowed' some feed bags and some oats, which seemed to keep the horses satisfied. Neither Hoyt nor Willie had counted on the tent meeting lasting 3 hours. The preacher kept an eye on them the whole service. They were trapped and could not leave. The preacher would point at Hoyt and Willie and preach about 'lost young men' every time they even thought about getting out of their chairs. Finally, everyone stood up to sing a hymn. They ducked down low, crept out to the horses, mounted and took off in a flash.

"Well, Hoyt. What do you think? Is religion going to take?"

"I don't know, Willie. Seems like they spend a long time talking and shouting," said Hoyt. "Not sure if I'm ever going back."

Flash forward over 60 years later. I had just gotten my driver's license. Uncle Hoyt asked me to give him a ride to church. He said I wouldn't have to stay. Someone would bring him back. I helped him out of the car and he crept along on his crutches. A greeter opened the door and what should I see inside but a bunch of Pentecostals with hands raised, dancing around the church. That was a little too much at that time for this Presbyterian born and bred 18-year-old. But, Uncle Hoyt had the biggest grin on his face you had ever seen. He was welcomed even though he smelled like Budweiser and King Edward cigars.

Willie (by this time, I only knew him as Uncle Bill) had moved to Chicago to study art. He became a successful commercial artist. His big national account for years was Lennox Heating and Cooling. I enjoyed visiting him and getting to see his office, high in a Chicago skyscraper.

Uncle Bill's dad and my granddad, Joe Willie Clark, was a Deacon in the Mart, Texas, Presbyterian Church for decades. My dad, T. Clayton Clark, the youngest of Joe Willie Clark's children, served as a Deacon at Westminster Presbyterian Church in Waco, Texas, for decades, also. Uncle Bill mentioned that he tried to keep up his average for going to church by at least attending on Christmas and Easter. His level of involvement with the church or his faith is unknown. I was visiting Chicago and I remember someone bringing up the name Jesus and there was a dead silence.

So regarding my great uncle, Hoyt Coon, 'religion took' on some level.

Regarding uncle Willie 'Bill' Clark, it was hard to see where 'religion took'. In fairness, after Willie's wife died a slow, painful death from cancer, he didn't seem to have much use for God in his life. I hope I'm wrong.

Pictured above: My father pauses from his work for a moment to have his photo taken with Aubrey Clark and Havana Clark from the balcony of our downtown Tulsa office. Dad, editing this book has been one of the hardest things in my life to do. I think I need to just start editing this book from Atwoods.

Chapter 21

IS THIS THE BEST MAN YOU'VE GOT?

In the 1970s and 80s I worked in the furniture business as a salesman. The owner of this furniture store was a very intelligent man. And if you didn't believe it, he would be happy to tell you that he was and explain to you why he had a superior intellect. This owner, a.k.a. "My Boss", just simply loved to argue. No matter what you said, he would take the opposite position.

Our company was going through an expansion, which required building extra display room space as well as extra warehouse space. My Boss had a degree in electrical engineering; consequently, he designed every feature of the electric wiring for the expansion.

The electrical contractor we used was well known in Tulsa and was very reputable and they tried to send the same electrician over each time. When the day arrived to begin the installation, My Boss stood at the door waiting for the electrician to arrive.

The moment the electrician set foot inside the building, My Boss jumped out in front of the electrician. He looked like one of the crazy managers of a baseball team that is having an argument with an umpire. He shuffled his feet side to side so he could stay in front of him the entire way as they walked to the electrical junction box. No matter which way the electrician turned, My Boss would jump in front of the electrician with his nose no-less than a foot away.

My boss then began to go through the entire electrical circuitry schematic to verify that the electrician understood every feature that was built into the schematic and he told him how he wanted them labeled. He also explained what type of wiring he wanted.

Oddly enough, the electrician did not seem fazed in the least by the borderline ranting and raving that My Boss was engaged in. The more My Boss carried on in an agitated manner, the more the electrician seemed to relax and smile. The more the electrician smiled, the angrier my boss became.

Then the electrician held up his hand to indicate that he wanted My Boss to stop for a moment so that he could examine the junction box. The electrician opened the electrical junction box, took a step back, folded his arms and said in his best Gomer Pyle imitation, "Golly. Look at all them wires. Shazam, this must have been really complicated to draw."

My Boss began to shake with rage as he thought the electrical firm had sent the village idiot to our location to install this complicated schematic. He then ran down the hallway and called the electrical company to start raising Cain with them about why they would send such an obvious idiot to install the system.

As My Boss ran down the hallway to his office to make that call, the electrician looked over his shoulder at us, smiled and said, "Works every time."

Then, several sales staff and I quickly ran to the office to hear him yell, "What do you mean that you sent me your best man?"

This electrician had learned long ago that he could reduce our boss to an apoplectic state such that My Boss would eventually get a headache and have to go lay down on the sofa in his office. Then the electrician said, "Now, I can get some work done."

Pictured above from left to right: Havana Clark, Thom Clark (my Dad), Annie Moore (my mother-in-law), Scarlett Clark, Laya Clark, Vanssa Clark, me (Clay Clark), Aubrey Clark, Angelina Clark & Mary Clark (my mom) take a photo at our annual Christmas party. I don't put a lot of photos of my father up around my office because I can't ever deal with the fact that a man so good suffered such a horrible death. Dad, we miss you.

Chapter 22

JIMMY - JIMMY - JIMMY, WHAT WERE YOU THINKING?

I played on the 1965 Waco Northern Little League baseball team. We played 10 games to win the state championship of Texas, two games for the regionals in Norfolk, Virginia, and three games at the Little League World Series in Williamsport, Pennsylvania. We finished third after losing a game 1-0 in the rain. Flying across the country for the first time, standing as observers (try doing that today) in the control tower of the Washington DC airport, going aboard aircraft carriers in Virginia that were down for resupply, going to a New York Mets/San Francisco Giants baseball game and seeing Willie Mays hit his 49th home run that season, and going to The World's Fair in Flushing, New York was a trip in a series of events that we carried with us all these years. Except, for the one player who quit because he preferred to deliver newspapers and to swim in the public swimming pool. Bad move Jimmy. Bad, bad move.

It is believed that James Guerra really was standing by the side of the street with his basketful of newspapers watching us as we drove by on the way to City Hall to receive the key to the city and special proclamations honoring the success of our baseball team.

Pictured above my father and mother visited our 1100 Riverwalk Terrace office in Jenks, Oklahoma. Every time my father visited the office I would have a complete and total breakdown when he would leave. I could not stop crying and now as I'm adding captions to these photos he's doing it to me again!

Chapter 23
JULIO FRANCO
(46 JOKES ABOUT THE ONLY MAN TO HAVE PLAYED BASEBALL WITH MOSES)

Julio Franco played for 7 Major League Baseball teams over a 23-year span. My sons and I didn't pay much attention until he reached 40 years of age. We laughed and marveled at his ability at his advancing age for a baseball player. Hold onto your head. Julio has made a comeback as a 55-year old player / coach for the Fort Worth Cats. The following are rejected jokes for David Letterman's top ten when Julio played for the New York Mets at age 48.

Julio Franco's Major League Baseball spanned from 1982 to 2007. During this Epic career he averaged a .298 batting average, hit 173 home runs, and amassed 2,586 hits. Julio Franco is the oldest Major League Baseball to "officially" hit a homerun at the 48. He was the oldest player to hit a grand slam and the oldest major baseball player to hit a pinch-hit home run. Julio had a very unique batting stance that was often referred to as a "whip-like" batting style. Throughout his career Julio was named to the All-Star team three times and he won the "Silver Slugger" award five times for being the best offensive player at a given position on a Major League Baseball team.

Ladies, you are welcome to skip this blog. Guys, I leave it up to your judgment. Should I approach Letterman again about having Julio on Late Night with David Letterman?

1. Julio Franco was the victim of Ben Franklin's practical joke when he was given a quill pen dipped in disappearing ink. Had it not been for this joke, he would have been the 57th signer of the Declaration of Independence.

2. His favorite pet as a child was Dino, the dinosaur.

3. Franco's rookie card was made of stone. Paper had not yet been invented.

4. Julio Franco's rookie card is very rare. Only 50 of them were ever chiseled.

5. Early in Franco's career, the players didn't go to strip clubs. Mankind had not started to wear clothes.

6. The club house boy responsible for cleaning uniforms would take Franco's uniform after games to beat it on a rock.

7. Franco not only knows the names of each president, he has their personalized autographs.

8. One autograph says, 'Julio, never lie about your age. Signed, George Washington."

9. Julio isn't impressed by the post-game buffets. After all, it's tough to top the Last Supper.

10. The west coast trips were real killers during Julio's early days in the league. It was almost impossible to sleep on a stagecoach.

11. Franco not only remembers when they discovered King Tut's tomb, he remembers the opening day when Tut threw out the first pitch.

12. During Franco's early days in the league, running the bases was chaotic. Players didn't know where to go until the invention of numbers.

13. Back then, Julio had to paddle the water himself if he wanted treatment in a whirlpool bath.

14. Before the term Long Ball was used, Harry Carray referred to Julio's home runs as pre-Cambrian Clouts.

15. Julio's frozen rope line drives got their name during the Ice Age.

16. During Julio's early years, relief pitches rode in from the bullpen on mastodons.

17. Julio never faced a knuckleball pitcher during the first half of his career. Pitchers were still dragging their knuckles on the ground.

18. It is much easier to quantify Julio's success following the invention of arithmetic.

19. Gloves in the early days of baseball were much smaller and had no padding. Julio's first glove could have been used for prostate exams.

20. After a few years in the league, Julio bought a first baseman's mitt when he changed positions. He got a signature series mitt autographed by Moses.

21. Recent anthropological findings have proved conclusively that Julio Franco was playing second base when Babe Ruth hit his 643rd home run.

22. Julio will undergo Carbon 14 testing to determine his real age.

23. Bud Selig's first ruling as Commissioner was on the legality of Franco using petrified bats.

24. The Dead Sea Scrolls were found to include Julio's stats from his first five years.

25. There was no need for an alcohol policy when Julio came into the league. Jim Beam and Jack Daniels hadn't been born yet.

26. High and tight back in Julio's early days was the location of a pitch, not the condition of a player.

27. It was a big day for Julio when his number, XXXII, was retired by the baseball commissioner, Julius Caesar.

28. Julio remembers the opening day when the calendar changed from BC to AD.

29. Julio dated Wilma before she met Fred Flintstone.

30. Adam and Eve ate the apple in the Garden of Eden and learned the difference between good and evil. Julio ate the cumquat and learned the difference between balls and strikes.

31. Julio once beat Ty Cobb in a foot race...of course, Ty was 3 years old at the time.

32. Julio was watching a Geico commercial one day and thought, 'Wow, I think I dated that caveman's sister during my rookie season.'

33. Like Ted Williams who missed several seasons to military service during his prime, Julio missed several years during his prime while stowed away on Noah's ark.

34. Whereas Babe Ruth's career spanned the dead ball and home run eras, Julio's career spanned the Paleolithic and Mesozoic.

35. Julio is an eyewitness to evolution. He has seen Barry Bonds evolve from baseball player to mastodon.

36. Julio's teammates didn't chew tobacco until Columbus brought it back from the New World.

37. During Julio's early years in the American League, the post-game chicken dinners were catered by Private Sanders.

38. Moving the batting cage into place was made much easier with the invention of the wheel.

39. Julio remembers when before the invention of the protective screen, batting practice pitchers used to throw the ball and duck behind a rock.

40. Julio gave some thought to switching from second base to catcher, but only after the invention in 1885 of the protective cup.

41. Julio was partially responsible for Pete Rose's all time hit record. He planted the tree used to make Pete's bat.

42. Julio is familiar with several Bush's.........George H.W., George W., and the burning bush that he pointed out to Moses.

43. Julio believes today's cowhide covered baseball is juiced up compared to the brontosaurus covered baseball.

44. Julio has hit for the cycle in baseball nicknames...........kid, fella, pops, and gramps.

45. Julio's goal is to be the first player to play with his great, great, great, great, great grand-son during the father-son game.

46. In the early days of the league, Cleveland had cheerleaders for their baseball team. Julio dated a cheerleader named Pocahontas.

Chapter 24
LINKING–CULTURES / COMPUTERS / SPELLCHECK

I lived for 13 years in Minnesota. I became acutely aware of the number of communities that were formed by European immigrants. The county in which I lived, Wright County, had a population of approximately 30,000 of which more than 20,000 people were from Finnish descent.

The Texas County in which I was born, McLennan County, at a high percentage of Scottish settlers. The local junior college, McLennan Community College, commonly referred to as MCC, has as its mascot a Highlander. This is a reference to people from certain areas of Scotland.

Further south in Texas, there's a high German population in such towns as New Braunfels and Fredericksburg. If the monologue from a tourist guide in San Antonio is to be believed, the official language for the state of Texas missed by one vote of being German instead of English. If that were true and Texas had kept German as an official language, we would be much like Canada today in which French and English languages coexist as official languages. As late as the late 1960s, I had a conversation with a co-worker in which he stated that he went to a "good Lutheran church." I asked the man what was the difference between a good Lutheran Church and a bad Lutheran Church. He said it was simple to recognize a good Lutheran Church because everything spoken word was in German, not in English.

While living in Minnesota, my family attended a church that is formed as part of the Swedish Lutheran church. The Constitution of their church and various Bible verses inscribed on the walls were all in Swedish. It occurred to me that I have gone to a cousin's wedding in Clifton, Texas, which was held in a Swedish Lutheran Church. Another cousin referred to Clifton as the Swedish capital of Texas. Perhaps another influence, even within my family.

My first name is spelled T-H-O-M. According to my father, this is an abbreviated form of Thomas, as it would be spelled in Scotland. Somewhere along the line, the 'E' was dropped by some relatives in North Carolina who had migrated originally from Scotland. One side of my family was named Wallace. There is no proof of it, but we enjoy saying we are related to William Wallace (the famous Scottish Knight portrayed by Mel Gibson in his epic classic movie, Braveheart). So it is fairly well established that I am Scottish. To set the record straight, my name has been spelled T-H-O-M for all of my 61+ years and my father was rather dedicated to maintaining this Scottish heritage.

Why am I giving history lessons and the background of cultures? Let's just say that things in life are tied together and come back to mind for the oddest of reasons.

Example: The librarian at North Waco elementary was insistent that I was not spelling my name correctly when I wrote Thom instead of Tom when checking out books. I explained to Ms. McCartney, the librarian, that I spelled my name Thom. She disagreed vigorously and stated that arguing with her showed that I had a bad attitude. Not knowing the rules of engagement between first-graders and librarians, I simply stated that she was wrong and didn't know what she was talking about. Not a very persuasive way in which to convince Ms. McCartney that I knew what I was doing. Then Miss McCarty pulled what she thought was the trump card. She said she was going to call my parents. To which I responded, "Go ahead. They named me Thom." At which point she just about blew a gasket!

Miss McCartney was true to her word. She called my house and my father answered the phone. She explained the situation and told my dad what he should do to punish me. My father proceeded to tell her that we are not Hispanic. We do not spell Thomas, T-O-M-A-S. We are Scottish and we spell Thomas, T-H-O-M-A-S. Therefore, the contraction of my son's name will be spelled Thom.

Of course I was young enough and stupid enough not to know better than to rub it in next time I checked out a book at the library. I checked out the book of my choice, signed it T-H-O-M, turned to Miss McCartney and said, "see, I told you so."

Fast-forward about 40 years. Computers are ubiquitous. And they all seem to share one common attribute-spellcheck. And wouldn't you know it, for the first year that I had my Mac computer it changed my name from Thom to Tom every time I typed my name. I have subsequently trained my computer to type Thom instead of Tom. This little episode gave me the idea of possibly naming my computer: Miss McCartney.

Chapter 25

LIVING UP TO EXPECTATIONS

My Dad, Clayton Clark, had a unique ability that I am sad to say that I lacked, he could follow directions. When it came to putting things together, he simply read the instructions. It was apparent to me that he read instructions from beginning to end before he began a project. He assembled all the parts or found substitute parts before he began working on a project. I unfortunately start with step number one and push through full speed ahead. Oh, I should also say that he had patience. In my eyes, he could fix anything.

Cousins would limp into Waco with their 'old beater cars' and ask Dad if he could fix it. Dad would just say, "Let's take a look and see what we can do." And, it seemed like he could always get their old cars running. I'm sure there were some cars that should have been shot and put out of their misery, but Dad would somehow work a miracle.

At our small church in Waco, Dad would repair all manner of plumbing and carpentry problems. Dad repaired a wall that had been deteriorating due to a water leak. He fixed the plumbing. Then he didn't just repair the exterior wall, he rebuilt it. The project was rather large and Dad did it all by himself.

The interim Pastor was admiring Dad's work and asked, "Do you do this type of work often, Mr. Clark? It looks great."

"Well, this job and my next one will make two."

Dad could make some neat stuff. Like all young boys from Texas, I had a hankering at one time to be a cowboy, which included roping stuff. Dad made some sort of contraptions with hooks and handles. He set one of the 'things' at one end of the house and the other at the end of the hallway that ran the length of our house. He proceeded to run cotton strings back and forth between the wooden things with hooks. I'm not sure how many balls of string he used, but he was able to weave a rope out of the balls of string. The rope was ½ to ¾ of an inch thick. It was flexible, but also strong enough to tie from the bumper of one car to the bumper of another and be able to tow a dead car (Don't ask how I know this and we will stay friends).

When the winds were whipping around during the spring of the year, I thought it would be neat to buy a kite and take it out to fly high in the sky. Dad did better than that. He took paper grocery bags and some lightweight pieces of wood left over from some window repair and made a kite. Of course I had to write and draw all over the paper after he assembled the kite. We took it to our cousin's place out in the country and flew it high up in the sky. For a little kid, it seemed like it was a mile high.

In Mr. Farney's sixth grade science class, we were studying electricity. Dad came up with an idea to show how heat generated by resistance could cook a hotdog. He ran two nails through a wooden base that he cut out, sanded, and finished with lacquer. (Did I mention that Dad could be obsessive in doing things right?) He cut a groove in the woods where he was able to split an electrical cord, running the ends to the nails. The nails were driven up through the wood and bent so that the tip of the nails pointed at each other. And, they were just the right distance apart so that the ends of a hotdog could be stuck on each end of the nails. All that was left was plugging in the electrical cord to an outlet and like magic, the hotdog began to get hot and cook to perfection. The sizzling dog should have been evidence enough that electricity was running through the hotdog. Unfortunately, Ann Haney was a skeptic who wanted proof. She touched the hotdog.

Surprisingly, she still spoke to me at our High School reunion despite having been almost electrocuted 50 years ago.

Mom told the story of a guest dropping something and breaking it. I was a little kid, but I assured the guest that, "It's okay. Daddy fix." Dad was supposed to have just rolled his big green eyes at my declaration. As far as I was concerned, Daddy was perfect and he could do anything. Now, that is a lot of pressure to live up to those expectations.

Skip forward to last week when I was driving my granddaughters (4-year-old twins, Laya and Scarlett, and 6-year-old Angelina) home from Wednesday night church where the girls are in a class that most people would refer to as being like Sunday School in our younger days.

The twins, Laya and Scarlett, were anxious to tell me about the Good Samaritan. I wasn't aware that a story could be told from the end and work back to the beginning. It was amazing to hear Laya and Scarlett's descriptions.

Then Angelina asked everyone to be quiet because she had something to say.

I said, "Okay, everyone quiet. Angelina has something important to say. Don't interrupt her. Go ahead, Angelina."

"I have decided that I want to get married."

"Okay, Angelina. That sounds like a big decision."

"When I grow up, I will get married and not live at home."

"I see. I thought you weren't going to get married because you wanted to stay home with your Mommy."

"No, I have decided that I want to get married, but only to someone that I know."

(Does it strike you that there are some deep truths in Angelina's last statement?)

NOTE: *It blows my mind how common it is for people to marry people with whom they do not share values and goals.*

"14 Be ye not unequally yoked together with unbelievers: for what fellowship hath righteousness with unrighteousness? and what communion hath light with darkness?"

— 2 Corinthians 6:14

FUN FACT: "78 percent men admit to having cheated on their current partner" - Five myths about cheating (https://www.washingtonpost.com/opinions/five-myths-about-cheating/2012/02/08/gIQANGdaBR_story.html)

"Well, Angelina, I think that is a smart decision. You are smart to only marry someone that you know."

"I know. It would be dumb to marry someone I don't know."

"I believe you have put a lot of thought into your decision, Angelina. Do you have any idea what your husband will be like?"

(Are you ready for it.............?)

"I want him to be just like you, Papa."

Thank you, and ouch at the same time. I was overwhelmed by the confidence that she showed in me. And, I was reminded immediately that the image she has of me was the image that I had of my Dad at the same age.

I tried to explain to Angelina that I am far from perfect, no matter how hard I try.

"Angelina, you need to talk to God. HE is your heavenly Father and HE is perfect. If you will talk to him a lot, God will show you the right man for you to marry. But in the meantime, I want you to keep talking to me."

Angelina is the middle of 5 siblings. Sometimes she gets frustrated when she can't be heard over the whole group. I noticed her frustration and made a promise to her.

Anyone can walk up to Angelina anytime and ask her, "What does Papa do?" and she will always give the same answer, which was my promise to her.

"Papa always listens to me."

If God can listen to my precious Angelina, so can I.

NOTE: This is why my Dad is a better person than me. You are my spiritual mentor and you are not even ALIVE physically on Earth. Dad, I appreciate and miss you.

"²¹ Not every one that saith unto me, Lord, Lord, shall enter into the kingdom of heaven; but he that doeth the will of my Father which is in heaven. ²² Many will say to me in that day, Lord, Lord, have we not prophesied in thy name? and in thy name have cast out devils? and in thy name done many wonderful works? ²³ And then will I profess unto them, I never knew you: depart from me, ye that work iniquity."

— Matthew 7:21-23

Pictured above is my mom (Mary Clark), my dad (Thom Clark) and I. This photo was taken at our 101st and memorial house.

Chapter 26

MEETING ROY ROGERS, KING OF THE COWBOYS

One year, Roy Rogers was slated as the featured star of the "Heart of Texas Fair and Rodeo" in Waco, Texas. To see Roy Rogers and his fabulous horse, Trigger, in person, was almost more than any five-year-old could bear.

I watched him every Saturday morning on television. Roy and Dale Evans, his wife, defeated every bad guy in the Wild West while never firing a shot. It was unbelievable. Even more unbelievable was Roy's sidekick, Pat Brady, who didn't ride a horse. He drove a Jeep named Nellie Belle. If I can suspend reality to accept time travel in movies, I can accept a jeep in the Old West.

Thinking back more than a half-century later, I suspect my father was not Roy Rogers biggest fan. Shall we say… there were other things to do besides taking his son to a rodeo, with or without Roy Rogers. Taking a five-year-old to see Roy Rogers on a weeknight was more a labor of love than any desire to revisit the Old West.

Roy was great. He sang songs. He told stories. He did rope tricks. Trigger did tricks that made him seem more human than a horse. Roy even brought Pat Brady and Nellie Bell with him. And of course on cue, Jeep, Nellie Belle, died in the arena. I turned to my dad, an auto mechanic, and asked him why didn't he go down to the arena and fix Nellie Belle (I'm sure a few parents sitting next to us got a good chuckle out of that). What can I say besides it was a perfect night.

Then to top it off, Roy took a lap around the arena to shake hands with all the boys and girls. Of course, I pestered my dad to go down to the arena. He didn't even try to fight me. He carried me down the stairs and walked through a holding pen to the edge of the railing. He held me up and I was able to shake hands with the one and only, Roy Rogers, King of the Cowboys.

There had also been cattle and horses in the holding pen before we got there. Cattle leave behind droppings, a.k.a. cow pies. My focus was on getting to Roy Rogers, not on where I stepped, and I found a cow pie. My dad didn't realize that until he lifted me up to shake hands with the King of the Cowboys. Too late! The inch-thick coating of cow manure was scraped off the bottom of my shoe into dad's shirt pocket. I was oblivious to what happened. I just stared at the hand that had just shaken the hand of Roy Rogers. We drove home in our old Volkswagen. I ran in the door to tell mom the good news about meeting Roy Rogers. Dad immediately took off his shirt. He stopped in the kitchen to get something out of the drawer then headed for the bathroom. Mom wondered what he was doing. I looked down the hallway as she looked into the bathroom. I have never heard such loud and uncontrolled laughter in my life. She laughed until she cried. She had to sit on the floor and hold her sides while Dad dug the crap out of his pocket. This was made worse by the fact that dad did not find this to be very funny.

I had met the king of the Cowboys, Roy Rogers, and my dad had learned a very important lesson—never take your pocket protector out of your shirt pocket unless you are going to church.

Pictured above is my father (Thom Clark) and my mother (Mary Clark). My father was an incredibly diligent and consistent father when it came to teaching me how to write legibly and in "ALL CAPS." My father had a beautiful signature. He loved the Eagles, the Doobie Brothers and playing the drums.

Chapter 27
MOM'S OBITUARY

My Mom and Dad believed in crossing every t and dotting every i. They left nothing to chance. Consequently, when Dad died in 1990 my sole job was to take care of Mom. Four years later when Mom passed away, she also had her entire funeral planned saving me from picking out songs for the service. I knew that she intended to plan out her entire funeral and all financial arrangements as well. "I've written out everything that needs to be done, so don't you dare change a thing. Do you understand me?" she said. "Yes, Ma'am. I understand completely."

My dear friend, Jack Frazier, went with me to the Funeral Home as moral support while making the final arrangements, which basically consisted of selecting the day, place and the time for the service and burial. I handed a package to the gentleman at the funeral home, which listed everything that Mom wanted done. He then proceeded to offer me upsell items such as a casket that would last for thousands of years. I said, "I don't mean to be rude, but I have to explain something to you. And I also want you to know that I'm not trying to be cheap. But, if I deviate by one iota from Mom's plans, she will find a way to reach out of her grave and wring my neck. Then, when she's done with me, she'll be coming after you. So, just follow her plans as listed in this file." Jack almost hacked up a lung laughing, which he unsuccessfully tried to hide. I told him to go ahead and laugh. Mom would be laughing too, if she were here.

Then, I decided to deviate from Mom's plans, but only slightly. I asked the gentleman about getting a flower display for the casket. He asked, "Are you sure?" I told him I was going out on a limb as far as Mom's wishes were concerned, but "Go ahead with the flowers. I'll take a chance."

The funeral home representative offered to deliver Mom's obituary to the newspaper. Of course, Mom had written her own obituary. All I had to do was list the date of death. Not that I wasn't interested, but grief was a little too much for me at the moment to bother reading her obituary. After all, what were the chances that my perfectionist Mom would have any typos? I wish I could say the same for myself. More about that later.

I suspect everyone is somewhat uncomfortable at a funeral. Mom had a little more reluctance than some people. She would rather be in the kitchen preparing a meal for the family after the funeral than to attend the funeral. I discovered that my Grandmother, Bland Augusta Hollan Wallace, had died giving birth to twins, a boy and a girl. Grandmother had an arm around each baby as she lay in the casket. Mom, at age 5, was horrified at the sight. It is only speculation, but the sight of her Mother, brother and sister in the casket could explain why she seemed so uncomfortable at funerals. Again, it may be my runaway imagination, but probably not.

Mom's obituary said that she was born in Chalk Bluff, Texas. I didn't know that.

Granddad worked for the railroad and he was somewhere between Waco and Chicago most of the time. I had asked her where she lived after her Mother died. Mom said with her maternal grandparents, the Hollans. "But they were too old to take care of us." The 'Us' Mom referred to was her oldest sister, Henrietta (Aunt Hen to me) and her brother, W.G. (which stood for W.G. (there is a history on both sides of my family of not getting around to naming children), and Elizabeth (Aunt Libba to me) and of course, my Mom, Dorothy Pearl Wallace Clark (call her Pearl and you had better be ready to put on boxing gloves. The doctor that delivered Mom liked the name Pearl (Mom never did like that doctor).

I asked Mom to tell me about the Hollans. I got my first, "None of your business").

So, the next logical question was, "where did you live if not with the Hollans?" They couldn't take care of themselves. At best guess, Hen was 9, W.G. (aka,

Bubba) was 7, Mom was 5 and Libba was 3. The answer to where they lived was another resounding, "None of your business."

Mom wrote in her obituary that she and her siblings grew up in the Disciples of Christ Orphanage in Fort Worth. I didn't know that.

That seems to explain why Mom worked at the Methodist home for almost 40 years. She had a particular affinity for children whose parents had died. She must have been effective at helping kids in need. I was born in 1953. The lady that my son Carson met would have lived at the Methodist Home somewhere between 1950 and the 1960s. She knew that Mom took some time off when I was born. Mom made enough of an impact on her that Mom was remembered over 50 years later. Working at the Methodist home was a ministry for Mom.

One day my grandfather drove to the Fort Worth to pick up the kids. He had a surprise with him...........a new wife/mother for the kids. So, how well did that go? My Dad told me rather unflattering things about Mom's stepmother. I was 41 years old when Mom died. She never mentioned to me a single time anything about her stepmother. Dad told me never to ask.

Mom did tell me about her brother, Bubba, punching out their Father when Granddad got abusive. I asked her what that was all about. Her answer? (I'm sure you've guessed it.) "None of your business."

There were other minor things I learned in Mom's obituary. One thing was for sure. She was one tight-lipped lady when it came to the past.

As for her siblings, they had a remarkable way to deal with adversity. In one word.......Humor. The Wallace girls laughed so hard at even the most insignificant things. Never, never, never get them laughing at the dinner table because food would fly and milk would come out the nose. We went to a drive-in movie with my Aunts when I was a little kid ("Come September," with Rock Hudson and Gina Lolabridgida). They laughed so hard and loud at the movie that people would gather around to watch. Then they would start laughing. They were contagious when it came to laughing.

Their brother, W.G., whom they called Dub, was eventually named William George Wallace, not by the family, but by the Navy. He was boarding a ship to go to the fighting area of the Pacific Ocean during World War II.

The officer checking the sailors as they boarded the ship asked Bubba his name. He said, "W.G. Wallace."

"What does the W.G. stand for?" demanded the officer.

"W.G.," he replied.

"Don't get smart with me, sailor. What is your name?"

"Uh, William George."

For the rest of his life, he received his VA benefits and Social Security communications directed to William George Wallace.

And as for Uncle Bubba's humor, imagine Tim Conway from the Carol Burnett Show. He would say outrageous things with a straight face and cause his sisters to go into convulsive laughter.

So, that is the story of my Mom's obituary and her siblings. As mentioned, Mom was meticulous. Write her a letter and she would summarize your previous letter before telling the news about her life and what was going on in Waco. She would even comment on misspellings (I would have died to have had spellcheck back then).

Mom had a heart attack following surgery on April 21, 1994. She was moved to ICU and remained there for several hours. Shortly before midnight, her doctors came out to tell me that she seemed to have turned the corner. Her condition was improving. The doctors went back through a swinging door as is often found in restaurants. Within 10 seconds, the nurse came out the swinging doors and asked me if I wanted to execute the directive not to resuscitate.

Mom and I had this conversation. She was very clear that she didn't want any extraordinary medical treatment. I remembered that conversation, paused and told the nurse to 'let her go.' I had done as Mom said, but I felt like I killed her. I was able to put that out of my mind for a few months, but I then had the mother lode of depression. Only by the grace of God did I get out of what I called the 'Big Blue Funk' (actually stole that phrase from a friend because it seemed so accurate).

It has been 20 years since Mom died. I have a big problem. Mom had her heart attack around 3:00 p.m. in the afternoon on April 21, 1994. She died at 12:07 a.m. on April 22. Knowing how meticulous my Mom was, I don't know if I can face her when I get to Heaven, because the headstone has the wrong date.......... April 21, 1994.

Pictured above is my mother (Mary Clark) and my father (Thom Clark). My father loved talking about Hawaii and taking mom to Hawaii.

Chapter 28
MY DAD—CONTROLLING A TEMPER

Mark Twain once said that at age 14, "When I was a boy of fourteen, my father was so ignorant I could hardly stand to have the old man around. But when I got to be twenty-one, I was astonished at how much he had learned in seven years."

It is easy to speculate why some people act the way they do. I prefer to think that my father, Thomas Clayton Clark Jr. underwent a dramatic change in his temperament over the years. I regret that I was so immature that I was not able to comprehend the changes in my dad's life. Many people considered my dad to be a kind and gentle man. But I want to tell you; he could tear you up in a fight in a heartbeat. As a matter of fact, he was a fighting machine as a young man.

My dad was born July 25, 1914, in McGregor, Texas. Somewhere around the year 1919, my grandfather's postal carrier job was transferred to Mart, Texas. This involved putting everything the family-owned in a flatbed railcar and riding on the railcar from McGregor to Mart. It is another story entirely that I've written about previously in other posts, my father had no given name until they moved to Mart. He was simply referred to as Sonny. My dad made the transition from McGregor to Mart and he met his lifelong friend, Jack Drinkard. He also met a set of brothers with the last name Caton who felt that it was their life's mission to make my dad's life miserable. Just as Jack had been dad's best friend, it appeared that the Catons were destined to be dad's worst enemies. They would find my dad after school and would, as a group, beat up my dad. This really upset dad's brother, Otho Clark. God sent Otho to be my dad's protector at exactly the right moment. My dad had gotten his father's 22-caliber rifle and was looking for the Caton brothers. Otho happened upon my dad and took the gun away from him and told him, "we're going to take care of this right now, the right way." In all honesty, it is difficult to say that Otho used a Godly method to stop the harassment by the Caton brothers. Nonetheless, it worked.

Otho asked my dad where the Caton brothers were. When dad told Otho where they were, he said, "let's go fix this once and for all." When dad and Otho found the Caton brothers, Otho put a headlock on two of the brothers and said do my dad, "Sonny, you know what to do." My dad proceeded to beat the first brother into submission.

Otho then let go of one of the brothers whom he had just beaten (he was the Canton brother who had recently beat up my dad). He continued with the headlock of the second brother and it began all over again as dad began to beat the second brother to a pulp.

And then Otho let go of the last brother and told my dad to finish the job. Which he did!

All three of the Caton brothers went home as bloody messes. When Mr. Caton found that my dad had beat up all his sons, he came calling on my grandfather, Joe Willie Clark, and demanded to know what he was going to do about my son beating his three sons. To which my grandfather answered, "I guess Sonny will have to beat them up all over again if they lay a finger on him. Your boys have been ganging up and beating up my son and I'm not going to tolerate it. So if you don't take control of your boys, my son is going to beat them up over and over again until they get the message. Now, get out of my house."

At this point, Granddad turned to Otho and said, "good job, son." Then he turned to my dad and said, "Sonny, sometimes you are just going to have to stand up for yourself, and Otho and I will help you if you need us." The Caton brothers never bothered my dad again. And, Otho never told granddad about the rifle that dad had with him.

As an aside, my dad went to the 30th reunion of his high school class. I guess no baby sitter was available. I went with him. Dad was 48 years old and I was eight years old at the time of the reunion. Three men came up to my dad and expressed extreme happiness in seeing my dad again. I asked my dad who they were and he said they were the Caton brothers. And that's when he told me the story about keeping control of your temper because if his brother had not stopped him, it would not have been a fight. It would've been a murder.

When I was playing in the Junior Teenage Baseball League, some parents who had children playing on both teams that night got into an argument. The argument escalated until there were a number of people involved in the argument, which finally escalated into a brawl. My dad who was then 54 years old and virtually crippled with very bad knees, grabbed one of the combatants in the brawl and put a wrestling hold on him called a full Nelson. The young man who I would guess to be 25 to 30 years old started trying to kick at my dad's knees and ankles. My dad's response was to speak in a very slow and controlled tone and told the young man, "you need to stop kicking or I'm going to have to hurt you. And I really don't want to do that." The guy kicked at my dad's legs again at which point my dad began to bear down on the young man's neck to the point that he began screaming and crying.

Dad let the pressure off and told him, "just be calm and we'll be fine." I didn't know what to make of a 54-year-old man pulling a young man half his age out of a brawl. Even more, I didn't understand the self-control exhibited by my dad.

Another time when I was in Little League, a couple of players got into a shoving match that was working its way toward a full-fledged fight. My dad stepped between them and told them to cool off, there wasn't going to be a fight. The father of one of the young combatants was encouraging his son to continue with the fight. My dad in a cool, calm voice said, "I don't think we are here to train the boys how to fight. We're here to train them how to play baseball."

The father of the young player in the shoving match told my dad that, "we should show them how to really settle this," as he took off his watch, sunglasses, and a hat.

To which my dad responded by taking off his glasses and saying, "I don't think that would be a very wise idea." Dad just stood there and stared at the aggressive father who wanted to fight.

"What's the matter? Are you afraid to finish this?"

In a low voice and a calm tone, dad said, "No, I'm not afraid. But if you want to finish something, you may find out why it's not such a good idea." At which point, dad simply stared and never said another word despite what the aggressive father was saying to him.

Somewhere in the middle of the taunting, the aggressive father noticed that my dad was 6 foot four and about 240 pounds. Dad's fists were virtually the size of a sledgehammer. The aggressive father surmised that perhaps this wasn't a really good idea after all to have a fight. He mumbled something about, "Oh, forget about it."

Then my dad extended his hand to the other father and said, "I think you're being a very wise man today and you have taught these boys an invaluable lesson. And I just want to thank you for that."

And who knew that over the coming years that my dad and this other aggressive father will become friends.

I have to believe that it is a supernatural peace and wisdom that comes from knowing Jesus Christ that allowed my dad to handle these situations and diffuse conflicts. Without intervention by God, Thomas Clayton Clark would not have become my father. Instead he could've been a seven-year-old murderer.

NOTE: My son Aubrey Napoleon-Hill Clark recently recalled a time where my father (may he rest in peace) absolutely lost his mind while attempting to place an order while going through a Braum's Ice Cream and Dairy drive-thru which is hilarious to me because I always have recalled my father being so calm.

I'm wearing my father's headphones in this picture. I love wearing headphones and listening to my father's Chicago records while wearing his headphones and drawing cartoons and baseball players.

My father smiles for a quick photo. My dad always had long-form stories to tell and a way of relating those stories to current events. Dad, here is the situation on earth and my on-going issue. I miss you.

Chapter 29

NOT...SO...FAST... CLARK

It has been determined that the slightly illuminated spot on the adrenal gland atop my right kidney is indeed a cancerous growth. It is small. It is not growing. It is just there. My PET scan confirmed that the formerly described blemish on my right adrenal gland that was hardly detectable is a cluster of cancerous cells/ tumor. The radioactive material injected prior to the PET scan that causes the tumor to light up confirmed its presence. My CEA (Carinon Embryonic Antigen) test is the blood marker measurement that indicates the presence of cancerous tumors. The count is extremely low. That indicates no active growth of cancer cells within my body. My understanding is that this tumor is not aggressive.

My oncologist, in whom I have great trust, indicates that it is just a matter of waiting and watching. I have been moved from monthly blood tests to every three months. My surgeon has moved me from a three-month checkup cycle to six months. And, my gastroenterologist has moved me from a one-year cycle to three-year checkup cycle. All input from my doctors indicates that I am functioning well and the cancer is not an imminent danger.

So, my take on the situation is this: God is still in control.

As if I could ever read the mind of the God of the universe, I think I have a small understanding of what is going on. Having a small, non-aggressive tumor gives me a pause........pause to stop and listen to God instead of getting too busy with life. This situation makes me more reflective. That is good.

I decided long ago that I was going to be positive throughout this process. So, if any one is looking for me to be morose and depressed, I will continue to disappoint you. That would be unproductive in my walk with God.

The long-term stuff (defined by my oncologist as being five years) doesn't bother me at all. The issue with atrial fibrillation takes a bit more effort to consciously put into God's hands. The risk of stroke, heart attack, or embolism (which claimed my Dad's life) is very real. The side effects of the medications are enough to make one's hair stand up if allowed to dwell on them. So, my request from my friends is prayer that my sleep apnea will be cured with the use of a CPAP (continuous positive airway pressure) machine. I am told that this is the possible cause of my atrial fibrillation. Perhaps I will have a bit more energy if this keeps me from waking up every 4 minutes all night long like I did during the sleep test.

God has been faithful, just as He promised. Thank you my dear friends for all your prayers for me. They are systematically being answered. My goal is to dance with my granddaughters at their weddings. Seeing as how the twins are a few months short of being 5 years old, I have much living yet to do.

By the way, it is not too soon to RSVP for those weddings. Depending on the responses, we may need to get a bigger ballroom.

My father Thom Clark and his long-time friend (and the legendary best-selling author and entrepreneur) Clifton Taulbert pose for a photo while sitting in Doctor Robert Zoellner's over-sized throne room chairs. Clifton was always there for my father as my father battle cancer and then Lou Gherig's Disease. Thank you Clifton for being my father's true friend to the end.

Chapter 30

PART 1 - THE SUMMARY FOR THE PAST YEAR (THE CANCER STORY)

Hello friends. I have been 'out of circulation' for a while which is a euphemism for recovering. I have thought of some more pithy stories to retell, but didn't have the energy to sit down and write them. Losing memory and concentration is supposed to be a sign of aging. If that is true, I aged 50 years in the last 16 months. Let me warn you that you are about to encounter another one of those "end of year summaries." The theme for this letter is God's faithfulness.

The reality is that I just came along for the ride. I didn't do much. I physically wasn't able to do much. So, I made a decision to trust God no matter which way last year turned out. The good news is that last year turned out to be very good. This posting, letter, blog (whatever you want to call it) is pretty much for my benefit. I wanted to put into writing what happened last year so that I can refer to it whenever I am tempted to be depressed about the mundane things of life.

NOTE: I didn't look my father in the eyes enough. I should have done that. When I had to assist my father with 100% of my strength to help him use a restaurant restroom in Waco, Texas, while attending his last high school reunion after ALS had devastated him I made eye contact with him and it was TOO much for ME. He looked at me with eyes that said, "Son, THANK YOU for helping me and I'm sorry that you have to see me like this." Dad, I miss you. I'm sorry I didn't look at you in the eyes enough. Please forgive me.

2014 was a great year in spite of some "challenges," such as type II diabetes, cancer, and heart failure. This year reminded me of taking a final exam (you will pardon me if I find the terminology using the word 'final' as being somewhat offensive to me, because the tests from last year bordered on being absolutely final). Going through challenges was an opportunity for me to see if I really believed what I had professed. It is also an opportunity to see if God is trustworthy.

NOTE: Dad, what you went through during the last year of 3 years of your life forever impacted me. Thank you for saving me. I will not depart from the LORD, although I am not at your level. Dad, I 100% believe that Jesus Christ died for my sins.

Let's start with the cancer story. First of all, don't be an idiot like me. I was 60 years old and never had a colonoscopy.

NOTE: Dad, that seems like a good move. The idea of having a colonoscopy is not a positive one.

In September of 2013, I began having symptoms that were similar to a case of the flu with intestinal distress. It felt like a case of the flu that wouldn't go away. I thought my grandchildren were passing on a case of the flu to me over and over and over, again. By the time it reached Thanksgiving in November, the symptoms only got worse; I finally figured out that it wasn't the flu. I spent 2 weeks in December mostly flat on my back. So, you would think by now that I would have the good sense to see a doctor. Finally, I did go to the doctor before Christmas. As he was running tests to rule out viruses, bacterial infections and the like, I began having the most unusual intestinal cramping. It was the beginning of an intestinal blockage. Pain was a definite symptom. The other symptom was downright strange. The cramping would begin on one side of my abdomen and move across to the other. It looked like a snake underneath my skin crawling across my belly.

After ruling out a variety of causes for my distress, my gastroenterologist performed a colonoscopy on January 15, 2014. The results: a tumor the size of my fist (now you see why I said don't be stupid about getting a colonoscopy when recommended. Much of my distress could have been avoided by being smart). The visual examination of the tumor suggested cancer.

The subsequent biopsy confirmed the tumor to be malignant. Fortunately, a CT scan showed the tumor had not metastasized to any surrounding organs.

So, it was time to see a surgeon about removing the tumor. I was scheduled for surgery on January 27th, my birthday. But as they say, 'Not so fast, Mr. Clark.' There were other complications. The pre-op exam revealed atrial fibrillation, slow pulse, and an irregular rhythm. Now it is time to see the cardiologist. Since I had no shortness of breath and could walk a couple of miles, the doctor cleared me for surgery. A change of surgery date due to the heart issue, change of insurance plans, and availability of the surgeon moved the surgery schedule to February 10th. Only, I didn't make it that long. A 100% intestinal blockage occurred on the evening of January 31st. I didn't know that my wife had the skills of a NASCAR driver until that ride to the emergency room. My surgeon called on me Saturday morning, February 1st. He changed the surgery date to Monday, February 3rd and ordered me to consume nothing but ice chips until noon on the day of surgery.

(THE PRECEDING TEXT WAS INCREDIBLY BORING. CONGRATULATIONS IF YOU HAVE MADE IT THIS FAR. I TRUST THE BACK STORIES WILL BE A BIT MORE INTERESTING).

Back Story #1

I suggest that you search on Google for 'The Last Lecture' by Dr. Randy Pausch: a phenomenal lecture and display of courage by a wonderful man. He had pancreatic cancer and has subsequently died. In his 'Last Lecture,' he made a statement that I have subsequently stolen from him. "If I don't seem sufficiently depressed or morose, I'm sorry to disappoint you." Dr. Pausch's religious faith is unknown to me. But as for me, I had to decide if God was in charge regarding my colon cancer. I chose to make my decisions and actions a reflection of my confidence in God. Live or die, would He let me down? No. He would always be with me. So, I may have seemed a bit brash in terms of my own personality. Some people might think I enjoyed having cancer based on my manner of reacting. The answer to that is, No! I did not want nor did I enjoy the attention from my cancer. Rather, I decided to act upon my faith. In essence, "If I don't seem sufficiently depressed or morose, I'm sorry to disappoint you."

Back Story #2

Many people have written to me to say wonderful things that I really appreciated. But I have to correct one that was said a lot to me via email, I was not and am not an example of bravery. The reality is that I worked my way through the recovery while mostly in a fog of fatigue and diminished mental capacity during and following chemotherapy. I was physically and emotionally wiped out a vast amount of the time.

It was my wife, Mary, and sons, Carson and Clayton that kept me functioning at a level resembling normal. How can I ever repay Mary for her devotion and willingness to care for me while still meeting the obligations of her job? Answer: Can't be done. Carson virtually moved in with me at the hospital while I was really out of it. He stayed in my room, sleeping on a miniature sofa with his 6'4" frame, and enduring the wake up calls every 2 hours from the nurses as they checked my vital signs. Clayton, ever the 'fixer' (and I say this with only admiration), was the confirmation that I was on the right path for treatment. He called and told me to drop whatever doctor I had lined up as my surgeon, and call Dr. Marc Rocklin. Clayton had called his business contacts that were doctors. They 'all' agreed that the only surgeon that they would consider for this type of surgery for themselves or their family was Dr. Marc Rocklin. Clayton called me with this information just minutes after I had scheduled an appointment with Dr. Rocklin. Is that confirmation or what?

Back Story #3

I had multiple opportunities to make some difference in some people's lives. What I did, I don't know and may never know. In the pre-op exam, the nurse said something to the effect of, "pardon me, but do you know the severity of your condition?"

"Yes, ma'am. I do."

"Well, you don't appear to be terribly concerned."

I repeated the quote from Randy Pausch, listed earlier. Mary was there with me. She told the nurse, "We may be surprised by events in life, but God is never surprised. We have just chosen to believe that God is real and that He is in control. We'll let Him handle the worrying."

Not that it makes much difference, but we learned from the nurse that she was the daughter of a Lutheran Minister and she was from Minnesota. Having lived in Minnesota for 13 years, we were able to make some small talk. The nurse had to leave the room, as she got misty eyed, so that she could regroup. We don't know what nerve that touched, but the nurse was obviously moved by something we said.

Back Story #4

How do you begin to thank everyone that prayed for us, prepared meals, sent encouraging notes and supported us in a very real way?

For all my wordiness, there are a lot of things that I prefer to keep private. I tend to believe that it was a 'God thing' in choosing to disclose my cancer diagnosis and information about treatment. It was an opportunity to publicly express our faith and confidence in God. Call it witnessing if you wish. So, I began putting updates on Facebook. It was also a way of letting people know that I was not dead or dying. It isn't gossip when people are repeating directly from me.

So here goes a Big Thank You.

For people from my class at Waco High that I haven't seen since graduation night in 1971 and who prayed for me............thank you.

For the people at Christian Chapel who kept us 'well fed' and continually prayed for us while I was recovering.........thank you.

For my boss who paid me, even when I wasn't able to work, and sent me home (with pay) to recover while I was almost brain dead from the after effects of chemotherapy.........thank you.

For Randy Willis, a classmate in Mrs. Dudley's 1st grade class, who drove up from DFW to Tulsa, to spend some time with me while I recovered (Randy, also a cancer survivor, was with me at the doctor's office when I was told that the cancer had spread and I was in Stage 4). That was a tough day and I can't express enough how much I appreciated Randy being there...........thank you. *FYI:* I am not a doctor, but even I could see that the glowing cancer cells showing on the PET scan were spread all up and down the right side of my back.

For Eddie and Debbie Sherman who drove many miles out of their way to visit us in Tulsa. They even took us out to dinner. *Another FYI:* our Little League team would not have gone to the World Series if not for the greatest shortstop in all of Little League Baseball, Eddie Sherman. Then he broke his hand and we came in third instead of first......thank you.

For Pastor James Weaver, who has more friends than George Bailey from 'It's a Wonderful Life?' To present Pastors Chris Dow, Greg Dave and former Pastor Richard Exley. I really counted on their power packed prayers ...thank you.

For Curtis Neimeister, who discovered that he had cancer at about the same time that I did. Curtis did not survive. Instead, in Curtis' own words, "I'm going through a bump in the road only to fall into the loving arms of Jesus. Not a bad deal, don't you think?" Curtis mentored me all throughout his final days. To be brutally honest, I was more than a little afraid of death until Curtis ministered to me. He gave me more than I ever gave him........thank you.

For Dr. Muhammed Janjua who on December 29, 2014, told me, "You are bad for business. There is nothing else I can do for you........because you are well." And for Jim Nitz, a fellow cancer patient, who sat and talked about everything in the world while we underwent chemo together *(FYI: Jim is also in remission)*...thank you.

Given the time, I could thank a couple of hundred people. Thank you to everyone who prayed for us and blessed us during 2014. You made it a really good year in the Clark household.

Last week on December 29, 2014, I received the following report:

- PET Scan using an injected radioactive-like dye—no cancer cells can be detected.

- CEA test that measures for serum created by cancer cells—I'm between 4-5 times lower than the average person.

- My colonoscopy showed no signs of cancer or polyps. My recheck date was moved back to 3 years instead of yearly.

- That was the cancer story from 2014. I suspect that you are tired of reading this, so I'll start another posting regarding the heart condition. Bye for now.

"And he said unto me, My grace is sufficient for thee: for my strength is made perfect in weakness. Most gladly therefore will I rather glory in my infirmities, that the power of Christ may rest upon me."

— 2 Corinthians 12:9

The verse quoted above had particular meaning for me last year. I was not a brave soldier fighting my maladies. Rather, I was sleeping on duty.

I did not battle for my health; God did it for me. I really and truly was in a mental fog following chemotherapy. The fog was a result of a slowing pulse, which resulted in me getting about half the amount of the required oxygen to my brain. I was too weak to function. So, God gets all the glory. All I did was try to focus as best I could on who was really in charge. God did all the rest.

God is good! He has brought me through Stage 4 colon cancer into 8 months of remission for which I am enormously grateful. Now if you will indulge me, it is time for the story of my heart issues.

As I mentioned, my surgery for cancer was delayed while I was checked out for atrial fibrillation. I was deemed healthy enough to proceed with surgery after which I would meet with my doctors to determine a plan of action regarding atrial fibrillation (AF).

I completed my last chemotherapy session on July 3rd. A month later I met with a cardiologist. He explained that my body is allowing itself to develop blood clots which lead to heart attacks, strokes, or embolisms (okay, doc, you've got my attention. Dad died of an embolism). My heart condition did not appear to be a result of cancer treatment, but rather a matter of an increase in the irregular rhythm of my heart. How that works together, I don't know or even claim to fully understand. I just know that I was first made aware of an irregular heart rhythm during a physical at the 1965 Little League World Series. I got a grim look from the doctors, but they allowed me to play when I told them that I did not have dizziness, shortness of breath, or fainting spells. Every sports physical after that was the same story. The doctors always let me play. I suspect that a younger body can just compensate for a problem in the heart better than an older body can.

For Your Information (FYI): I did pass out 3 times in the locker room during my senior year of high school. I blamed it on the heat. Only one time was anyone else there. I just claimed that I had slipped. The problem never appeared again after I was done with competitive sports.

Following the end of chemotherapy, I felt tired and lethargic. My pulse rate was generally 40-45 at doctor appointments. Reading was getting difficult because it was getting harder to keep words in focus when I read. I was making mistakes at work over the simplest things. I originally believed that it was just a hangover from the recently completed chemotherapy.

There were problems with my heart: heart rhythm, and pulse rate. My doctor recommended that I take medication to help correct the heart rhythm. After 4 weeks on the medication, he wanted to perform a cardioversion to shock my heart back into rhythm. On August 14th, I went into the hospital for the cardioversion (i.e., shocking the heart with electrical paddles). My cardiologist that worked with the physiological condition of my heart put an instrument, which I understand to be like an ultrasound device, down my throat while I was anesthetized. He found a blood clot in my heart and told the other cardiologist that worked with the electrical function of my heart that the cardioversion was cancelled (good deal for me. I was told that a shock to the heart would have been potentially fatal).

So what was I to do now other than begin taking a blood thinner to allow my body to reabsorb the clot? Should I stay home? Could I travel? What was the danger of traveling by car? The general answer was that the blood clot could fragment sitting at home or traveling. Or, nothing at all could happen. So, Mary and I decided to make the trip to Minnesota for our niece's wedding on Saturday, August 16th. That apparently risky decision resulted in saving my life.

On the way to Minnesota, I became very ill and had to stop at the emergency room at Mary Greely Medical Center in Ames, Iowa. I checked my iPhone for symptoms of a heart attack while Mary drove. Nine of ten symptoms were present. That is when I told, Mary that I had to go to the ER.

They found no evidence of a heart attack. Enzyme levels were normal. But, my pulse was down to 30, occasionally reaching 35-37. Dr. Chai, the cardiologist on call, took my medical history and list of medications. It seems that the medication prescribed for heart rhythm by my 'electrical' cardiologist in Tulsa was actually depressing my pulse. It was slowing my metabolism (no kidding! I gained 2-3 pounds per week since I began taking that medication). Dr. Chai told me that I had to stop taking that medication now. I asked why? He told me that it could prove fatal if I continued taking that medication. Ok, doc. I got your message loud and clear! They hooked me up to some fluids and practically forced me to continually drink water. I would describe this as trying to flush the medication from my bloodstream. That may be an inaccurate description, but I know I practically lived in the restroom for the next 18 hours.

FYI: I am a type II diabetic who is able to control my glucose levels with diet. That was until I took that prescribed medication. My numbers were sky-high no matter how closely I watched my diet. They even had to administer an insulin injection at the Ames, Iowa hospital.

During that night in Ames, Iowa, my heart rate began to go lower and lower until it reached 23 beats per minute. At about 2:30 a.m., bells and lights went off lighting up the room and making all sorts of racket. Frankly, I wouldn't have noticed the noise and lights if the staff had not rushed into my room dragging a crash cart behind them. The nurse, a tall beautiful and strong woman from Jamaica, woke me up by shaking me like a rag doll. She asked, "Are you okay, Mr. Clark?" To which I answered something to the effect, "I was okay until you woke me up......and you can call me Thom." No electrical shock was needed. And the answer is YES to the other question; will the sight of a crash cart increase your pulse?

By morning, my pulse had stabilized at 40+ beats per minute. Dr. Chai wasn't too thrilled about me checking out of the hospital, but he thought I was significantly improved. So, I asked what would have happened if my pulse had gone below 20 beats per minute. All he would say was, "nothing good."

We continued on to Minnesota, arriving one hour before the wedding. I was pretty much grumpy and tired. Mary did all the driving. When I got home, I was somewhat functional, but still did not feel 'right.' I had an appointment with my cardiologist set for September 25th. I never made it to that appointment.

On the morning of Saturday September 6th, we took our dog to the vet for a skin rash problem. I felt rather 'blah' that morning. After returning home, Mary asked me to go to Wal-Mart with her. I suddenly realized that I didn't have the strength to get out of my recliner without help. I tried to focus enough to take my pulse. The highest reading that I could get after finally getting up and shuffling around was 32 beats per minute. I tried to make excuses for not going back to the emergency room. I called a young man that worked for my son's company whose father was the cardiologist that discovered a blood clot in my heart. I asked him to call his father to ask what the significance of 30 beats per minute and what should I do. The young man called back and quoted his father as saying, "get your butt into the emergency room NOW."

Mary took me to the ER. I told them my pulse was about 30 beats per minute. Within 15 seconds, a nurse opened the door, put me in a wheelchair, and hustled me back to the examination room. The ER doctor was able to record a pulse of 30-35 at which point I was admitted to cardiac ICU. The doctor on call that Saturday morning was the partner in practice with my cardiologist in charge of the heart's electrical function. I had already met him while at an appointment with the cardiologist that prescribed the poison for me. He recognized me and recalled the discussion I had with his partner. He took one glance at the monitor and turned to me immediately to say, "you are getting a pacemaker tomorrow morning." I asked if he meant Monday. He indicated that there was an emergency implant being performed on Sunday morning and he would add me to the schedule that consisted of one other guy and me. "It's no problem. The surgical team is already going to be here, so there is no problem adding me to the schedule." What he didn't tell me was that I was an emergency, also.

I had trouble sleeping because my pulse rate and rhythm were completely out of sync. They had to turn off the lights and sounds of the monitor in my room because it sounded like a 4 alarm fire in progress. My nurse, the sainted Mary Lou, told everyone at the nurse's station that they would have to watch out for her other patients because she had to track my monitor exclusively. Fortunately, my dog was sick and I told my wife to go home, take care of Bob (my dog's name is Robert Joseph Dole—most commonly referred to as Bob Dole) and get some rest. I say fortunately because I began to have heart failure twice that night. Mary got to miss the rush of people into my room. They had already attached electrical pads to my chest and back in case the needed to revive me (Do they use Gorilla Glue on those pads? They removed the top layer of skin off my chest and back, including an approximately 1 inch square of skin. Yikes, that hurt! Still have a scar for a souvenir). Mary Lou, my wonderful nurse, was able to shake me like they had in Ames, Iowa, which proved enough to increase my pulse. Twice my pulse drifted down to the low 20s before Mary Lou applied what felt like a roller coaster ride. I didn't sleep much after the last shake. Mary Lou came in to prep me for surgery somewhere around 7:00 a.m. She told me she couldn't wait for this shift to be over. I had worn her out by having her watch over me so intently. While I was changing in the restroom, Pastor Chris Dow had entered my room. When I came out, he slightly startled me (Maybe my pulse increased 1 beat per minute. That's about as much as extra pulse as I could generate at that point). I really look up to Chris for two reasons: 1) he is a great Pastor and 2) he is taller than me. He prayed for me and left for Sunday services at Christian Chapel. I believe that Mary Lou must have given me something via an IV. I remember my wife coming into the room and I have a brief recollection of being in the operating room. Other than that, I have a blank memory for at least the next 10 days or so.

I called my dear friend, Steve Alley, about 2 weeks after surgery to ask him if he had heard that I had a pacemaker implanted. He said, "yes, I was in your room before surgery and talked with you." Oops. My brain was not working right. I have people that have told me they talked with me at church and I sounded okay. Folks, I was a walking zombie. I remember nothing for at least 10 days. If I were a football player, they would have taken away my helmet.

I'm joking somewhat when I say I forgot how to type. In reality, I couldn't focus. Errors at work and forgetting things was a way of life. Bless her heart, but Mary had to be the most frustrated person in the world. Whatever someone said to me might register after the third time it was said.

After watching a show about concussions, I think the lack of oxygen to the brain is like a concussion. It really dumbed me down. I have enough grasp of reality now to recognize that I am maybe 80%+ back to normal (I used to be able to multiply two 3-digit numbers in my head. Okay, I'll concede that is not normal, but now I am barely able to do simple addition using pencil and paper). Was the cause lack of blood flow or chemotherapy? I don't know. Maybe both. The good side is now I am able to focus enough to read the books again. I read two last week. I can run up a flight of stairs at work (all 16 steps……..and remember without a note why I had gone up stairs). At one point before the pacemaker, I often sat in my chair at work for 2 hours trying to summon up the strength to walk 50 yards to my car, then waited another 30 minutes before driving home (think someone should have taken my keys?). I wish I were exaggerating about the time, but I'm not. I've got witnesses to that.

The good news is……the fatigue is gone. I remember things much better now, not as good as before, but better. I run up the stairs sometimes as many as 20+ times per day without having to sit down and rest. The world is brighter, literally. It was like having a dimmer switch turn the lights from 100% to 30%. The stamina is getting better. Losing the weight I gained would be helpful. I can't blame the medication that I was on for keeping the weight on. I never changed my eating habits, which inhibits losing weight now and facilitated gaining while on that killer medication. My job performance reminds me of the days when I was called into service as a drummer, after a 30-year hiatus, for worship services at my church in Minnesota. I can truthfully say I am rapidly approaching adequate.

THANK YOU IF YOU HAVE MADE IT THIS FAR. LIKE ANDY DUFRESNE SAID TO RED, 'IF YOU HAVE COME THIS FAR, COME A LITTLE FURTHER.' I HAVE THE BACK STORIES TO THE HEART ISSUE, WHICH SHOWS WHERE GOD WAS WORKING BEHIND THE SCENES OVER AND ABOVE THE OBVIOUS. And I ask your forgiveness for the reference to the 'Shawshank Redemption' (Well, sort of ask for forgiveness. I like that movie).

Back Story #1

Marshall Morris was a DJ for my son's company, The DJ Connection, and I was the warehouse manager for the company. Marshall mentioned once while loading out equipment that his father was a cardiologist. Dr. Edward Morris is the doctor that discovered a blood clot in my heart and cancelled my cardioversion. He probably saved my life by informing me via Marshall that I needed to go to the ER immediately.

Back Story #2

I had a Medtronic pacemaker implanted to keep my pulse always above 60 beats per minute. Medtronic employed me for 5 years, as a calibration tech. Part of my job was to calibrate the equipment used to make various components of pacemakers. The wires/leads must be insulated and cured within specific temperature ranges. I calibrated many temperature-measuring devices used in the bradycardia area (pacemakers for slow heart rates). The bradycardia lab was on the floor above me for 5 years. Who knew?

Back Story #3

Our niece was getting married in Minnesota. Her mother, Bonnie, is Mary's sister. Bonnie called to ask if we would be willing to pick up her college roommate, Carole King Liston, in Joplin, Missouri, and bring her to the wedding with us. We already had our granddaughter, 6-year-old Angelina Clark, traveling with us on the trip. We told Bonnie and Carole, "Sure. We'll be cozy, but why not?" That decision turned out to be a 'God Thing.' Carole had some experience related to heart issues, which proved to be immensely helpful. She can now be called Angelina's best adult friend. Carole calmly cared for Angelina in the back seat while making calls to our health insurance company as Mary, NASCAR's gift to I-35, drove directly to Mary Greely Medical Center (MGMC) in Ames, Iowa, as if she had been there before. No detours, just directly to the emergency room. All the while, I was having nausea, cold sweats, and muscle cramping in areas that might be signs of a heart attack, or worse, signs of a blood clot broken loose. We were trying to stay focused and calm. It wouldn't have happened without Carole being with us. It was a God thing.

Back Story #4

My heart condition consisted of three things; low pulse rate, atrial fibrillation (AF), and irregular heart rhythm, with a blood clot thrown in for good measure. Dr. Chai at MGMC had reviewed my tests and medications. He concluded that my most pressing issue was the low pulse rate. I am fairly smart, but it can be difficult to follow all the medical terminology. Dr. Chai explained clearly, with minimal technical terms, what was my main priority. He also pointed out that one medication that I had been taking for 4 weeks was contributing to my lowered pulse rate. Given that my pulse was in the mid-30s, Dr. Chai directed me to stop taking that medication immediately. Another couple of weeks on that medication could have been disastrous.

Dr. Chai had me checked into MGMC for observation. It was a good thing that he did. As I mentioned before, this was the first time I had begun having cardiac arrest. What would have happened if I hadn't stopped at MGMC? What would have happened if I hadn't stopped taking the prescribed medication? What would have happened if I had been sleeping without a monitor alerting someone to make me wake up? It is quite probable I would have died, either at home or somewhere while on the trip, had it not been for Dr. Chai and the staff at MGMC.

Back Story #5

Strother Martin, the Captain from 'Cool Hand Luke,' would have told me that I "needed to get my mind right," because my mind was anything but right on September 6th. Don't ever listen to a person who is in a daze. Do the right thing. Take away the keys and get him/her to the hospital. Mary did that. All the while, I was trying to talk my way out of going to the ER, even though I couldn't get my pulse above 32 beats per minute after walking around. Per Mr. Rogers, "Can you spell STUPID? I knew that you could."

As mentioned before, the staff at Saint Francis Hospital wasted little time evaluating me in the ER and moving me to Cardiac ICU. It was shocking to me how fast the Doctor determined that I had to have a pacemaker implanted. "On a Sunday morning," I said. "You've got to be kidding me." What were the chances that an operating team would be already giving up their Sunday for an emergency surgery? And, that I would need the same surgery? What would have happened if I had not given in to the sound advice of my wife and my doctor? Do you think that maybe there is an unseen hand guiding this entire process?

I was a bit startled the next morning when I was rolled into the operating room to discover that I was the only person having surgery that Sunday morning. One of the few things I could remember out of the 10 days or so following my surgery was asking how the surgery went for the guy that was scheduled in front of me. Without any elaboration, all the operating team members would say was, "He didn't make it." I asked if they took me first because he was late or something. Again, "He didn't make it."

I think I knew what they meant. And, they came very close to saying the same thing about me.

Chapter 31

THE SINGER OF 'WHEN A MAN LOVES A WOMAN' (PERCY SLEDGE) IS DEAD

Percy Sledge, singer of "When a Man Loves a Woman," died last week. His song was burned into my memory because the repetition with which it was played on one occasion at the Lions Club Swimming Pool in Waco, Texas. The following is a 'replay' of the assorted memories around that time and place.

The following is my response via email to radio personality, Don Shelby, on WCCO in Minneapolis regarding what he called "Anthems of Summer," songs that had special meanings for a period of time.

~

Dear Don,

My special song was, "When a Man Loves a Woman," by Percy Sledge. Every time I hear that song it takes me back to the summer of 1966. I remember spending many days at the Lions Club Swimming Pool on 42nd street in Waco, Texas. The air smells of chlorine. There are 10-15 buddies hanging out together. The sun is turning us the color of ripe tomatoes. I can taste the strawberry malts that I bought at the concession stand. My Schwinn bicycle is in the rack by the pool entrance, ready for the last minute dash to baseball practice...6 miles away and with less than an hour to get there. Could life have been any better?

The reason that I associate the song with that place in time is that one particular idiot would fill the jukebox with dimes and then play "When a Man Loves a Woman" over and over and over and over on the sound system...to the point of nausea. But that's okay, that song helped me to burn vivid images into my mind of two special ladies.

One image was of the lovely, older, and completely unapproachable Emily. She was a high school freshman and I was a goofy 8th grader. Emily radiated a 'bigger than life aura' that was equal to the spell that Bo Derek cast over Dudley Moore in the movie entitled "10." Unlike Dudley, who felt an emotional let down when he discovered what Bo Derek's character was really like, my situation was just the opposite. Emily was as lovely a person as she was a good-looking Babe. She was unapproachable because her beauty intimidated the 10-15 guys who were hanging around at the corner of the pool. She would smile and say hello to us...a shamefully obvious group of gawkers. We would have a collective cardiac arrest when she spoke to us. How else do you respond to a goddess?

I didn't get to know Emily except as a casual acquaintance in high school. She was a senior and I was a sophomore. Emily was stricken with cancer sometime near the beginning of her senior year. Still, she was a cheerleader, homecoming queen, and graduated with her class. She was the picture of grace and courage during an unimaginable time. When she graduated, I lost track of her. I assumed that she had passed away; because the last I had heard was at that she wasn't doing well. To my surprise, I discovered over 20 years later that she had survived the cancer. Emily married. I don't know any details, but the names listed in her obituary indicated that she had a lot of family and friends. The article sent to me said she was involved with many civic activities. It would appear that she had a wonderful life. Sadly, Emily was only 48 when she passed. She was mentioned at a gathering of high school friends that she reminded us of, not in appearance, but in style to Grace Kelly, Princess of Monaco. Grace, style..... and a Babe to the end.

On a more personal note, the other image of that time in my life was my 'first girlfriend,' Kerry Urban. She would come to the pool on occasion with her friends and sisters to hang out. Who knows what she saw in me? I was a painfully shy, socially awkward, a 6'5" 13-year-old, a geek that looked like a stork...what an appropriate description. All I can say is, "Gee, it was great being in love for the first time!"

Kerry and I broke up, as is expected of young teenagers. But, an unusual thing happened. Her parents and my parents became great friends. They would get together occasionally for special events, like a birthday, or an anniversary, etc. Dad and Bob, Kerry's dad, would get together and work on their cars, true shade tree mechanics. Mom and 'Emma,' Kerry's mom, would call each other and sometimes do stuff together. I'm not sure what they would do, perhaps just hang out.

Emma's real name is Lynn—but I told her she looked like Emma Peele, a good-looking babe on the "Avengers" TV show. Was I trying to score points or what?

When both my Dad and Mom died, Kerry was there. I found out later that those were particularly inconvenient times to leave work, but she came anyway. Kerry called on a Thursday morning to tell me that her Dad died. She just wanted to tell me personally about Bob. My family didn't expect me to make the trip from Cokato, Minnesota, to Waco, Texas. However, I was there Friday night for the wake. Someone from Minnesota asked why I would drive 1,200 miles on such short-notice..."Because I lost a Dad, too," I said. Emma told me that I was her favorite son. Considering that she only had girls, I guess that was a compliment.

I can't hear "When a Man Loves a Woman" without thinking about the 'Style and Grace' that was Emily, or the second family that I found with Kerry's family. Can a summer ever get any better? Even if that idiot did put $5 worth of dimes into the juke box........THAT'S 50 CONSECUTIVE PLAYS OF THE SAME SONG, FOR CRYING OUT LOUD!!!!!!!!!!!!!!!

Thank you, Percy Sledge for helping to save those memories.

My father poses for a photo with his dog. My father loved dogs. I now love my dog, Davis. I'm not sure when it happened, but I now value photos more than money.

Chapter 32
STRIPING THE FOOTBALL FIELD

Cheap labor was easy to find at North Junior High School. All you had to do was ask the boy's physical education teacher to put the students to work. When Coach Smith was at North Junior, he always asked for volunteers to carry out a special assignment. "The only requirement for the assignment is that you have a size 44 jacket and a size 1 hat." Never had problems getting 'volunteers' because we knew it meant that we didn't have to run laps. Even with size one hats, we could still figure out that this was a way to avoid running laps.

One of the assignments was to mark the football field with chalk for the 7th and 8th grade teams. The gang of "line markers" were given a roller device filled with chalk.....but with no other specific instructions other than, "Eyeball it and get the lines as straight as you can." This was a perfect recipe for mayhem. Without a string to layout plumb lines on the field, one can only imagine the results.

When the visiting teams got off the bus, their coaches were somewhat aghast by the imperfect lines, which resembled 'a lazy S' in some places. It takes 10 yards to earn a first down.

Depending on the side of the field where you stood, or where the line marker bowed in the middle, the yard lines could be anywhere from 9 to 11 yards between markers. This rendered the use of chains/first down markers for all practical reasons useless for measuring a first down.

No one knows what agreement the North Junior Coach and visiting Coach arrived at for determining first downs that were close. The officials were high school students who were members of a club that taught officiating. It is a pretty good assumption that many aspirations of becoming a football referee were dashed after their experience at North Junior.

On one occasion during a 7th grade game, the play started with the ball lined up evenly with the first down marker. The play called for the halfback to run a slant off right tackle. Butch Clements hit the hole off right tackle and broke to the sideline before being knocked down a couple of yards past the chain that measured the 10 yards necessary for a first down. But.......he was still a half yard short of reaching the chalked yard line marker.

I have no idea how the coaches came to an agreement as to what constituted a first down. All I know for sure was that we turned the ball over on downs to the other team despite moving the ball past the chain that measured for a first down.

Some traditions are hard to break. When we got to the 9th grade, it was our turn to mark the field. And, there were some 1st downs that were 9 yards and others that were almost 11 yards. Oh, well!

The only other thing goofier than the yard line markers was the football that was changed out on 4th down as we were preparing to punt. It was raining, so they put a new, 'clean' ball into play. Unfortunately, someone had forgotten to inflate the ball. How do you kick a 'flat' football? We had to burn a time out to get another ball into the game, this time with air in it. You would think we would at least send in a deflated ball when the visitors were getting ready to punt. Let them burn a time out instead of the home team. Geez!

My father visits his father-in-law and my grandfather, Ben Meinhardt. Ben was a faithful follower of Christ, a skilled electrician and a lifetime self-employed entrepreneur. My Grandpa Ben would often recite the following poem which has always inspired me. I loved shadowing my Grandpa Ben during the summers and just riding along with him in his work truck (pickup) and watching him go from job to job fixing electrical problems while selling, managing a team and pondering deeply about the Bible.

Chapter 33

"TO BE OR NOT TO BE...... OLD"

* * (I DEDICATE THIS CHAPTER TO LARRY BIRD WHO WORE #33 AND WHOM MY DAD LOVED)

Mary and I decided for our 50th birthdays that we would celebrate in the 50th state, Hawaii. Our birthdays are only four days apart. We wanted to do certain things on Mary's birthday and on my birthday. Mary wanted to be on Waikiki Beach overlooking Diamondhead on her birthday. I wanted to bicycle down Haleakala Mountain in Maui for my birthday. Mary did a lot of research and picked a tour that would put us on the right place on the right date. Little did I know that being a part of a tour would become an interesting look at human behavior. In essence, it taught us how to be old.

We were the children on the tour. Everyone else was anywhere from 75 to 85 years of age. We discovered quickly that one of the signs of being more "mature" was to tell everyone about your medical history. One gentleman gave me the complete textbook definitions for all aspects of heart surgery. But, in his mind he was still young because he would go to the old folks home to play the accordion every week. By the end of the week I knew all about knee replacements, hip replacements, heart bypass, stents, medications for blood clots, treatment for aneurysms, treatment for strokes, the best places to buy durable medical equipment, and every way possible to get senior discounts. I began to feel old just listening to all the stories. But hey, I'm just a strapping kid at 50 years of age.

Another sign of impending old age according to my 15-year-old niece is the increased number of noises made by old people. According to her, it is impossible for an old person to get up out of a chair without having some sort of popping sound in their joints. The popping sound is accompanied with a grunt when trying to stand up and with a deep sigh of relief when sitting down. My niece also informed me that old people can't be quiet when they're eating. Her example was the noise of approval or disapproval after taking a bite of food. Something good tasting was always followed by a long and prolonged sound of "MMM MMM MMM."

On the other hand, something that did not meet the approval of the old person's taste buds was followed by testimonials of the way that they don't make food the way they used to. "They use too much garlic. They use too much salt. They use too much pepper. What in the world is poi? The spices are too hot. There is too much of this and there is too much of that, yada yada yada."

I began to take inventory of my life and realized the unthinkable...... I'm getting old. My posts on Facebook the last year have been almost exclusively about health. I thought I was being informative. Wrong! I was just getting old. When I stand in line at the bank to make a deposit, my ankles pop. I turned around in the chair to look behind me and my back sounds like a rifle range with all the pops. So I have come to the point of making a critical decision. I'm going to turn back the clock. I'm going to live like Merlin the Magician from Camelot who lived time backwards. I'm going to think of projects and activities to expand my mind. In other words, I'm going to create the fountain of youth for myself by thinking young.

So how do I do this you might ask? Well first of all, I'm going to get all the medical history stated as clearly as possible. I still don't know what I'm going to do about the joints that pop. I'm going to stop making judgmental sounds about the food I eat. I'm going to stop grunting and sighing as I get up and down out of chairs. It's going to be a whole new me. But first, I have to cleanse myself of old thoughts by acknowledging where I am regarding my health.

In 2014, I was diagnosed with stage IV colon cancer. As of June 2014, I have been in complete remission. Praise God, he gave me some great doctors. In August 2014, I had a pacemaker implanted. It has worked like a charm ever since. I also developed atrial fibrillation and a blood clot in my heart. Both of those seem to be under control now. Beginning on our anniversary date of May 17, in 2015, I almost had a heart attack, but they were able to clear a 99% blockage and I appeared to be well on the road to recovery. About six weeks later we did the same thing all over again for a 95% blocked artery. Then six weeks later we did it all over again for a 70% blockage of the artery commonly known as the widow maker. In total I had six stents implanted and was feeling pretty good.

Now I ask you, doesn't all this information about health issues drive you nuts? Well, stay tuned there's more.

I began to have weakness in my arms that progressed to my back beginning in September 2015. Eight months later I was diagnosed as having ALS (a.k.a., Lou Gehrig's disease). I have an unusual type of ALS in that it has a rapid onset. Normally a person lives three years after diagnosis. I have deteriorated to the point of someone who has had ALS for two years. So, my prognosis is not good. I am undergoing some alternative therapies that may help, but they are a long shot at best.

From this time forward I will only give information about projects or uplifting activities—focusing on bad medical outcomes accomplishes nothing. As I have said before, if I don't sound as depressed or morose as I should be…sorry to disappoint you.

I have some projects with which I'm involved that will fill my days. The Lord has been gracious to us caring for our needs far beyond I can possibly express. Friends from over 40 years have come to see me and on some occasions traveling long distances to do so. I am a blessed man. The wife of my youth is the wife of my later years. Mary and I have been married 42 years, which is a blessing beyond anything I can possibly explain. My sons Carson and Clayton have been a blessing beyond what I can express again. Carson's wife Alicia is a wonderful new addition to our family and we treasure having her in the Clark family. Clayton is married to the only woman on the face of the earth that could put up with him and prosper with him. Vanessa, you are a gift from God to our son Clayton and to us.

Regarding our five grandchildren I am immensely blessed. Havana, Aubrey, Angelina, Laya, and Scarlett have given me more kisses and messed up my hair, and given me more tickles and laughter than anyone should be afforded in a lifetime.

I have been blessed and will do my best to pass on the blessings I received to others. This will require that I focus on things that are yet to come. I hope to express my deeply held belief in the saving power of Jesus Christ my Lord.

There you have it folks. I will not be commenting on health issues anymore but I still intend to be writing. Thanks to voice-activated devices, I will still be able to write. Mary will be providing health updates from time to time.

I've been so deeply blessed that I can hardly contain the love that I have for all of my friends. You have been wonderful. I love you. And probably the greatest thing of all, at our 45th high school reunion, I was kissed by more women—in front of my wife—then I could count. What was especially interesting was that I was kissed by several ladies that I had wanted to ask out in high school but was too shy to ask them. But I guess you could say everything has worked out the way it should.

God bless you all.

Chapter 34

WHAT IS THE REAL STORY?

What was Great Grandfather Thomas McCrander Coon really like? Another good question goes unanswered but there are clues.

First clue: he was Scottish.

My great grandfather (my grandmother's Dad), Thomas McCrander Coon, was born July 6, 1858, in Roanoke, Virginia. Records show that his mother died when he was very young—probably an infant—and his Dad died when he was 9 years old. The first 6 years of his life coincided with the Civil War. Need there be any doubt that great grandfather Thomas McCrander, 'Tommy,' Coon had a turbulent childhood.

Second clue: He would be described as always 'on' as a comedian, only less animated than Robin Williams.

My Dad was 23 years old when his Grandpa Tommy passed away, so he knew Grandpa Tommy as an adult, not just as a kid. Dad spoke of Tommy Coon several times over the years. All discussions started with the description of him being a 'cut up,' always looking for the humor in everything. We know that Tommy Coon moved to central Texas from Virginia at age 19. Where did he grow-up and where did he live from ages 9-19? We don't know. He did mention something to my Dad about spending some time in St. Louis as he headed west. My Dad guessed that Tommy Coon lived on the streets and hustled for any type of work he could get in order to eat. He always had a funny story to tell instead of talking about his background.

Tommy Coon settled down in Moody, Texas, and married Hattie May on November 12, 1879. It was surmised that Tommy moved to the area because of a job with a railroad. He later went into farming and raised livestock.

Dad told the story of his Grandpa Tommy telling him not to get into a corral with a particular bull.

Well, Dad along with his friends and cousins had been hand-feeding cattle all the time, they found it was possible to make friends of the livestock. However Grandpa was right about the bull. The bull began chasing Dad and the others around the corral until they were able to slide under the bottom rail and escape. Grandpa Tommy came running to see if the boys were all right. He said, 'I told you not to go in that corral with the bull. He could have killed you.' My Dad replied, 'How was I to know that you were serious. You are always joking about things like that' (Another example of clue number two).

In rural Texas, peddlers traveling by horse and wagon selling household items were quite common. Great Uncle Tommy was known to give peddlers bits of misinformation. As an example, he would tell the peddler that the lady on the next farm was a recent widow. The peddler would go to that house next and would offer his condolences for her recently deceased husband. The 'widow' then turned back to the house and yelled out, "Harold, are you dead yet?" Let's just say that it was a bit awkward.

Even Great Grandpa Tommy's wife was not off limits to his 'humor.' He stopped a peddler by the road to tell him that the lady on the next farm was named Opossum. 'And whatever you do, don't call her Coon. She will really get mad.' The truth was that great Grandma Hattie was not known for her sense of humor, that especially extended to being called 'Possum.' It is part of the family legend that she chased that peddler back to his wagon while swinging a frying pan at him (example two of clue number two).

Third Clue: his past was private - no exceptions.

According to my Dad, Great Grandpa Tommy was very reluctant to tell how he made his way from Virginia to central Texas. His standard answer to the question 'Where did you come from?' was, 'I was hatched out of an egg.' All that we know about his travels across country came from Great Grandma Hattie.

In a church class one evening, a man told a story about a relative. I believe it was his uncle. The man was full of humor and loved to take family members fishing. The man was described as being very genial and uplifting to be around. Only years later, did the man from our church learn that his relative/uncle had suffered for years with depression. That sounded a bit like it could have been my great grandpa, Tommy Coon.

Many years ago, there was a television special honoring the great comedians of this century. It was so long ago that Georgie Jessel was still alive (If you know who Jessel was, you are older than me. You might have had a dinosaur as a pet). They had Bob Hope, Alan King, Rodney Dangerfield, Milton Berle, George Gobel, Steve Allen and many others that have long since passed away. Johnny Carson was one of the younger comedians. Anthony Newley wrote and performed a song dedicated to the 'funny men' entitled 'The Man Who Makes You Laugh.' Most of the lines were aimed at the career of comedians, but the bottom line was: their humor was what helped them cope with life. It was strange to see the 'Masters of Comedy' crying as they listened to Newley's song.

So, what is the real story? I know that I got my first name Thomas from my Great Grandpa, Thomas McCrander Coon. I know that he was viewed to be a 'jovial Scotsman.' I know that from a childhood of great pain he emerged as a funny man that was always good for a joke, a quip, or funny story. I know that my Dad adored his Grandpa Tommy. I know that my Dad had this quiet affinity for some things Scottish, such as the contraction of my name being T-h-o-m, not Tom. Was Great Grandpa Tommy fighting depression his entire life? THAT, we will never know. It would be easy to make a case for it, but that is purely conjecture.

~

But there is something I have observed, the relationship that my grandchildren have with me, their Papa Thom, is the same relationship that my Dad, Thomas Clayton Clark Sr. had for his grandpa, Thomas McCrander Coon.

Opportunity by Edward Rowland Sill

This I beheld, or dreamed it in a dream: —
There spread a cloud of dust along a plain;
And underneath the cloud, or in it, raged
A furious battle, and men yelled, and swords
Shocked upon swords and shields. A prince's banner
Wavered, then staggered backward, hemmed by foes.

A craven hung along the battle's edge,
And thought, "Had I a sword of keener steel —
That blue blade that the king's son bears, — but this
Blunt thing!" — he snapt and flung it from his hand,
And lowering crept away and left the field.

Then came the king's son, wounded, sore bestead,
And weaponless, and saw the broken sword,
Hilt-buried in the dry and trodden sand,
And ran and snatched it, and with battle-shout
Lifted afresh, he hewed his enemy down,
And saved a great cause that heroic day.

Chapter 35

WHERE DO YOU GET THE IDEAS FOR THIS STUFF?

I was asked where do I come up with ideas about things to write. Most of the ideas come from looking at the world with the same sense of humor as my uncle, Bill Clark. Born Willie Hoyt Clark in McGregor, Texas, in 1902, he changed his name to William H. Clark believing it to be a better moniker for a commercial artist from Chicago, Illinois. Uncle Bill was the life of the party when it came to telling stories. It has been 50 years in some cases since he told his stories to ever laughing siblings and their spouses and to me, his little nephew from Waco, Texas.

What could possibly be funny about buying cigarettes? Let the master, Bill Clark, tell the story and it became hilarious. Printed words can't convey the Cajun accent of the store clerk and the erudite man from Chicago, but I'll give it a try to retell this story from over 50 years ago. While visiting family that lived in Louisiana's cajun country, Bill, a lifelong smoker (so much for the Surgeon General's report—he lived longer than any of his siblings), stopped at a small country store to buy cigarettes.

The store shelves were stocked with many cartons of Picayune Cigarettes and some Marlboros, but none of Bill's preferred brand of cigarettes.

"My good man, I would like to purchase a pack of Dunhill Cigarettes, please."

"Say what?"

"Dunhill Cigarettes."

"We've got Picayune and Marlboros. Even some Marlboros in a hard pack, but I ain't never heard of Dunhill. Even have some loose tobacco and papers if you want to roll your own."

Bill looked over his shoulder at his brother, my Dad, and gave him a wink. Dad always told me that Bill got 'that look' when he was up to some mischief.

"Oh, my goodness. I deem this to be totally implausible."

"Say what?"

"Look here my good man, don't you have any rich people in this Parish of the Sovereign State of Louisiana."

"Say what?"

"I'll have you know that rich people in Chicago only smoke Dunhills."

"They do?"

"Yes, it is both a blessing and a curse because one is able to determine the financial wherewithal of a customer simply by hearing whether or not they smoke Dunhills."

"You from up north in Chicago?"

"Indeed, I am."

"And you smoke Dunhills?"

"That is correct."

"So, does that mean you're wealthy?"

"Forgive me my good man, but modesty prevents me from answering that question. I guess I'll purchase a pack of Marlboros.......in the hard pack if you don't mind."

As Bill and Dad were exiting the front door, the store clerk asked, "Hey big shot, if you're so rich, who's the big guy walking around with you?"

"He's my chauffeur."

Uncle Bill had an impish sense of humor that made even buying a pack of cigarettes an event worthy of a story. Though seldom displayed, my Dad could also make a simple event into fodder for making a story out of nothing.

My dad, Clayton Clark, was 6'4" and about 240 pounds that made associating him with a Volkswagen Bug seem a bit of incongruity. Despite the apparent small size of a VW Bug, the domed roof and deep floor cavity, created by the placement of the engine in the rear, made the car quite roomy for the driver and passenger. Our 1957 Coral Red VW was a beauty despite not being the color that Dad had ordered. Oh well, it looked great. And it was the perfect size for me. At age 4, I could lay flat on my back on the back seat with an inch clearance both below my feet and above my head. When we went to visit our family in Louisiana, Dad took us for a ride with Dad driving and Uncle Leslie in the front, Mom and Aunt Mabel in the back seat, and my cousin, Nancy, and me in the well behind the back seat (I couldn't fit my shoes in there now). There were only 25 VW Bugs in Waco, a town of 100,000 plus. So, we were quite a novelty to see driving down the street.

But the most surprising thing to people back then was the fact that the engine was in the rear, not under the front hood. Thus, the story begins.

~

One Saturday afternoon, we crossed over the Brazos River into east Waco to buy a watermelon at the Farmers Market. The watermelons they had were from

Gholson, Texas, which were consistently the largest and best of their type, not to mention that the Farmers Market kept them chilled in a walk-in cooler.

Dad may have bought a couple of melons, which was his usual want. As he lifted the front hood to put the watermelons inside, a small kid who looked like Buckwheat from the Little Rascals two reel movies walked up to Dad and asked, "Mister, how come you don't have an engine in your car?"

"It doesn't have an engine."

"It don't?"

"Nope."

"Then, what makes your car go?"

"It runs on watermelons."

"It do?"

"Yep, it do."

"You mean that watermelons make your car go?"

"That's right. I ran out of watermelons in my garden, so I came down here to get some more. When my next crop comes in, I won't have to buy any watermelons."

"You sure your car runs on watermelons?"

"Yep. Watch, I'll put the watermelons under the hood and I'll drive away."

So Dad put the watermelons under the hood, got in the VW, started it up, and drove away."

The little kid ran over to an older lady that was probably his grandmother, pointed at us and yelled, "That car ain't got no engine. It's running on watermelons."

Dad and Uncle Bill could make good stories out of nothing. I was about 7 years old when Dad pulled the watermelon stunt. And I can still remember Uncle Bill telling his stories fifty years later. I admire storytellers that can find humor in the most mundane of events. That was a gift that I believe my Uncle Bill shared with Mark Twain.

Chapter 36
WHICH ONE IS HE?

Sorry, folks. This has nothing to do with high school, but it is a story related to me about the Meinhardt family (my wife is Mary Clark, née Meinhardt) as they watched the 1987 World Series between the Minnesota Twins and St. Louis Cardinals.

~

All the family crowded around the television to watch as the Twins played in the World Series.

Each person had their own 'Homer Hanky' that they waved, especially when sluggers Kirby Puckett, Tom Brunansky, or Kent Herbek came to bat. Grandma Laura Meinhardt was there with the family enjoying the game, or at least enjoyed having the family all together for the evening.

Grandma M seemed to especially enjoy the boisterous nature of the evening. But, Grandma started to show some signs of being rather agitated as the game went on. Everyone thought that maybe she was getting tired. After all, she was 93 years old. Maybe it was the noise when everyone started waving their Homer Hanky's and yelling as a Minnesota Twin player marched up to home plate to take a swing at the St. Louis Cardinal pitchers.

Granddaughter Tina asked, 'Grandma, are you okay?'

'Yes, I'm fine, but I want to know which one he is.'

'Which one is who, Grandma?'

'You know. The one they keep cheering for.'

'I don't who you are referring to, Grandma.'

'Yes, you do. I heard all of you cheering for him. What is his name? Tina, would you please show me which baseball player is Homer Henke?'

It seems Grandma M was wondering if Homer Henke was any relation to her son-in-law, Elmer Henke.

(With thanks to my father-in-law Ben Meinhardt, for relating the story to me).

Chapter 37

MY FAITHFULNESS IS A SHIELD

I am faithful.

I am good.

Nothing takes me by surprise.

I am with and by and above.

I am holding.

I am grieving.

I am faithful.

I am good.

My love is trustworthy.

It's true.

My love is holy, consistent, unchanging.

My strength is perfect in weakness.

When you don't understand,

I'm still holding.

I'm still loving.

I'm still faithful, always good.

I am near to the brokenhearted.

In my presence there is rest.

Even when everything crashes,

there is hope.

There is love.

There is faithfulness and goodness.

I am here. I've never left.

I have not abandoned or forgotten.

I have not misunderstood.

My faithfulness is a shield.

My glory is a garment.

I will be a protection, a fortress where you can run and be safe.

I am steadfast.

I am faithful.

I am good.

Don't let the truth of who I am be clouded by your perception
of me, or by grief.

I am the same. The same. The same.

I am loving.

I will walk with you.

I will go before and behind.

I will be strength, peace, and comfort.

I will be love.

When you feel like you've been left, you are not alone.

You are mine and my right hand is steadfast upon you.

You will know my faithfulness and goodness.

You will know me forever.

Pictured above my father (Thom Clark) would occasionally shave his beard just to freak us out! Who is this guy? Whenever my father shaved his beard I always found it to be very unsettling. It was like seeing Mickey Mouse smoke.

Chapter 38

HE CHOSE TO BE (SCREENPLAY AND PLAY)

Father's Day – "He Chose to Be"

SCENE I

(Jack's been dealing with anger issues over losing his father and has been 'acting out.' Jack's friend Tim was over playing ball when the conversation got heated and Jack put a bat through a window in the house. Now Mr. Stanton (Jack's step-father) is addressing the situation from inside the house.)

Mr. Stanton:	Jack, I would like you to tell me what happened here. (points to broken window)
Jack:	It's broken.
Mr. Stanton:	I see that. I also see your bat lying on the floor under the window. Would you please tell me how this happened?

Jack: I don't have to tell you anything; you're not my father!

Mr. Stanton: Jack, I didn't ask because I was trying to be your father; I asked because I care about you. I believe in you, so I came to hear the truth—from you.

Jack: (Defiant silence)

Mr. Stanton: Let me tell you about a choice I made when I was your age. One day at school, a group of boys came up to me yelling that I wasn't very smart, and certainly not very strong. They called me names and made me angry. They dared me to prove I was smart and strong by doing something my father would not want me to do. I thought if I did what they said—just once, they would see they were wrong and they would leave me alone. So I did.

                    You've gone with me to set up live traps for squirrels, Jack. Remember the time we watched how it worked? We put something in the trap the squirrel thinks it wants, then we set the trap and put it in a place that looks safe to the squirrel. When the squirrel goes in to get what he thinks he wants, suddenly the trap closes and the squirrel is caught.

That's just how I felt after I disappointed my father. I thought I wanted approval and peace with those boys who were being nasty. Then I realized that to get their approval, I had to become like them. And when I made that wrong choice, I didn't like them *OR* me. And I had broken the trust of someone who was very important to me. I lost a *lot* with that bad decision.

While I was thinking what a loser I was, and that maybe those boys were right—I wasn't smart or strong—Dad came to talk to me. He asked me what had happened. Well, right off, I had to make another decision. I could tell him the truth or I could lie. In my heart I knew which one was right, but the right decision was also the hardest. And what would Dad say when I told him the truth?

Jack: What did your dad say?

Mr. Stanton: It's funny how owning up to something we don't like in ourselves can help us grow so much better. Dad said he'd known all along. What I did wasn't right, and we needed to work through that together. Then he said something I don't think I'll ever forget. He said that my telling him the truth meant a great deal to him and he believed I was a good son.

Jack: (Looks at the floor)
The kids at school make fun of me because they say I don't have a real dad. You're nice and all, but first Dad left and died, then you came and took Mom, and I don't know if there's anybody left for me.

Mr. Stanton: Jack, let me tell you a secret that's true. A man is not a father because of who he is; a man is a father because of what he does. And the best fathers are fathers because they want to be, not because they 'happened' to be or 'have' to be.

No one will ever take the place of your biological dad. Even if they looked exactly like him, that wouldn't be possible; God made your dad unique and one-of-a-kind.

There are a lot of people who love you, Jack; not because they have to, but because they want to. And you know what that means? You can have the best family in the world—if you let those people love you.

Jack: Uh.....about the window....

Mr. Stanton: (Goes and stands beside Jack; puts
                his hand on Jack's shoulder)
                Let's go outside and have a look. Then
                we'll figure out how to work through this
                together.

http://www.grahamkendrick.co.uk/songs/sound/mp3_
edits/Father%20Me%20Edit.mp3

SCENE II

(Jack Brown is sitting on the curb waiting for his Dad to come home when his friend Tim Gordon walks up)

Tim: What you doing Jack?

Jack: Waiting for Dad to get home. What are you doing?

Tim: Nothing much. Mostly just hanging around.

Jack: Sit down, if you want to.

Tim: Thanks I think I will. What time does your Dad get home?

Jack: Usually about 5:30. He should be here any time now. What time does your Dad get home.

Tim: It varies. He's a very busy man, you know.

Jack: No, I didn't know that.

Tim: Yes, it's true. I went to work with him once. You wouldn't believe how many people depend on him. People came from all over the building to ask him questions. Someday, I want to be just like him.

Jack: That sounds cool.

Tim: What does your Dad do?

Jack: He works hard making sure our family is taken care of.

Tim: No, I mean, what type of work does he do?

Jack: To tell you the truth, I don't really know.

Tim: You don't know?

Jack: Some sort of technical stuff that I don't understand. He told me not to worry, it would make sense soon enough.

Tim: Okay, if you say so.

Jack: Actually, I think he has more fun being around us than being at work. At least it seems that way.

Tim: That sounds great, but my Dad is really an important man. I want to be just like him when I grow up.

Jack: Yea, that's what you said before. Good luck with that.

Tim: Jack, you mind if I ask you a question?

Jack: Sure, why not?

Tim: It's kind of personal.

Jack: On second thought, maybe not…………Oh, go ahead. Shoot. I'll answer if I can.

Tim: I heard your Dad isn't your 'real' Dad.

Jack: Oh, that.

Tim: I'm sorry. It's just that the other guys talk a lot and that's what they said. Is it true?

Jack: In a way, that's true?

Tim: I don't get it.

Jack: My biological Dad is dead. I was 5 years old when Mom married Dad. That was just before we moved here.

Tim: So, why do you call him Dad if he wasn't around until you were 5?

Jack: Because, he is my Dad.

Tim: How can he be your Dad?

Jack: Are you proud of your Dad?

Tim: Of course.

Jack: Do you want to be just like him?

Tim: I already told you that.

Jack: Well, I want to be just like my Dad, too.

Tim: So, the man who adopted you is your Dad?

Jack: I'm not adopted. My last name is Brown. His name is Stanton. But, he is my Dad.

Tim: I don't get it.

Jack: It doesn't matter if you get it. I do.

(Jack's Dad walks into the scene)

Mr. Stanton: Hi, Jack. Hi, Tim.

Jack: Hi, Dad.

Tim: Hello, Mr. Stanton.

Jack: Dad. Want to play catch?

Mr. Stanton: Sure. We'll have to go inside to get the ball and gloves.

Jack: Beat you to it.
               (pulls out gloves and ball hidden
               behind him)

Mr. Stanton: I think you set me up.

Jack: Got that right.

Mr. Stanton: Tim, would you like to join us?

Tim: No thanks. My Dad will be along in a
               few minutes.

Mr. Stanton: The offer is still open if you change
               your mind. Come on, Jack. Let's go
               over to the park.

(Jack and Dad disappear. Tim waits a few moments,
then his Dad arrives.)

Tim: Dad!

Mr. Gordon: Hey there! How's my buddy?

Tim: Great. How was your day, Dad?

Mr. Gordon: Busy, busy, busy.

Tim: Can we play catch?

Mr. Gordon: Gee, Tim. I would love to, but I have to answer some emails right away. They are at a critical point in the construction project that I was telling you about. They will fall way behind if I don't get to this right away.

Tim: I understand, Dad. They are really lucky to have someone like you there to help them.

Mr. Gordon: Thanks, Tim. You are really understanding.

Tim: No problem. That's what I'm here for.

Mr. Gordon: Tim, I'll tell you what. Tomorrow we'll play catch when I get home.

Tim: Great!

Mr. Gordon: We'll have a great time then.

(Light fades to black. Spotlight comes up on singer. 'Cat's in the Cradle.')

Link to the song: http://www.youtube.com/watch?v=paYHs8RhJqc

SCENE III

(Fast forward to high school. Jack and Tim are seniors, waiting in front of the Principal's office.)

Tim: Well, what are you in for?

Jack: In for?

Tim: Yea. What crime did you commit?

Jack: What are you talking about?

Tim: We must have done something wrong or we wouldn't have been called to the Principal's office.

Jack: Would you knock it off? I haven't done anything.

Tim: Neither have I. All the more reason to
                be suspicious.

(In walk Mr. Stanton and Mr. Gordon)

Tim: Dad. What are you doing here?

Jack: And you, too, Dad.

Mr. Gordon: Tim, what is going on? Mr. Evans,
                the principal, called. He said there is
                something very important happening
                and that I need to drop everything and
                get here immediately. I had to cancel
                three appointments to be here.

Tim: You did?

Mr. Gordon: Of course, I did. You know I'll drop
                everything when I can. Your mother
                isn't answering her cell phone, so here
                I am.

Mr. Stanton: Jack, do you know what this all about?

Jack: Sorry, Dad. I don't have a clue.

Tim: I can't think of a thing that we've done.

(Door opens. Out walks Mr. Evans, the Principal)

Mr. Evans: Well, I can.

Mr. Gordon: Mr. Evans. What is going on here?

Mr. Stanton: Is there anything wrong? You sounded very serious on the phone.

Mr. Evans: I should say so. There is something very serious and important going on here. But, I need to talk with your sons about this for a few minutes. Please have a seat. We will only be a few minutes.

Mr. Gordon: Can't you handle this all at the same time with all of us?

Mr. Evans: No. And I notice that your wives are not with you.

Mr. Stanton; Well, you caught us a bit off guard. My wife is out of state looking after her Father. He had a stroke a while back and needs some help from time to time.

Mr. Evans: And your wife, Mr. Gordon?

Mr. Gordon: Sorry, Mr. Evans. She didn't answer her cell phone.

Mr. Evans: Very well, then. Young men, come with me. Mr. Gordon, Mr. Stanton, please be seated.

(Mr. Evans, Tim, and Jack walk into the office and close the door.)

Mr. Stanton: Excuse, me. I'm Phil Stanton. I've known Tim for a long time, but I don't think I've had the pleasure of meeting you.

Mr. Gordon: What? Oh, I'm sorry. I'm Arthur Gordon. You can call me, Art. Please forgive me. There is so much going on that I've sort of lost my bearings for a moment.

Mr Stanton: That's completely understandable. I wish I knew what this was all about.

Mr. Gordon: I guess we'll learn soon enough.

Mr. Stanton: It won't be anything serious. I'm sure of that. They are good young men. You can be proud of Tim. He is a fine young man.

Mr. Gordon: Do you know Tim well?

Mr. Stanton: Fairly well. Tim has come with us on a few family outings. I'm sure your wife told you.

Mr. Gordon: I'm sorry. I didn't put it together. Isn't Jack's last name, Brown?

Mr. Stanton: Yes, it is. I guess I would officially be called Jack's stepfather.

Mr. Gordon: Then you're not Jack's father?

Mr. Stanton:	I like to think of Jack as my real son. I just got a later start. His biological father was killed in a helicopter crash while flying for the Marine Corps. Jack was 5 years old when I married his Mother.
Mr. Gordon:	I'm sorry. You must find me to be nosy. I just always assumed that your name would be Brown since Jack always referred to you as Dad.
Mr. Stanton:	Well, I'm really glad to hear that. I guess wearing this paid off.
Mr. Gordon:	WWJD. Doesn't that stand for 'What Would Jesus Do?"
Mr. Stanton:	In most cases it would. In my case, it stands for 'What Would Joseph Do?'
Mr. Gordon:	I don't understand.
Mr. Stanton:	Well, I'm not comparing Jack to Jesus, but sometimes a man is called to step up and be a Dad. That's what Joseph did. I'm just trying to follow his lead.

Mr. Gordon: I must compliment you for that, Phil.

Mr. Stanton: Thank you, Art.

Mr. Gordon: Why didn't you adopt Jack?

Mr. Stanton: The Browns are fine people. I wanted Jack to know his heritage. It is a sticky wicket when it comes to knowing the right thing to do. The fact that he calls me, Dad, is all I need to know.

Mr. Gordon: Excuse me. I have to take this call. Art here. What? How soon? Oh, no! Can't Dave take care of that? Yes, yes. I know. All right. I'll be there in 30 minutes. Okay. Good-bye.

Mr. Stanton: Trouble?

Mr. Gordon: There is always trouble. I shouldn't say that. It's just that there is always someone who needs my help and I don't have a back-up to fill in for me. Would you do me a favor?

Mr. Stanton: Sure, if I can.

Mr. Gordon: Tell Tim that I got called back to work. It was an emergency. He can call me on my cell phone. I'm sure that there isn't any problem here. So, just have him call me. Tell him we can get together later.

Mr. Stanton: Sure, no problem.

Mr. Gordon: I really enjoyed talking with you. We'll have to get together when we can find the time.

Mr. Stanton: That sounds good, Art. It was a pleasure talking to you, also.

(Mr. Gordon departs. Mr. Stanton sits. Suddenly there is a big yell from the Principal's office. The door opens and out walks a smiling Tim, Jack, and Mr. Evans.)

Tim: Where's Dad? No, don't tell me. There was an emergency at work and there was nobody there that could fill in? And, he said to call him on his cell phone. And.......that we would get together later.

Mr. Stanton: Yep, that pretty much covers it.

Jack: Tim, aren't you mad?

Tim: Are you kidding me? My Dad is a mover and a shaker. I love it when I see how everyone throws themselves at his feet. I told you a long time ago, Jack. I want to be just like him. And, I meant it.

Mr. Evans: Now that we have called roll and found one missing, perhaps you would like to tell Mr. Stanton about the purpose of our meeting.

Mr. Stanton: Hurry up. The suspense is a killer.

Jack: Dad, Tim and I are the co-valedictorians of our graduating class.

Mr. Stanton: What?

Tim: He's trying to tell you that we tied for first place at the top of our class.

Jack: Mr. Evans reviewed every class we taken for the last 3 years and we are a dead even tie.

Mr. Evans:	This is the first time this has happened at our school. I thought that it would be good for the parents of Tim and Jack to be here to congratulate them for an amazing accomplishment.
Tim:	Don't worry, Mr. Evans. Dad will make it up to me.
Mr. Evans:	I certainly hope so. Good day, Mr. Stanton. Thank you for coming on such short notice. And, my congratulations again to both of you. (Turns and goes back into his office)
Tim:	Sorry to run, guys, but I have a call to make. (Tim runs out)
Mr. Stanton:	Jack, I can't begin to tell you how proud I am of you.
Jack:	Thanks again, Dad.
Mr. Stanton:	We have to get your Mother on the phone and let her know.

Jack: Sure, let's do that. But I want to tell you something first.

Mr. Stanton: What's that, Jack?

Jack: Do you remember what Tim said?

Mr. Stanton: What was that?

Jack: He wants to be just like his Dad.

Mr. Stanton: I can understand that.

Jack: Well, I know what I want to be.

Mr. Stanton: Do you want to be a 'mover and shaker' also?

Jack: No, Dad.

Mr. Stanton: Well, what do you want to be?

Jack: Some day, I want to be half the Dad you didn't have to be.

(Link to Brad Paisley — 'He Didn't Have to Be' — http://www.youtube.com/watch?v=iVFmHHxXCVg)

SCENE IV

(High School Reunion 10 years later.)

Jack: Well, if it isn't Tim Gordon!
            (Extends a hand to shake Tim's.)

Tim: Jack Brown. You 'old man,' you. You're
            looking pretty good!
            (Extends his hand to shake Jack's.
            Gives him a bear hug.)

Jack: Old man, nothin'! Here, give me a
            mirror and I'll hold it up for you!
            (Sigh.)
            Isn't it weird? High school was so long
            ago, but it feels just like yesterday.

Tim: Yeah. Strange. I guess that's what
            growing up gets you. Hey, is that the
            wife?
            (Points.)

Jack: Yeah; that's Teresa. She's holding
            Elizabeth, and Phillip's running around
            here somewhere. How about you?
            Wife and kids?

Tim: Yes and no. Stephanie—I met her in college—needed to go be with her mom. Her mother's not doing well all of a sudden. But no kids—yet.

Jack: Ah, I remember—you always wanted to be a 'shaker and mover.' Well, one of these days, Tim, you'll have to make room for rattles and rug rats. There's just nothing like 'em!

Tim: Yeah; been thinking about that. Steph and I have talked, but it just doesn't seem to be happening—if you know what I mean. Steph's ready for alternatives, but I-I'm just not sure. Was kind of hoping to talk to you about that—you know, with your Dad and all.

Jack: Funny you should mention that. Before I met Teresa I had my name legally changed to Brown-Stanton. I did that because I wanted to. The way I figure, Phil became my Dad because he wanted to. So I legally became his son—because I wanted to.

Tim: Does it really work like that, Jack?
Didn't you ever feel disenfranchised—
like you were a big outsider?

Jack: Well, at first I did. But you name me
one human being who has NEVER felt
like that at some time in their life.

Tim: Good point.

Jack: I discovered the issue wasn't how I felt
about that, but what I did about it.

Tim: What do you mean? You just can't
change the way you feel.

Jack: No, but I can change the way I think.
And when my thinking changes,
my feelings will naturally follow...
eventually.

Tim: Okay. I didn't realize there was such a
philosophy to this.

Jack: I don't know so much about the philosophy of it, but I do know about the truth of it. There's a wise saying that goes, "As a man thinks in his heart, so is he."

Tim: You mean the mind controls the heart?

Jack: Think of it this way. The mind is like the lid or cork on a bottle. The contents of the bottle cannot change unless the lid (or cork) opens to allow the change.

Tim: Is this sort of like 'positive thinking?'

Jack: It's deeper than that.

Tim: Can you explain?

Jack: Here's how I began to understand it. Dad explained that the best fathers were fathers—not because they HAD to be, but because they WANTED to be. He also told me I could have the best family in the world if I decided to let people love me. So I took a chance and tried it. Dad was right.

Tim: So you're saying you made a decision to allow your stepfather to become your family?

Jack: Exactly. It took some adjustment, but it worked—probably because Dad had already decided to love me before I took the chance to let him. You might say he was practicing what he preached.

Tim: Hmmm. That's definitely food for thought.

Jack: For what it's worth, I didn't figure out what Dad did until Phillip was born. Holding him in my hands... looking into his tiny wrinkled face... right then and there I knew I was going to love him— even before he could understand what that meant.

Tim: But what if a child decides to not let you in? What if they don't change their mind?

Jack: That's a risk of love. Most kids don't have a clue what love is. My children have no idea what Teresa and I sacrifice for them. But they respond to love—every time. Sometimes it takes a while. And so will a child that you and Stephanie decide to love.

Tim: Do you really think so? What about that 'real birth parents' stuff? You hear so many stories about how kids are driven to find their birth parents. Doesn't that get messy?

Jack: I suppose it can. But part of that depends on how you look at it, because it will influence how you handle those curiosities.

Tim: What do you mean?

Jack: Kids are naturally curious. I remember Phil telling me that no one could take the place of my real dad. Eventually I realized real love doesn't displace people—it picks up where they left off and covers.

Tim: Wow. Your dad had a lot of courage.

Jack: Phil didn't try to take my real dad's place, but he backed his decision to love me by consistently demonstrating that in his behavior. He eventually became my father.

Tim: I think I understand what you're driving at.

Jack: Probably better than you know; it's how God works with us. When we first meet Him, it's pretty obvious we're nothing like Him. But because He made the decision to love us first, if we respond to that, He really does become our Father.

Tim: Guess I've never looked at it that way before. I see where it's more than wishful thinking; the whole premise of what you believe has to be based on a truth.

Jack: Yep. Actually, the whole adoption thing is God's idea. I think He uses that illustration to draw pictures for those of us—me included—who don't get it any other way.

Tim: You're hilarious. I can see that you're a good dad.

Jack: Tim, you have a lot to offer in that department. Don't sell yourself short. Some of the best moving and shaking you can do is to get inside the head and heart of a child who is all turned around and help them figure out life's most important things.

Tim: Do you really think so?

Jack: Yes I do. You have what it takes.

Tim: Thanks, Jack. That's a big encouragement. I need to schedule a long talk with Stephanie.

Jack: You do that. Let's stay in touch. I'd love
                 to hear how it goes.

Tim: Thanks. I will.

(http://youtube.com/results?search_
query=when+love+takes+you+inandsearch_type)

Chapter 39

HOW NOT TO BE A MISSIONARY (SCREENPLAY AND PLAY)

Pete Brooks

Section 1 - Childhood

The cold, cold northern city in Minnesota, Bemidji, was the place where God saw fit to have me born. Bemidji was on the southwest side of a lake some twenty miles in diameter. It is the northernmost point of the Mississippi River.

I remember a day in my early childhood when the thermometer registered 65 degrees below zero on the Fahrenheit scale. Sledding, skiing and skating were all a part of my childhood and youth. And quasi-frozen fingers, nose and toes were part of the pain to be endured.

My first years are hard to remember. My father's death when I was three does not register, though I do remember the "round house," a sort of round porch in the yard of the house where we lived at the time and where we played in the summertime. I also remember the licking I got when I threw my deceased father's Bible down the stairs from our upstairs bedroom hall. Another spanking was mine when I found a medical book in a trunk in the attic showing a cut of a pregnant woman and was caught looking at it. Back in those days storks delivered children and it was a secret that they came from their mother's womb. Anything related to sex was prohibited to children.

My father had been a farmer's helper. When he came over from Holland at 17 years of age, he went first to Canada. I understand he worked for a time for a furrier's firm, for back in those days there was still a lot of trapping of wild animals for fur coats and collars. At what time he came down from Winnipeg to Minnesota, I do not know, but he met and married my mother in 1920 and they settled in Bemidji. He worked for a farmer, a Tom Smart. At some time when he was still single, he suffered a motorcycle accident that injured his thigh. After he was married for a few years, he bruised this same thighbone while plowing and it festered and became an open sore. This eventually worsened, and led to his early death. Mother said it was TB (tuberculosis) of the bone, but I suspect that it was some type of cancer. He was 33 when he was taken from us.

My father became a believer in Christ Jesus while still in Canada. He wrote some very urgent letters to his family in Holland about the need of accepting Christ and being prepared for the soon coming of the Lord. That is almost a century ago. My mother was the daughter of a Salvation Army captain, and early in her childhood accepted Christ as her personal savior. She became a cadet in the Salvation Army, a very attractive young lady in her uniform. Her faith endured through hardships and poverty unto the day of her death in 1986.

My religious background, as you may see, was fundamental, and probably holiness or Pentecostal from the start, certainly Arminian in doctrine. There was no eternal security for us, so we had to be faithful unto the end to be saved. I remember how the testimonies of those believers scared me as a six-year-old child! Faithful unto the end! Me?

Extreme poverty was our lot. My father was young when he died, living in his brother's house on the outskirts of Bemidji, and working as a hired laborer. Mother had a washing machine, so she began to make a living by taking in washings. I remember that old fashioned machine with it's square copper or brass body, and the motor and mechanism exposed underneath and the rubber wringers to squeeze the water from the clothes. Dangerous for little children they were, so different from the washing machines today.

In those days everyone was expected to make his own living, not to become dependent on the government with its social security programs. However, mother was a frail creature, and it soon became necessary to find help. The government did have a program called ADC (Aid for Dependent Children), otherwise called Widow's Pension, and she was able to obtain help from that fund. I recall her receiving twenty dollars a month, which at that time was about twenty days of a poor man's wages. Rent was about five dollars a month, as I recall, though I believe some of the houses we lived in were rent-free.

Water was from a "pitcher pump" in the kitchen, water obtained by driving a "sand-point" directly into the sandy soil, where the water level was close to the surface. Electricity was very cheap, so there was enough money from those twenty dollars to keep us fed, and clothed, though I remember having but one pair of pants to wear to school. We ate ground meat (hamburger) once a month, but peanut butter was a cheap staple that substituted meat. Mother was a hard worker and always got a small lot from some friendly neighbor to plant. We then had fresh vegetables in the summer and canned vegetables and fruit in the winter. We all had to hoe weeds on hot summer days. But the memory of fresh peas, corn, carrots, onions, potatoes, beets, beans and cabbage is sweet. Apples and pears were cheap in the fall and mother would also can them for wintertime. Sophy reminds me here of blueberry picking and canning every summer, also. We always enjoyed blueberry "sauce" in the wintertime. The local creamery plant would give away skim milk, so I remember going there with a gallon pail to get some free skim milk. Breakfast was usually of cream of wheat, oatmeal, or cornmeal with milk and sugar, and mother's delicious homemade bread. Cornflakes were an unusual treat, as also we always thought bakery bread was such a treat! Spuds were our staple at every main meal. Macaroni and tomatoes, pancakes, all the common cheap foods were our diet. But apparently we were healthy, for we were seldom sick.

Childhood memories also include being burned twice on stoves in the cold of winter, trying to keep warm. The first time, we were living in a house in the country, near the Scribner School where we studied. I was probably in second grade. On a cold winter morning I got too close to the hot kitchen stove (called a "range") and burned a large round spot around my navel. It was a fairly deep burn and took months to heal. We had moved into Bemidji proper by the time the last scab fell off.

The second time I was eleven or twelve, and taking a bath near the living room heater in the cold of winter, and accidentally got my "bottom" too close to the hot steel barrel and burned another round spot on my buttocks. It was hard to sit for a time, but neither of those incidents left a permanent scar on my body, though even if they had, they were in spots not usually displayed.

Another incident of winter cold involved a small round, glass aquarium of goldfish and a wonderful lesson on prayer. We attended North School, where sister Sophy's teacher let the kids take the aquarium home for overnight, and her turn was in the early fall. There was a hard frost that night, unexpected, and the goldfish bowl froze solid on the dining room table, since there was no fire in the stove. When we awakened, there were the goldfish, frozen in the ice! Sophy cried, and the two younger ones cried with her. Mother, however, had us kneel and pray, and then warmed the small round glass aquarium on the stove in a pan of water. She then put a pinch of salt in the water and stirred the fish around. They came to life, and we all were very happy and thankful. God has answered our prayers!

We were also "church tramps" due to our frequent moving. I'm not sure that I can remember all the churches, but a Mr. Vaughn, a lay preacher, bald and mustache, and always smiling, dedicated me to the Lord in a small house church. I believe it was "Jesus Only" doctrinally. I'm not sure at what age we attended the Salvation Army, but I suspect it was very early in my lifetime, for about all I remember is a street meeting and a preacher predicting that Mussolini was the anti-Christ. For a period of time we attended the local Baptist church about the time I was in kindergarten. I also remember beating the bass drum in the Church of the Nazarene when in kindergarten or first grade. We attended a chapel at Harley Lake when I was six or seven. My personal acceptance of Christ was in the Nymore chapel of the Swedish Mission Covenant church in a children's service directed by a missionary to Japan, a Miss Ruth Larson, when I was about eleven. The pastor, a Rev. Johnson, lived neighbor to us. He had a son, Donald that was my age. Nymore was a subdivision of Bemidji that was part way around the lake. It was while living there that the Assembly of God came to Bemidji, and it was only natural that my mother, who had spoken in "Tongues" as a child, should take us there. From then on the Assemblies was my church until I graduated from Bible school and spent a year helping start a church in Eveleth, Minnesota, on what was called the "Iron Range" due to the rich deposits of iron ore.

I also remember attending the principal Mission Covenant Church near the center of Bemidji as well as the Assemblies of God there when they moved from Nymore to build a building nearer the center of town.

A very friendly and reasonably wealthy man entered our lives when I was about five. He was a handsome man who owned a tourist resort a few miles out of town, and who earned a fortune selling gravel to the state highway department from some hills on his property. He was Pentecostal, and became very friendly to us, bringing us gifts and special food. That is the first time in my life I remember eating steak. Of course, in my innocence, I did not know the why's and where-fore's, but when my mother took us all to Northome to her sister's house and gave birth to a baby boy, it later became obvious. To me it was great to have a baby brother, I being seven years old, and I think there are still some pictures around of me pushing him in a sled on a snowy day. He was fully accepted by all three of us children, and became a welcome member of our family. After his birth we returned to a house near Harley Lake, and then moved in to town. Mother took a long time to fully realize that God's forgiveness was total and complete for all her sins.

In retrospect, I would say that my childhood was very good. A godly mother, freedom to play, study, work a bit, and witness the goodness of God to us, in spite of our poverty and the loss of our father, was our privilege as He watched over us. Our frequent moving gave us a taste of town and country and a variety of friends.

Section 2 – Housing

Another aspect of poverty was the constant moving from one house to another, always seeking a house that was a bit warmer (and probably cheaper) to face the terribly cold winters. My brother Reuben made up a list of the houses that we lived in according to mother's remembrance, and I found one house missing from that list. But there were at least twelve houses we lived in from the time of my birth until Mother was able to build her own little wooden house on a corner lot on the same street that I was born, several blocks distant. I must have been in my late teens at that time, already in Bible school. Reuben didn't get the dates down, but I have some favorite memory associated with each house.

Uncle Aries' house where I was born had that round porch-like place for us to play. We must have moved within a year after Dad died.

In my mind, after Father died we moved to a house on Norton that was closer to town. While living there, we three got on mother's nerves so badly that she packed her suitcase to leave us. As she went out we all set up such a howl that she came back on the promise that we would behave. I don't think our good behavior lasted very long, for I remember her repeating this act more than once! It was at this house that she took in washings for a living. I do not find this house on Reuben's list.

Our next house was a little house on 18th or 19th street surrounded by trees, with a field of delicious tomatoes planted across the street. The owner let us eat big, red tomatoes. It was here that a neighbor boy and I "played" the piano by jumping on the keys. Sophy thinks it was Grace and I, because she was "babysitting" us. And a man named Robert DePugh proposed to Mother, but she did not accept, thinking that he might not treat her children with patience and love (Sophy's version is that the marriage did not take place because Robert's mother opposed his marrying a woman with children, and that he simply disappeared from mother's life, even after she had purchased a wedding dress). Also, there was a gravel pit nearby where we sledded down the decline in the wintertime.

I can't be sure, but I believe that the next house was on 12th street just off Park Avenue. Here was where the goldfish bowl episode happened, I learned to ice skate with clamp-on skates on the ice rink made by the fire department when they drained the hydrants in the cold of winter to keep them from freezing solid. And I believe it was here that Sister Sophy began to call me Peter instead of Brother, my nickname. I hated that! I was losing my identity. I was probably five, in my second kindergarten class. Here we played Parcheesi with a neighbor boy who cheated. I still remember his name. Also it was while at this house that I experienced God's protecting hand in a special way. Some of us had gone uptown Bemidji to see a "spider man" climb a bare brick wall. While there I got lost in the crowd, so after the great event, I ran home. When running across a street near home, a car hit me, and I found myself sitting on the front bumper, hanging on to the radiator cap. Not a scratch on me, just a small bump behind my ear was the result. The driver got out of the car all excited, thinking I had been injured, and warned me to never, ever run across a street again without looking both ways. I don't believe I ever have since!

The next house was on the corner of Seventh and Irvine where sister Grace, who had a mean streak, threw the rag doll she had given me down the toilet hole to make me cry. I was still about five. It was probably while living here that I played the bass drum at the Church of the Nazarene and got off beat because I was trying to hit the letters in my name. The pastor stopped and asked me what I was doing.

We moved up one square to a very small house in the 600 block on America Avenue. I remember how cold it was and also skating in the rink across the street that I believe later became the Northland Apartments where mother lived after she retired. Sophy reminds me that in this house was where I provoked sister Grace so much that she chased me with the kitchen knife to put an end to my life. I must have been a terrible tease. And also, I must have been faster than she was, running for my life! It was here that we had the mumps or chicken pox, or maybe both.

The year or so at Harley Lake, our next residence, was wonderful. The lake was fairly small, but had two peninsulas we called Islands. There were wild grapes growing on one of them. I remember us boys swimming nude from one of the islands. We fished perch and sunfish in the summer, though I almost drowned before I learned to swim. Wolves howled at night, and I had my first motorcycle ride over a hundred miles an hour on the highway that ran in front of the gas station where we lived. A family moved in about a quarter of a mile up the highway. The children had lice, and for the first, and only time in my life, I caught lice. Mother bathed my head with kerosene to get rid of them. The older boys taught their younger brother to swim by taking him out to the deep in the rowboat and tossing him into the water. He learned fast! Daisy Glick swallowed a moth when going from the chapel to her house carrying a gasoline lantern. Toby the dog loved to chase cars on the highway and finally was killed by one. The gas pump at the station where we lived caught fire, and a man who was passing by yelled, "Use sand! Use sand!" The fire was put out with sand! A bachelor who lived nearby brought in a Sears Roebuck or Montgomery Wards catalogue one day, slamming it on the counter in the gas station, saying, "This is my Bible!" Jessie, Harley's daughter my age and I would run around the tourist camp with the chrome rings from an old car's headlights pretending they were steering wheels. We were driving our cars. And one day, I got in one of Harley's cars that were always parked on a hill to get started on the downhill run, and had Jessie take the block from in front of the wheel. I was six and unable to steer the thing, so when it got going, it hit a tree and stopped rather suddenly. My two front teeth were broken, and my bottom well warmed with a strap. It was here we tested the new ice formed on the lake in the fall and from here we trudged to Scribner School through the woods on icy cold winter days. And. Then there was a time in the summer when some robbers came to the tourist camp and stayed for a few days. They were very nice to us kids, but I believe they threatened the adults to keep silence as to their whereabouts. I remember one of them showing me his revolver. There was a pretty, young lady with them. I also remember the telephone we cranked to call out. Our ring was one long and four short cranks. Also, Harley had a battery light system with a motor-generator for lights at night that was a marvel to us kids. We could hear the wolves howl at night when the lights went out.

The time at Aunt Mary's house near Northome where Reuben was born was marked by two or three incidents besides his birth. One was the male turkey that I was afraid of. The other kids chased him, but he chased me. He knew I was afraid of him. And there was the time the girls got into the backhouse and dared me to peek in the cracks. While I was doing so, Uncle Alfred, returning from the field, came by and picked me up by the ear and carried me into the house to be punished. Uncle Alfred would buy Corn Flakes for himself while all the rest of us would have to be content with oatmeal. After Reuben was born, I pleaded with Mother to let me hold him, but as a six-year-old forgot and let him roll off my lap onto the floor. Mother got very excited! He cried for a while, but is still living and healthy at this writing!

The next house I remember is the one not on Reuben's list. When we returned from Northome to Bemidji, we did not stay at Harley Lake very long, but moved to a house somewhere between the resort and Scribner School. There was a nice row of raspberry bushes in the yard, and that was where I burned my belly on the kitchen stove on a cold winter day. That was the year I skipped a grade in the country school with eight grades in one room. Bob Glick, who had been a year ahead of me, became my classmate, and there were now two of us in third grade.

From that house we moved into Bemidji to 912 America Avenue. It was either a corner house or next to an empty lot on the corner. I remember coasting up and down the sidewalk in my red wagon, and it was here that George Thorobrugger gave me the log cabin set. Sophy remembers the following: "There were neighbors that had 2 boys that were always fighting. One threw a hunk of coal at the other and hit me instead. I got 2 black eyes."

The next house was Beckstrand's, a large house on the south side of town in Nymore. I think we lived upstairs. The church met in the basement. The railroad tracks ran nearby, and the freight trains rumbled by, pulling over a hundred boxcars. We would sit and count them. Also, that summer the temperature rose to well over a hundred degrees, and we would sleep outside on the ground hoping for a breeze to cool us. There was a junkyard nearby, where the man would pay us two cents a pound for copper. We would search everywhere for old armatures and copper wire to earn a few cents. At a gas station nearby the price per gallon was nineteen cents.

From there we moved to 610 Central Avenue in Nymore. My memories there include the Wednesday evening when Grace and I got into a scrap, and I defended myself by hanging onto her long hair until she quit. She cried for at least two hours so that I would get a licking from Mother who had gone to prayer meeting. She was mother's pet, and I got my licking. Dear Grace! The last time I saw her before she died of cancer; she hugged me and asked forgiveness for all her meanness. I told her I would forgive her if she would also forgive me mine. I was no angel. One day I got mother upset and she chased me out with a broom. When she swatted me on the back with the broom, the handle broke in half! It was cross-grained and very weak. It was also when living at this place that I learned to "whistle double." One of the young men from the church would pass by whistling double, so I asked him how he did it. He replied that it was by moving the tongue up and down while whistling. I learned to do it by persistence. It was in this house that our "male" cat surprised us with a batch of kittens behind the kitchen stove, and where I pestered mother for a mouth organ until she finally gave in and bought me one from the pittance she received from ADC. A whole dollar! Also while there, a neighbor kid and I stole a batch of nickels from another kid's den, and when we were found out, we had to face the boy, his father, and my own Mother. I don't remember ever stealing again. (Sophy says, while at 610 Central, "Peter went to the outhouse with a black boy to see if he was black all over"). In the backyard was the old iron pump, and one very cold winter day, Sophy induced me to put my tongue on the pump handle. It froze on very well! I don't remember how it got "unstuck," but I'm sure I left some skin behind. Funny, Sophy was usually very kind. I'm sure it was all in fun.

It was also while at 610 Central that I got my first real lesson on the misuse of Tongues and Interpretation. A Mr. Peters frequented the prayer meetings. He worked at the box factory in Nymore, a poor man with quite a family. In a prayer meeting some lady gave a "message in Tongues" and another interpreted, telling him he should leave Bemidji and go out to a certain city in Oregon to evangelize and establish a church. I don't recall all the details, but know he left his job, sold his things and packed his wife and family into an old car and went out to Oregon, a long, tedious drive. When he got there, he looked for the city specified in the message in Tongues, and there was no such city in Oregon! He arrived back defeated and disillusioned.

We moved from the house at 610 Central to the Akre Store building on the same avenue. I don't remember much about this, but believe that the Assemblies of God had rented the building and was using the store area as a meeting hall, and we lived in the rooms in the back. It was here I burned my buttock on the living room stove while taking a bath in the cold of winter in one of those round wash tubs. Here at the Assemblies of God building, a guy died during an evening service. Sophy had this to say, "Holbrook had a heart attack and died in Grandma's bed (He got sick and was taken to lie down on Grandma's bed). Grandma wouldn't sleep in that bed until Daisy Glick slept there one night and then Grandma slept there again." I believe also that it was in this building that my mother got sorely offended when Reuben was fussing a bit and the pastor very undiplomatically said quite loudly, "Will SOMEONE please take that child out of here?" Here in Brazil, I adopted a tactic quite different. When a child was crying or running up and down the aisle, I would stop and remark with a smile that the child was so much better looking than I that it was distracting everyone's attention. Usually the parent would try to get it under control.

From Sophy again, "Every house we moved into had to be fumigated for bed bugs and we couldn't move in until the place was aired out." Which brings back the memory of Aunt Mary's log cabin outside of Northome. When we were there the nights were bad because the bedbugs would come out of the crevasses between the logs and torture us. And we always took a new load of bedbugs back home with us. Also at Aunt Mary's her husband, Uncle Alfred, liked an occasional joke, so one day gave me a bottle of homemade chokecherry wine to drink. It was delicious, but when I'd had enough so that I could no longer stand, he had a great time at my expense!

Our next move was to the north side of the city, the Carver Store building on the corner of 15th and Park Avenue where we stayed from then to my graduation three of four years later, the longest we ever stayed in one house. I must have been twelve then, in the eighth grade. My memories include becoming a paperboy, beginning to attend movies against Mother's will, the old radio someone on my paper route gave me and listening to the Grand Ole Opera on Saturday nights as well as Opera music on Saturday afternoons and symphonic music on Sunday afternoons in the cold wintertime. I remember the struggle Mother had trying to get me to split wood for the stoves before it got dark in the wintertime, and her going out to do it, to my shame. The months of summer I would spend out at Uncle Arie's farm with the cousins, driving his "bugs" (home-made tractors) to swathe and bring in the hay for winter. He never paid me a cent nor bought me clothing, but I did learn to work hard. It was at this house that the cat ate our canary and I shot the cat. While we lived here, Sophy got her first buck when deer hunting with her friends. And she left us upon graduation to do a teacher's course in Walker, Minnesota. We lived there when I graduated from high school and went out to get drunk with some colleagues to whom I had promised to drink on graduation night. We drank and danced until the girls went home, and then we danced men with men. Not nearly as fun! When I got unsteady on my feet, one of the dear girls took me out to walk it off in the cool night air. Nice gal! We rented a cabin on Lake Bemidji to sleep off the effects of the whisky. When I walked in the next morning, Mother thought I'd been out to the outdoor toilet, but wondered why I was dressed up in my suit so early! Not until MANY years later did I tell her the truth!

This gives a total of thirteen houses in sixteen years that I remember as our home. I may have doubled up on one of them, and I seem to remember one more. It is not on Reuben's list, so I'll skip it. I find it interesting how in our poverty we moved so many times. It will be interesting in Eternity to see if Mother remembers the why of each move! We didn't appreciate her as we should have, children usually don't, but when looking back and imagining the struggles she had to keep us healthy and get us educated both intellectually and spiritually, she is to be admired greatly. I trust her house in heaven is a palace.

Section 3 – Education

Later on you will hear me mention that I went to the mission field practically ignorant of mission policy and practice. But the fault was probably much mine for I was never a good student.

My studies began early. When Father died and Mother had to take in washing to keep our souls and bodies together, my sisters were already in school, so Mother got permission to enter me in kindergarten when I was still only four. I was big and fat for my age, and my sisters had already begun to teach me to read. We had wooden blocks with letters that they used to form words and names, so these were also my teachers. Sophy, older than me by two and a half years, learned to read and write at our father's bedside when he was ill when she was three. He kept himself occupied with many types of beautiful handiwork, and I still have some with me in Brazil in 2005. Sophy was always brilliant and charming, as she still is at this writing, nearing her 84th birthday. Grace had a more difficult disposition, and we others thought that she was mother's pet. But both of them were my earliest teachers.

Because of my early start, I had to spend two years in kindergarten. My principal problem was that I lacked coordination and could only skip on one foot when all the other children skipped with both! But learning was easy, and by the time I was in second grade up at Northome when our little brother was born, I was called to the head of the class to correct the other students when the teacher left the room. I was proud of that!

We were living at the resort at Harley Lake when we had to walk some distance to the Scribner School. We plowed through snow on icy cold days, not too well dressed for those temperatures. At Scribner School, all eight of the primary grades were in one room. It was a typical country one-room schoolhouse. I believe we spent two years in this school. In second grade the male teacher had me also accompany the third grade work, and eventually I was graded as a third grader. This placed me a year ahead of my age group for the rest of my secular education and although it made no difference for me scholastically, it was not good for me socially. Sophy had the same problem in school, for she graduated from high school at fifteen years of age, about three years ahead of her age group. I don't believe this is practiced much anymore.

When we moved into town to 912 America Avenue, I entered the fourth grade, complex because I had come in from a country school to the large city grade school and also because we were so poor. I don't remember anything about my fourth year except the teacher's insistence in getting me to write with my right hand. The minute her back was turned, the pencil automatically returned to the left hand! She finally gave up.

Fifth grade was in Nymore on the southeast side of Lake Bemidji for we had moved to that part of the city. There I met a number of my classmates that would accompany me through high school. But as to the learning, the only thing I recall is that the teacher did not discern my problem in arithmetic. I had never learned to "borrow" when subtracting, so my math grades were poor. I don't remember that she ever looked at my arithmetic papers closely enough to see what the problem was. Someone else had to show me.

The Nymore kids were bussed to the high school in Bemidji proper, and for some reason or another, I was sent over there to attend the special sixth grade in the high school building. It was never explained to me whether this was for students especially bright or retarded, but we had an excellent, old, white-haired, strict teacher, a Miss Bernhard. Sophy had also had had her as a teacher, so she must have been for exceptionally bright students! She was very pleasant in spite of her age, but very strict. We were not allowed any horseplay. One very pleasant memory is that at Christmas she gave a whole box of chocolates to each student! And for a poor kid who seldom had chocolate, that was like heaven to me. Dear soul, she did a good job preparing us for junior high. I still love her and see her face as if she were present right here!

It was an easy transition to junior high, since it was in the same building, and I was used to going there. It was different because we moved from classroom to classroom and had different teachers. We also had electives and could choose some of the subjects we wanted to study. I was now eleven years old in the seventh grade, a bit big for my age, and my voice was already changing. By the time I was thirteen, it was a deep bass, much deeper than it is now that I am in my eighties. My joy and pleasure was to respond with a booming bass voice to someone who thought I was just a kid. Surprise!

As I look back, I can see at least three things that were harmful to my education. First, the lack of a father to give me orientation and encouragement; second, an inferiority complex due to poverty. I always recall the year I had to start school using a pair of summer pants dyed a chocolate brown because there was no money to buy a new pair. Also, remember walking the halls at high school with my hands crossed behind me to hide a patch on the seat of my pants. Thirdly, there was the lack of sufficient orientation or examination of capacities and desires on the part of the school system. The result was a lack of interest in the possibilities that education offered. I thought I was mentally incapable of getting a college education. I had no idea of what my talents were. As a result, I got mediocre grades generally through the junior high years. I had no intention of going to college. My electives were always based on what would be the easiest to pass. An example of the result of this was my choice of a class in auto mechanics and another in mechanical drawing, both of which served me well on the mission field. I was placed in a general math class, a non-prep course, instead of algebra. I took no language courses. I opted for plane geometry because I thought it interesting and easy. I loved English, especially literature, but my grades generally were mediocre until one fall day my buddy, Ken Meland, and I skipped school to attend a football game in St. Cloud, Minnesota, on a Friday night. That was an adventure in itself, but does not belong here. When we arrived back in school on Monday we were called down to the principal's office. I don't remember what Ken was told, but when the principal looked at my grades and my IQ, he simply stated, "Pete, I don't know what's wrong with you. You have a high IQ and get such low grades!"

Well, I left that office with a totally different attitude toward my studies and myself. So I had a high IQ! Why didn't some teacher told me that I was working below my capabilities? The end result was that I paid more attention in class, did my work with a different attitude and was soon on the honor roll, and, more important to me, an Honor Society member.

But back to the seventh grade for a moment; we had a class in music appreciation. In that class, a test was given to test the students' musical capacity, and my score was perfect! Rhythm, tone, the works! However, my teacher took the wrong tack, not knowing my background and lack of discipline, and put me on violin immediately. Violin requires much personal application and discipline, let alone a desire for it. I had none of these. Not until senior high did I get involved in music, and that only voice, since this required but an imperfect reading of music. I was offered free voice lessons and free piano lessons and rejected both, due to my false pride. I wasn't going to accept anything that was free. And to this day, I read music very poorly.

As to the high IQ, it brings back a funny incident that may be worth telling here. When we moved into town from Scribner, near Harley Lake, we were neighbors to a boy called George Thorbrugger. I'm not sure I am spelling that name correctly, but he was a great guy. He was a year older than I, but in the same grade. My first remembrance of him is his giving me a log house set. He was tired of it, and thought I might enjoy it. George also had a high IQ, so one happy day when we were already in senior High, the whole class was called out to take another intelligence test except George and me. So we intelligent guys were left in the classroom without anything to do. We decided we could find something to occupy our time, found a paper punch on the teacher's desk, and decorated the classroom floor with those little, round pieces of paper that a paper punch makes. Well, when the teacher and class returned to the room, the teacher looked at the floor and asked what that mess was all about. After we hemmed and hawed for a bit, she ordered us intelligent guys to get down on our knees and pick up each and every one of those little round dots! So much for our super intelligence! Needless to say, the class had a good time at our expense.

After high school I went to the Assemblies of God bible school in Minneapolis, North Central Bible Institute, now a college or university. I was already habituated to poor study habits, and didn't do much better in bible school. Oh, sure, I got good grades, probably among the best, but did not really apply myself, as I should have. I really didn't learn much. It would be interesting to find out what my grades were. I'm sure I had a 90% average or better, but this due only to natural intelligence, to no credit of my own. I did take a few Spanish lessons at another seminary just for fun, and really enjoyed it. I still remember the basic verb conjugations learned at that time. As to Missions, I belonged to the India Prayer Band, but had no idea of the HOW of Missions. Assembly of God Missions would be denomination related anyhow, not distinctly church related, as are Baptist Missions. At this juncture, I do remember that the more profound studies such as theology were more Baptist than Pentecostal. I'm sure that my attitude toward life in general and education specifically has always been more an attitude of enjoy and relax than work and get somewhere. The fact that I remember so little of my Bible school education tells me that I wasn't very studious.

The only further education I have had through the years has been special courses taken here in Brazil, especially aviation and education. These were to meliorate my capacity to serve better on the mission field. However, the fact is that I arrived in Brazil with very little knowledge of missions, its polity and practice.

Section 4 – My Spiritual Life

My own personal spiritual experience began early. Playing an instrument in the church services was very important. I was given a fine banjo-ukulele when about six, living out at Harley Lake, and learned to chord it to accompany hymns. Later, it was the mandolin. I had sufficient talent but no dedication to music, and that is true up to the present. Perhaps in heaven - - - - !

Both the Baptist Church and the Church of the Nazarene left pleasant memories on my early childhood. The Baptist Sunday school teacher was a lovely, fat woman who loved children (I believe her name was Mrs. Butts, but Sophy believes Mrs. Butts was a teacher at the Salvation Army Sunday school. Maybe she taught at both). The gospel choruses were a delight to me. The lively music at the Church at the Nazarene kept me busy as the bass drummer. At the age of six, out at Harley Lake, I thought I was a believer and wanted to be baptized. But when I saw the pastor submerging the folks, I got cold feet and backed out - happily, of course, for I was only really converted some five years later.

Our whole family was musical, the house full of instruments, including a piano. I believe Mother played the guitar-banjo, Sophy the triple-uke (?), Grace a mandolin, and I the banjo-uke. Singing was always great in the Pentecostal type services. My favorite as a six-year-old was sung in every service for any time the music director asked for a favorite I gave the hymn number of that hymn, "There is Power in the Blood." I didn't know the meaning spiritually, but loved the rhythm and music.

As a child I was never too much interested in the content of sermons, but always paid attention to the illustrations. This had an influence on my teaching homiletics years later in Brazil, when I insisted that every point of a message have an illustration for understanding and to keep people interested.

At some point in my childhood, I became very aware that I was a lost sinner and that when Christ appeared in the skies to take away his church I would be left behind. This worked on my mind so much that I remember I became very nervous to the point where I could hardly swallow my food. It was about this time that a future missionary to Brazil came to be our daily vacation Bible school teacher in the Nymore Mission Covenant Chapel. His name was Garnet Trimble, later one of the pioneers of Baptist Mid-Missions' work in the Amazon, being from Bemidji but studying at the Baptist seminary in Minneapolis. We were only two students, two very unruly boys, the pastor's son and I. But Garnet had us memorize chapter 53 of Isaiah in order to earn a plaster of Paris plaque of Stephen the

Martyr. He couldn't have chosen a better portion of Scripture for two boys that needed salvation. However, as I previously mentioned, it was not until perhaps a year later in a children's service in that same chapel that the Holy Spirit made so very real to me the great and marvelous sacrifice of Christ Jesus on the cross for me, a lost sinner. And that I was! When the altar call was made, as was the custom in those days, I rushed forward to accept the Savior as my own. The burden of sin lifted from my soul was so great I thought I could fly! I ran out of that chapel filled with joy and turned somersaults on the lawn at home. What a relief, to have that burden of sin lifted! (I believe we were living at 610 Central Avenue at this time).

Unfortunately, there was little or no help in churches for kids these days. It was pretty much taken for granted that we would grow spiritually on our own, so it wasn't long that we were back in the old rut, though we were more faithful in paying attention in Sunday school and church. No classes for new converts, no recognition of the decision made, and no baptism made available. It was only some two years later when I was thirteen that the Assemblies pastor baptized me in a lake somewhere south of Bemidji, probably at a church picnic. This was only recognition that I had accepted Christ, but no church membership involved.

Although my loud bass voice was probably the noisiest in the after service prayer meetings, the truth was that I was ashamed of the noise and fanaticism in the Assemblies. My voice developed early, so I loved to roll out loud "hallelujahs" to hear my voice thundering in my chest, but I don't think there was much real worship involved. And then there were the police visits around midnight, coming into the church building asking us to cool it because the neighbors couldn't sleep for the noise. When asked in school what my church was, I ashamedly called it the "holy roller" church. My best high school friend, Bob Hanson, was a Baptist and tried to persuade me to come over to his church where we had attended when I was four or five, but for some strange reason I did not do so, regrettably.

A Mr. Scherling, one of the local photographers, had quite an influence in my life when he introduced me to Finney's Theology. I believe Scherling was also a member of the Baptist Church (or was it the Free Methodist?), but did not manage to attract me there. I was very absorbed by Finney's practical outlook on Christianity and Bible interpretation. Finney had lived in the previous century, a great revivalist, and had been a lawyer. His theology is reasoning based on Scripture, but quite different and very appealing to the reasoning mind. For years Finney's interpretation of the Scriptures influenced my doctrinal beliefs.

As Pentecostals, we did not believe in Eternal Security. That means that we needed to find security in something else, and my impression was that I could find it if I "got the baptism," as is the expression used in reference to a supposed second experience of Grace called the "baptism of the Spirit." When I graduated from Bemidji High School, I had just turned seventeen. I graduated with honors, on the Honor Society, leading actor in drama, outstanding in choir and octet singing, but with absolutely no ambitions except drama. I had not prepared to go on to college and had taken what I imagined to be the easiest electives in the high school course. I never took a book home to study, finding the hours of study hall at school sufficient to do my homework. Being raised without a father, I had no orientation from home about studies, since my mother only finished the eighth grade. So, here I am, now wanting to go on to college to major in drama, with an inferior college prep course, and afraid to go that way because I might lose my salvation. The solution—get the "baptism!"

So, at seventeen I went to Lake Geneva Bible camp with the special purpose of receiving my "Spirit baptism" so that I might go on to college and major in drama with the idea of winding up in Hollywood and become a famous actor, but with my eternal salvation guaranteed! What a mixed up boy I was!

At camp, I made friends. Some beautiful girls, and especially a boy about my age who claimed to have the gift of speaking in Tongues. This was the evidence of the Spirit baptism! I asked him why he didn't speak in Tongues NOW, since it was such a great thing. He simply replied that it was because he "didn't want to." This added to my previous doubts about this "baptism" with Tongues as evidence, doubts that I had when in my home church the two "saints" who spoke most in "Tongues," were very jealous of each other, especially in reference to the single Assemblies pastor.

However, still believing to some extent in this experience, I spent my night hours in the camp prayer room after services, pounding on the bench, lying on the floor, groaning and moaning in good Pentecostal style. A dear saint of God who had been a Baptist kept people from hindering me, while I "tarried" for the Spirit. It dawned on me that I was lacking one thing—a real surrender of my life to the Lord! I recall getting out of that prayer room, going to the Bible school booth and getting an application form to Bible school, filling it out, giving up my idea of becoming an actor, and surrendering my life to God for the gospel ministry, the last thing in the world that I had wanted! Having surrendered my life, I returned to the prayer room to receive the "baptism." And I must confess that I did receive a baptism of God's love that moved me out of that prayer room with the same enthusiasm that my conversion moved me out of that chapel some six years earlier. I gave a quick hug to that woman who had watched over me as I prayed, saying, "Oh, Mom, the love of God!" and went out shouting "Oh, the love of God!" My heart was bursting with His love!

However, one thing was lacking. I didn't speak in Tongues, the essential sign of the "baptism!" And because I didn't speak in Tongues, in the eyes of the Assemblies of God I was not baptized in the Spirit. Faking speaking in Tongues was not my dish, so when I fulfilled my promise and went to the Assemblies of God school in Minneapolis that fall, I have to say that I had not received the "baptism," simply because I did not speak in Tongues on that occasion.

An interesting observation should be made here about my introduction to that woman who watched over me as I "tarried" for the Spirit baptism. I didn't know her from Eve, but when I went to Bible school, there she was in the Minneapolis Gospel Tabernacle where many of us students attended (and I later became the "best" janitor the pastor had ever engaged). She was a prayer warrior in that church and a mother to many students. I had called her "Mom" without knowing that this was the nickname that students gave her. She was a great help to many boys and girls while sojourning in school away from home. Her own grown boy was in the Navy serving during the Second World War, exactly during those years I was in Bible school. Both she and her husband, Emil Cambronne, were a great help to me, a boy away from home.

Observing the spiritual life of teachers and students at school, I became more cynical as to this spiritual experience demanded by the Assemblies to qualify as an ordained pastor. When my turn came to speak in chapel in my senior year, I was satiated with the false spirituality and spoke very frankly to the student body. The result was a breaking of spirit, and the day became a day of prayer. But in my own self, doubts about a number of Pentecostal teachings were brewing.

The pastor of the Lake Street Assembly of God was a gentleman named Frank Lindquist. A rather serious, stern fellow with a voice similar to mine, such that when we worked on the Iron Range some years later, someone told me I was an imitation of Rev. Lindquist. That had never entered my head, but certainly the effect of his ministry on me for three years influenced my style of messages and presentation. What affected me most was his humility. One evening I arrived early for the Wednesday night prayer meeting, and there he was with his coat and tie off, sleeves rolled up, mopping the prayer room floor. It took me by surprise, so I asked him what the score was, and he replied that since no one else was willing to do the job, he had to do it. The church probably had over a thousand members. That was when I took the job of janitor of that church and he told me I was the best janitor he had had in years. Little did he know that I would get up at three on Sunday mornings to vacuum, sweep, mop, and dust before Sunday school. Late, but left things fresh and clean! Thanks to his example, on the mission field it became a principle of mine to do whatever came to hand to do, be it little or big.

I was elected to the student council, and during my senior year in Bible school was asked to form a protest to the school board about the teachers' late arrivals and unpreparedness. Several days later I was called down to the president's office and asked if the protest was my composition. I said it was from the student body. But the president insisted, and I was obligated to say yes. "That's all I want to know," he then replied and dismissed me. I don't remember ever being marked because of this.

The school furnished nice, white towels to the students. There was a lot of soot in the city, and the white walls of our dorm room (the building was an old hospital building) would get rather black, so one day I accidentally took a used towel, filled a bucket with soapy water, and washed down the walls. The towel was very black, but I was sure that the laundry would get it white again. To my embarrassment, one beautiful day the school dean of men stood up in front of the whole student body, displayed MY black towel, wondering how it could get so black, and asking that the student responsible please come down to his office. Needless to say, I arrived there with a great deal of shame, but took the rap. I remember his surprise, saying, "YOU, Peter! I would never have thought this of you!" That was sufficient punishment!

Obeying school rules was never my strength, and during that first year when I was so madly in love with Genevieve, I sought every way possible to be with her. A freshman could only date once a month, if I recall correctly, and could not even see a girl home after service. My Genevieve lived and worked at a house at the end of the streetcar line. I worked at the Band Box, a luncheonette. The old, former hospital building had several fire escapes and many basement windows, so before going to church, I would see to it that windows giving access to the fire escape and also basement windows were unlatched, and then head out. Some nights I would see my girlfriend home after church, take the last streetcar and come back and find an unlocked window to get in and go up to the fifth floor to my room. But later, I developed a simpler strategy. I would simply go over to the Band Box and buy a sandwich, go up to the main door, ring for the night watchman, walk in, hand him a sandwich and go up in the elevator. He would make some remark, like, "Working late tonight, eh!" My answer was a simple "good night." An act of deception, but without verbally lying! Happily, after the first year my girlfriend threw me over so I had no occasion to deceive anymore.

Several memories of class events come to mind. One is the time a student asked one of the teachers just when did a sinning Christian lose his salvation. The teacher wrinkled his brow, thought for a moment, and replied, "There is a line drawn, known only to God, over which, when a sinning Christian steps, he loses his salvation." No Scripture, just an explanation without basis. A second event was when we were studying Roberts Rules and Orders about parliamentary procedures. The class was organized into an imitation church for learning purposes. On the sly a few students and I did a "special session" and modified everything that had been done, and in the following class after the "church" minutes were read, one of us stood and said there had been a special session and read our false minutes. Of course the "church" disciplined us and our rights to vote were taken away. I still remember the fun we had.

I don't recall graduating with honors though I did have good grades. I could not be ordained because I had not spoken in Tongues, but was licensed to preach. A fellow graduate and I, along with a number of graduates, went up to northern Minnesota to the "Iron Range" area previously mentioned, and he and I rented an unused theatre building in Eveleth, Minnesota, to begin "Gospel Services." It was an interesting experience, though I was not a skilled worker by any means. And I was passing through the experience of reading literature that was not Pentecostal, which brought me to the conclusion that I could not remain in the Assembly of God. I became a believer in Eternal Security, an unbeliever in the "baptism of the Spirit evidenced by speaking in Tongues," and had serious doubts about the Assemblies' teaching on the second coming of Christ. So, at the Presbyters' meeting in Minneapolis a year after graduation, I presented my resignation from the Assemblies. The pastors present pleaded with me to wait one more year and reconsider, but I could not. My new convictions were too firm. My own uncle was there, Rev. David Bruzelius, and I presented to him my basis for leaving—that there is no real biblical basis for a second Spirit baptism after regeneration, and, even less, a teaching in Scriptures that speaking in Tongues is the sign of such a baptism. Uncle David agreed, but terminated saying, "I believe it anyhow." Thus in 1945 I ended my association with the Assemblies of God. I had become a "straight" fundamentalist and a Calvinist. Where to now?

When I left the Assemblies I became a "man without a country," so to speak. Emil and Mom Cambronne took me in when I worked at a warehouse loading boxcars, and waited on the Lord's leading. Eventually this lead to my accepting the interim pastorate of a country church not too far from the Canadian border, seven miles distant from a small town called Kennedy. Their intention was to call a permanent pastor, and this gave me a year's experience in the pastorate. This church supported my missionary ministry until my total retirement in 2005.

The country church was a mixture of Swedish Mission Covenant and Swedish Baptist. Some were Calvinists, some Arminians and some legalists. With my Pentecostal background and a certain impression that "Open your mouth and God will fill it," I preached with enthusiasm but with little study. I don't know how they put up with a year of it, but they did. I had a fine catechism class of about a dozen twelve to fourteen year olds, and we had a lot of fun. One of the boys one day came in an old Model-T Ford, and we took time out to drive up and down the ditches in that. As far as I know, the majority of those youngsters remain or remains faithful to the Gospel.

On New Years Eve, 1945 or 6, a violent snowstorm developed, and all of the church people elected to stay home from the watch-night service, except a car full of young people and myself in my old Chevy. We fought our way out to the church building seven miles from town, sang, prayed and made merry until after midnight. I particularly remember one song we sang, even though that was way back then. It was "Oh, how sweet to trust in Jesus, just to take Him at His Word," a song with real meaning to us young people.

Snowstorms in the Red River Valley of the North where we were are particularly dangerous to those out on the road. The wide open spaces permit the wind to blow blinding streaks of snow across the roads at crazy angles, and one has to be extremely careful to not be fooled and led off the road. By winding down a window and maintaining a very watchful eye on the edge of the road, one can usually manage to stay on the highway. That is what we did on the trip back to town. About the middle of the trip we came across a car in the ditch with a couple in it, worried stiff about freezing to death in that dangerous situation. My little car was already full, but it was necessary to pack that couple in also, and like a can of sardines continue our trip into town. I haven't the faintest idea who they were, but they were very grateful. Tired of some of the older church members' legalism, I took time out to mow my lawn on Sunday afternoon, to show them that God does not send thunderbolts on those who do not keep the "Sabbath." I think this may have added to some anxiety on the part of this particular brand of member to see me leave. At the end of the year they called a very fine man to assume the pastorate permanently.

After leaving that church, I was invited to stay with the Field family near Stephen, Minnesota. They had a houseful of young people, so one more just made it that much better. There was where I learned a lot about mechanics. I got a job in the local hardware store in Kennedy, just a few miles up the road, and it was at that time that I was invited to be ordained to the ministry by the Wausau Bible Church in Wausau, Wisconsin. I had previously been there with one of my Bible school companions who also left the Assemblies about the same time I did and for the same reasons. He, Eugene Marsceau, and I were examined by a council and ordained on the same day, May 2, 1946. I applied for a number of different pulpits during this time.

Section 5 – A Call to Missions

It was in the church where I was ordained to the ministry that my interest in Brazil was first stirred. Missionary Horace Murfin, working in northeast Brazil, was there presenting his missionary work. During the afternoon when everyone was socializing, I glanced over in the corner where he sat alone looking at his slides with the tears running down his cheeks. I was impressed by this and went over to ask what he was thinking. He said he was just remembering his people in Brazil. His apparent love for the Brazilians affected me, and I got his prayer card and mission address and began sending him a monthly sum for his support. He in return sent me a monthly personal letter of thanks, but always finished it with the expression, "Come and see." This worked on me. Why not go?

I enjoyed my work at the hardware store, and the fellowship and fun at the Field household was out of this world, but something was lacking. Had I studied to sell hardware? Prayer and meditation led me to come to this conclusion: Doors are made to be knocked on. I decided to contact Horace Murfin's mission headquarters and ask for an application form to fill out for missionary service in Brazil. I was free from encumbrances, and if they accepted me, I would take it as a sign from the Lord that I should go. This must have been late 1948 or early 1949.

Filling out forms isn't always easy, and I decided to put on the request for recommendations the names of some of the persons I had offended with my fight against legalism and arminianism. But apparently these wanted me farther away still for I was well recommended and was soon planning to raise support and go down to Brazil. The mission was an interdenominational mission, by name the Brazil Gospel Fellowship. During my two years with this mission, I had no doctrinal conflict whatsoever, and was treated very well. To this day (2005) I have good relations with the members of this fine mission.

How to raise money as a missionary was an unknown to me, and I was not exceedingly successful. My notions of Missions were vague, including the idea that a missionary should be sent out and supported by a local church. My thought was just to get some support anywhere, get out to the field, learn the language and evangelize. My preparation for missions was practically zero. The one thing that I remember most about money raising was attending a missionary meeting in the Solway Chapel, west of my hometown, Bemidji, and hearing a missionary quote Second Corinthians 9:8, "And God is able to make all grace abound toward you, that you, always having all sufficiency in all things, may abound to every good work" (That verse is on my wall at this very moment in Portuguese, 56 or so years later).

What more could I ask? Why money if I had God on my side?

Missionary Horace Murfin had come back to the States to purchase a vehicle for use on the mission field. I do not think his choice was a wise one, but the important part is that he was in a hurry to get back and take me with him. So, with an uncertain amount of support, mostly by individuals, I packed my trunks and few belongings in an old trailer behind my 1934 Chevy and headed from northern Minnesota for the Brooklyn docks in New York State via Springfield and Chicago, Illinois, in late 1949. That was quite an experience in itself. I won't take time to tell much of it, but two things I remember in particular. The first was when the ball joint pulling the trailer gave out. I had cross chains from the trailer to the car, so the trailer followed right along, but the problem of getting to a welder and having it fixed was a hassle because I was on the Pennsylvania Turnpike. The second was when getting off the Pennsylvania Turnpike and heading into the capital, Harrisburg. The road signs were still a bit small and primitive, and I was looking for Federal Route 22, heading east. The famous Harrisburg Farm Fair was in full swing, and as I looked for road signs, I saw a sign pointing to the left, indicating the highway I wanted. When I awakened hours later (for I was dead tired), I was way back up into the Pennsylvania Mountains at

Lewistown going the wrong way! And being very tired, I decided not to drive all the way back to Harrisburg, but headed across the mountains going east on those small state roads. I don't remember the details anymore, but do know that it was necessary to stop and rest before continuing on to New York City. According to what I wrote in my article, "It Stands In the Book," it took twelve extra hours to get to my destination, and I had five hours of sleep in three days. When I got there and had crossed Manhattan Island and the Brooklyn Bridge, I stopped at a gas station, so tired I didn't know where I was, and asked the attendant how far I was from New York City. His reply was, "Buddy, you're in Brooklyn!" That was my destination! I was just a few blocks from the docks where the ship, JUTAHY, the freighter we were to board, was docked. In spite of the obstacles, the Lord had taken me right to my destination.

Another interesting memory returns—the disposing of my car. I had over-tightened one of the valve rocker arms and burned a valve, so I had come to the last part of the trip pretty much on five of the six cylinders. After unloading the baggage on the proper docks, I had to dispose of the old car and trailer. Calling a bunch of dockhands to come, I got up on the hood of my old faithful Chevy and auctioned it off. Obviously dockhands don't have a lot of cash in their pockets, and the most I could get was thirty-five dollars for the whole she-bang, but I got rid of it and went to a nearby Justice of Peace to pass the documents over to the buyer. It was a good old car, good radio, tires and motor. But it was a lesson that has stood me in good stead ever since as to material things. Don't get sentimentally attached to them. "You can't take it with you."

Leaving Brooklyn at night the water was calm when we fell asleep. The ship was a freighter with cabins for passengers on the rear end. They went up and down all night long on the high seas while we were sleeping, so we did not know what effect this movement was having on our sense of balance. I awakened in the morning and got up congratulating myself that I was not feeling seasick, when, to my surprise, whatever was in my stomach came up at once! Fortunately, the washbowl was near the bunk and I made it in time. I never felt quite right for the rest of the two-week trip.

My traveling companions, besides Mr. Murfin himself, were Ed and Jane Lieb, John and Leota Miller, and a single lady, Mary Hobaugh. John was from Bemidji, my hometown. Ed and Jane were from Pennsylvania and knew my future wife. Jane was pregnant, and her entire time onboard was spent in bed, as I recall. The food was probably good, but I couldn't stand the smells from the kitchen and dining hall. We ate with the officers who were very friendly, as was the whole crew. It was fun to watch the flying fish and the ocean spray, but we were anxious to get to Belem on the Amazon by the time a week has past. After two weeks it was such a relief to start up the Amazon River toward the city of Belem, so beautiful a sight, the green banks of the Amazon lined with brightly painted houses.

The JUTAHY spent a number of days in Belem unloading freight. We knew no Portuguese, but there were plenty of sights and smells to entertain us. The dollar had much more value than at this writing, so I was able to get a haircut for three cruzeiros, or about ten cents. Today, in 2005, I pay the equivalent of two dollars. That is DOLLAR inflation in 55 years. In the same time space, Brazilian money has inflated (or is it Deflated?) about a billion to one.

Belem being a river port, there were all types of boats docked along the quay. Buzzards by the dozens were eating dead fish and other scraps. Odors aplenty assailed our sensitive American noses. The street fairs, which eventually we got used to, had such a variety of strange, tropical fruits along with homemade artifacts that it was entertaining just to walk up and down looking. Especially different from the States were the strips of fresh meat hanging from poles. And fish, also.

However, the center of Belem was a modern, bustling city with beautiful parks. One thing our stop there did for me was to give me a desire to learn the language as quickly as possible.

We eventually boarded our ship and headed for Fortaleza, our destination in the "bulge" of Brazil closest to Africa. Fare from New York City to Fortaleza was $225.00. I don't know if the date on my Brazilian identification card is the day we arrived in Belem or the day we applied for our ID's in Fortaleza. It is dated January thirty-first, 1950 and listed as "Date of Entrance."

Fortaleza was very different from Belem, situated in what is called the "Polygon of Drought," Northeast Brazil. We were put up, or at least I was, in the home of a missionary couple, Ted and Dorothy Knectel. They were older missionaries, very interesting and active. After a few days in Fortaleza, Ted drove us interior to Sobral, our home for nine months of language study. Of that trip I only recall the strange custom that then existed of the drivers upon meeting a car coming the opposite direction flashing the headlights off and on, each giving the other the opportunity of seeing the road. Didn't their cars have a low beam? That custom died out later.

Finally I was in Brazil, a prospective missionary, with the simplest of a "missionary call," anxious to learn a new language and evangelize the lost, but with a very faint idea of how to do either. Happily, the Lord God who directs those who trust Him was there to care, and I was in the hands of caring missionaries.

Pictured above my father (Thoma Clark) and I pause to take a photo as I was presented with the 2007 Oklahoma Young Entrepreneur of the Year Award by the United States Small Business Administration. This photo was taken at the Summit Club in Downtown Tulsa which was at the top of the Bank of America Tower.

Section 6 – Language Study

Sobral was a bustling interior city, probably about twenty thousand population at that time, having a Roman Catholic seminary and many RC churches scattered throughout the city. Nearby was a mountain covered with fruit trees where Horace Murfin had a cabin to get away from the heat that at times became almost unbearable.He also had a cabin on a nearby artificial lake called Cachoeirinha, where we would go occasionally to picnic. Horace had been in Sobral for a number of years and had established an evangelical church that I am told no longer exists, but was quite active at that time. Horace died and was buried in Brazil many years later in Maranhão, a neighboring state.

Culture as well as language is one of the things missionaries have to adapt to, so the couple rented their own homes and began to not only study the language but learn to buy and bargain. The single lady and I were placed in the missionary's home. Very funny was the time that Edgar Lieb came in while we were playing dominoes, very excited because the new maid had just moved in and placed his chickens in the bathhouse for the night. His problem, of course, was trying to tell her that Americans don't keep their chickens in the bathhouse! His Portuguese was still very inadequate. Also, he wasn't yet acquainted with chicken thieves. Meanwhile, I was singing, "Chickens in the bathtub, singing for joy, living the life of Lifebuoy," a radio jingle used back then. I'm not sure that Ed appreciated it, however.

Getting used to the noises was also cultural. I wrote, "One other unusual thing about the city where I am now living is the noises. A city of 20,000 inhabitants, it sounds like a farmyard. In the morning bright and early the roosters begin to crow and soon one hears the mooing of cattle as they are driven down the city street out to pasture."

Extreme poverty was apparent everywhere. Of one particular home, I wrote: "After the service the lady of the house announced that Manuel had had a birthday and we were invited to have some refreshments in the kitchen. To get to the kitchen we passed through a couple of bedrooms whose furniture consisted only in hammocks and a few boxes to keep what few articles of clothing they had. Most of these people have not slept in a bed. The kitchen had a table and a few chairs besides the stove—an arrangement that burns sticks and heats water, though I don't know how. The refreshments were lemonade and cake. The lemonade was good, the water having been boiled because the natives know that missionaries like boiled water. But the cake was about like a devil's-food cake that no sugar had been added to, and had forgotten to rise. Still, we ate it out of politeness and congratulated Emanuel on his 15th birthday. But these folks in spite of their lack of material goods had found a happiness which only can be found in Christ Jesus." Fifty-five years has made a big difference in the poverty level in Brazil, but one still finds homes like these here in the northeast.

Maybe I should dedicate a whole chapter to culture shock. After leaving northern Minnesota with its wide open spaces and un-walled yards, especially in the Red River Valley of the North, where it is table-land flat for scores of miles, living in walled-in houses on narrow streets can be claustrophobic. Writing about going to the post office, I wrote, "We leave by the front gate since climbing over the fence is quite a task. It is about six feet high and very necessary to keep out thieves. Just last night one got in by piling bricks up against the fence, but judging by the dog tracks around where he landed, he didn't get very far before Lucky, the family pet and watchdog discovered him. Lucky is feared far and near around here, and if you saw him, you'd understand why, for he's "big as a house," and when he is coming at you he looks as if he could finish you in one bite." That was 55 years ago, and the situation is worse today than it was then as far as the necessity for isolation and precaution is concerned. I'm still not used to it!! Our dog, Ricky, is extremely playful, but when he comes at you barking, he'll scare you to death if you don't know him.

Another fact I have learned. After fifty-five years in Brazil at this writing, I am still an American. Things in the Brazilian culture still irritate me. Some Brazilian customs I still do not adapt to or am not sensitive to. Really, this is a pity, because I am sure that if I had really applied myself to "becoming a Brazilian" I could have done better. Just recently I came to realize that Brazilians always see a visitor to the door.

Now, back to language study, Sobral was very hot, but the rainy season that year was exceptionally hard, so that the river flowing along side the city invaded the houses along the banks. Poor folks from those houses soon appeared at our door begging, and I was highly frustrated because I could not understand them. This was more incentive to apply myself to the language.

A missionary couple from Fortaleza, the Percy Bellahs, came to visit Horace and Ida, his wife, quite early in our language studies. We were taken up the mountain plateau some miles away from Sobral to the city where they had worked or were working, São Benedito. My sensitive musical ear was already attuned to the different American "brogues" or accents in

Portuguese, and I was able to hear that Percy spoke Portuguese the best of all the missionaries I had heard. To myself I said, "I am going to speak Portuguese BETTER that Mr. Bellah!" Speaking the language without any American accent became my goal, and as a single man I had the advantage of being able to go visiting with the pastor, our teacher, more than the married fellows. I remember my jaws actually aching with the effort I made to imitate Brazilian speech. I can't understand it now, it is so natural to me, but it required lots of effort. The studies, no, they were relatively easy. We only had a grammar as a textbook, but the local pastor, Raimundo Paiva, was an excellent teacher and we had daily contact with the people.

I eventually moved out to the cabin on the lake, fished in the afternoon and studying at night in the light of a kerosene lamp. My effort paid off, and for many years I was known as the foreign missionary who spoke Portuguese most naturally. However, even today when I walk into a corner store or some place where I am not known, someone will ask me, "You are not Brazilian, are you?" There's still something there!!! Brazilians don't learn to speak from grammars, books and educated teachers. They learn at home, in the street, on the playground and in the market as little children who learn effortlessly.

My first message after six months of study was to be about the "Grace of God." However, I preached on the "Grease of God," and wasn't told about it until I was finished. I had made an "SH" sound instead of an "S" sound in the word "graça." I guess I thought it sounded more sophisticated, but it made quite a difference in meaning.

While in Sobral I had my first experience with the Brazilian knife, called a "peixeira." While taking a group of Christians to the lake for a picnic, along with the pastor and a young man, we were attacked by a drunken deaf man who apparently had it in mind to slaughter us all. Everyone ran, but I instinctively turned toward him as he came running down the path, thinking to protect the others, especially the women, girls and children. We men had picked up rocks for self defense, but suddenly my memory "rang" in my ears a comic strip from probably 15 years earlier where one of Little Orphan Annie's friends dispatched one of her many enemies, and returned saying, "Annie, if you ever have to fight a man with a knife, use your feet!" Right then and there I kicked as hard as I could when the man got close enough, getting him in the stomach. We both went over backwards, and after some exciting moments, I got his knife from him and all was well. I have the complete story in my writings for the Kennedy Star, "It Stands in the Book," a Swedish expression.

Something I mentioned earlier was the choice Mr. Murfin made of a car to bring to Brazil. One bright day he got it out of customs and drove it to Sobral. He was anxious to try it out on the back roads, so we started out, us men, on a trip to Camocim, a coastal city a few hours from Sobral on country trails. I think the car was a blue Plymouth, a simple passenger car. Somewhere down the trail, Horace went over a rock in the middle of the road and we heard a loud ripping sound. He stopped immediately, and when we looked under the car, the motor oil was running out of the oil pan! The rock had ripped a long hole in the pan. After Ed Lieb tried to stop the leak with his handkerchief, I yelled, "Grab the hubcaps!" which we did after prying them off with a tire iron. Back in those days, hubcaps were round like half spheres, fitting over the wheel bolts. Each was like a small basin, and we were able to save enough motor oil to get back to Sobral after plugging the rip in the oil pan with cloth and splinters. We strained the oil through one of my nice, white, new hankies. Reading the newspaper article I wrote, it appears we took the oil pan off to plug the hole. Mr. Murfin soon had a steel plate bolted under the car to protect it on the bad roads.

There are many other interesting things I could tell about those first nine months in Brazil such as my first scorpion sting, being bitten by a piranha, swimming in a piranha infested lake, eating and sleeping in the poorest of homes, teaching an English class of high society teen-age girls, vomiting blood on my first and only fishing trip on the Atlantic ocean, getting acquainted with a variety of snakes, poisonous and non-poisonous, and, above all, admiring the great beauty of the southern night sky with its billions of stars, so much more beautiful than the skies of the northern hemisphere.

Americans wonder about the piranha, the dangerous fish with the razor-sharp teeth. The lake where I spent my afternoons fishing was full of them, and also with the Brazilian lake trout, the tucunaré. I would fish until dark, catching a nice string of both. Most piranha were about sunfish size, although some bigger. One day as I was taking the hook out of the mouth of one of these, I let my finger get into his mouth, and with one quick snap, he severed a sizable chunk of flesh from my pointer finger on the right hand. Quickly I forced the flesh back into place and held it there with my thumb. I was on a raft close to shore, managed to get to the cabin and roll a piece of bandage or tape over the wound. It grew back into place, and today I can no longer see the scar. Since then I have caught hundreds of piranhas, but always with great care to keep my fingers out of their mouths! I always found it interesting that I could swim in the lake with the piranhas but they never attacked me. Seems they weren't hungry for Swedish or Dutch flesh.

Well, after nine months of language study, we were ready to go out and face the world. At least the married couples were. I had no working partner. I gather that Mr. Murfin had it in his mind that I should marry Miss Hobaugh, but she must have been at least ten years older than I, and really did not appeal to me. Besides, I had some years earlier committed the problem of love and marriage to the Heavenly Father, and was awaiting His direction, not Mr. Murfin's. For the present I was imagining in finding a male partner who would face with me the persecution I expected in those fanatical interior cities.

Section 7 – A Life Partner

This I hadn't mentioned, but somewhere along the trail I had learned to tune pianos. I wasn't a professional but tuned well enough for the average ear. This became known in Brazil, and Guy and Inez McLain, friends of the Murfins, came by Sobral to visit and invited me to go to Juazeiro do Norte where they lived to tune up an old piano. Having finished the language course we were expected to do, I was willing to go along. Meanwhile, Pastor Raimundo came up to me and took me aside to wise me up. He said they were taking me along to meet a single girl in Juazeiro, and remarked, "She is the only beautiful American that I have ever seen." Apparently most American missionary ladies were not very pretty in his sight. My reply to him was, "Fine. If this is what God has for me, I'm ready. If not, no problem."

My experience with girls in the States had taught me that I by myself was incapable of choosing a life partner if I was to serve the Lord. I had had all the normal experiences of a boy and young man. I remember when I was about five, one of the neighbor girls of my age and I showing our private parts to one another to see what the other sex was like! Once we saw, we were satisfied. The absolute separation in the American society of the male and female sex back in those days only served to increase a child's curiosity. Here in Brazil, sex is treated as normal, and little children often run around without clothing.

When I was about seven years old at Harley Lake Camp, a girl a few years older than I took me out to the woods to try to have sex with me. I don't remember much about it, but the excitement of the occurrence remains in my memory. It was also at Harley Lake that the older boys let me in on all the secrets about sex that my mother never told me. The secrets were illustrated vividly with jokes, of course.

Then, when I was about ten, living in Nymore, I fell madly in love with a beautiful little girl of about eight to whom I never spoke nor did she ever look at me as far as I know, but I would go out of the way to walk by her house to see if I could get a glimpse of her. One day when I walked by, a bully somewhat bigger than I was threatened to give me a beating. I ran through a neighbor's yard, and as I passed out the back gate, a German police dog jumped on me and bit hard on my back. I ran down the street to a corner bar where the owner or bartender washed my bleeding back with medicine and bandaged me up. I don't remember ever going to see my sweetheart again.

At the age of fourteen, a sophisticated girl from the Twin Cities met me on the beach at Diamond Point Park in Bemidji, and I discovered that she was a visitor in a home just a few blocks from ours. One evening we met and she said she was going to show me how to "neck," so right there on the front lawn in front of other people we sat embracing and kissing. But I don't think I really learned much that I didn't already know. Girls were not really my favorite pastime, but they gradually entered my life because of my dedication to drama. The plays I was in always involved a girl. Soon girls were after me, and expecting me to be as romantic as I had to be in dramas. As a Christian I had to hold back as far as sex was concerned where my high school companions did not. Going to a class picnic in a friend's car, a girl I had known since childhood literally threw herself on top of me in the car, and because I did not correspond, mocked me. I got as far away from her as possible when we left the car.

My first real love affair occurred in my first year of Bible school. We formed a gospel quartette and one of the members had a good-looking sister that I fell madly in love with. Genevieve. I highly respected her and never in the whole year I was in love did I make any untoward advances. We would attend free symphony concerts together, attend church together, all the things Christian sweethearts could do. My problem was that she was uncertain in her love for me. At times she loved me, at times not, and this uncertainty drove me wild. I actually got an ulcer from the stress this gave me. At summer camp, I finally took this passion to the Lord in prayer and after a hard struggle, He gave me victory and release from it. She had already said she wanted me no longer. However, after that she wanted me back but I was not interested. I recall the dean of women coming to me and inquiring about my relationship with her, questioning why I had given her up. It seems she was having some emotional or psychological problems.

"Necking" or sitting around hugging and kissing was the norm back in those days, though that was pretty much the limit for Christians. But the bad habit of young people to make "necking" a pastime ruined a number of good friendships because we could not keep on to the limit and had to cut them off. I had a number of fine Christian girlfriends before coming to Brazil, but the Lord held me back and taught me to wait for His leading in love and marriage. I recognized the need for divine guidance was such an important matter. So when I went to Juazeiro do Norte with the McLains, I was certain that if the Lord were not in the meeting with Louise Kinsel, nothing would come of it.

But something DID come of it! Louise was in Fortaleza trying to get her new kerosene refrigerator out of customs when I arrived in Juazeiro. When she heard that I was there she delayed her return for a week, expecting me to be gone when she arrived. On the long trip back to Juazeiro, about 13 hours, the men, Charles

Hocking, Jim Willson and Harold Reiner made it a point to tease her about the two single men around, including me, of course. She said she made every attempt to avoid meeting me, but was persuaded to go to a party on Saturday night, sometime around December tenth, 1950, knowing that I would be there. Some of us were outside talking, and when she arrived she would not look my way. Inside the house when I was able the first thing I said to her to break the ice was, "What pretty blue eyes you have!" I think that did it, for she gave me a nice smile.

The next day after Sunday school in the little Baptist Church hall downtown she came up to me and said more or less this, "Well, I suppose we have to get acquainted, for I have been invited up to McLain's for dinner." So, we walked up together, and began to get acquainted. In the afternoon we went visiting with the young people but were more interested in getting to know each other than anything else. We enjoyed each other's company until she went to her house. After she left, I went into the bedroom and knelt before the Lord, asking Him to remove the restraint I had been under for a number of years IF this were the woman He had prepared for me. And lift it He did! So that very night after service I walked her to her house and declared to her that she was going to marry me. She laughed at me, but the following night accepted. You might find interesting what I wrote to the Kennedy Star in my column, IT STANDS IN THE BOOK. Here it is:

"Louise had had a rough time of it. She was in Fortaleza with three of the men from this station attending to customs house business and when they heard that I was coming to Juazeiro she got a full week of nothing but razzing. Such things as, "Snooks hooks Brooks," and, "Be bright, be Burns, be Brooks," were composed for her sake (Burns was the name of a single missionary up the Amazon River who later married and whose wife died within 20 minutes of Louise's death). So she was pretty well set to ignore me.

"So, we met. Difficult situation. I was sitting along with Guy and Inez, the missionaries with whom I came to Juazeiro, out on the veranda in the cool of the evening when Louise came along with Harold and Ruth, whom I had already met. She was casually introduced to me but she neither looked at me nor shook hands but hastily mumbled, "how do you do," and went on with her conversation with someone else. And so it was for the rest of the evening until finally I made some statement that got her to look me squarely in the eye.

"The next day she was over for dinner and treated me less brusquely but quite ignored me until after dinner when with complete frankness I asked her if she'd been teased about me. That broke the ice and I found that she could be just as frank and free to talk as I. So we spent a happy two hours conversing and exchanging ideas before we went visiting the sick with the young people from the church. I believe it was then that something happened in the region of my heart, for I found that I had lost my appetite and I was strangely happy. A guy of my age (an old 26 years) falling in love!

"May I describe her? She's five feet two, eyes of blue—the prettiest, bluest eyes you could find. She has an oval face, a high, well-shaped forehead and a firm chin with a slightly sad mouth, all of which are molded into a picture that speaks of character. And what a hearty laugh she has! And that soft, expressive voice with twinkling, starry eyes!"

"Most of all in importance, she loves Jesus. In serving Him, she's not grown "stale" on that all-important theme, 'Jesus, Blessed Jesus.'"

That love affair lasted over 50 years.

Section 8 – The First Years of Marriage

Our courting was short. I was sure she was for me, and told her so about 24 hours after I met her. She agreed to marry me 24 hours later. She then said she wanted to get married as soon as possible to avoid gossip and also to marry before she turned 30. I hurried back to Sobral to get permission from my mission to work for a year in cooperation with the Baptist Mid-Missions missionaries in Juazeiro, and to get the few things I had brought to Brazil with me. While there I wrote the only love letters I ever wrote, and even tried my hand at a little poetry. Imagine! I, a poet, and didn't know it! Here is a sample, if you can bear with me, remembering that I was miles away, newly in love, and anxious to get back to her:

If I could hold Louise just now,

On my knees

And squeeze!

(Only a little!)

And steal a kiss –

WOW!

But I can't. Louise

(Bless you, child)

Is far away.

I must stay,

If you please,

Two whole weeks

Without her smiles

And kisses—

I'll be Wild!

On the flight back to Juazeiro and to her my heart was
singing the "Hallelujah Chorus" from Handel all the way.
Of course, I bought a diamond for her, and we had our
wedding rings made. I had a white linen suit tailored
and she got her gown and all the trimmings ready.
She was to turn 30 on February 19th, and we married
on January 21, 1951, about six weeks after we met.
Pastor Afonso and his wife Julieta, for whose wedding
she had been best maid, were our best man and maid,
and Charles Hocking did the knot tying. Sadly, Harold
Reiner's flash for his camera didn't function so we got
no pictures of the ceremony. We had our civil ceremony
in the afternoon and church wedding in the evening.
The wedding was at Louise's house, and I didn't really
recognize how blessed I was until just a few years ago,
around the year 2000, when I saw a young couple
struggling to get things in hand for marriage. I married
a woman, house, furniture and all!

The seminary invited me to teach a difficult class, Daniel and Revelation. My Portuguese was well pronounced but my vocabulary was still somewhat limited, so I had to dig to get lessons ready. I also began teaching in the primary school where Louise taught. These were good experiences and practical for my Portuguese learning.

But to a more personal subject, I had never had a role model at home to teach me how to be a good husband and father. A poor widow could not show a son how to be a good husband. I recognize now how much Louise must have suffered with my insensitiveness to her desires and feelings. They say the first seven years of a marriage are the hardest, and I remember Louise saying to me a few times that she would leave me were it not for the children. The same was true when the children came along. I wanted MY children to be perfect. I was cruel at times, and never very loving with the first ones after they got out of diapers. Perhaps having twins at the very start was a bit too much for me, but I was proud as a peacock of them. The third son was treated with more love, I believe, and of course, the last, our daughter, spent much time with me when a small child. I really enjoyed swinging in the hammock with the last two when they were small, singing a Brazilian chorus, "Meu barco é pequeno, tão grande o mar, Jesus segura minha mão" (My boat is small, the sea is big, Jesus holds my hand).

Sending our children off to the Fortaleza Academy
was cruel, but we were told we had to do it, so we did.
It wasn't so hard for the twins, because they started at
the academy while we were in Fortaleza caring for the
language school and First Baptist Church, but for our
third son, Bob, it was terribly hard. We left him crying,
and we cried, too. We had a hard time going home
without him, and were told that he cried himself to sleep
every night that first year. Louise always remembered
him playing on the kitchen floor in Assaré and saying
he would rather be a garbage collector than go out
to Fortaleza to become educated. Beth had it a bit
easier, for she wanted to go to be with her little friends,
fellow MK's (missionary kids). Years later at a mission
council meeting in Cleveland I testified of the problems
in parents' and children's lives caused by the mission
ruling that where there was a mission school parents
were obligated to send their children. The rule was
changed. Many parents and children have been saved
the agony of early separation by this change but many
MK's were severely damaged by this ruling. Some are
completely out of the Faith.

Before we married, Louise had agreed to come
to my mission, leaving Baptist Mid-Missions. When
senior missionary Guy McLain became ill and needed
treatment in Fortaleza, he asked us to take their place
for a second year at the primary school dorm. Guy was

the founder of the Work in the Cariri valley. I made a trip to Sobral to meet with the missionaries of my mission to request another year's leave. However, since I had already been lent to BMM for almost a year, they felt that I should return, and denied my request. Believing that it was the Lord's will that I go back to Juazeiro and serve for the coming year, I resigned from the Brazil Gospel Fellowship mission and, with Louise by my side, assumed the care of the children's dorm at the primary school, also teaching there, and continued teaching at the seminary. It was during this time that the twins were born. I learned that loyalty to a denomination or mission is secondary to loyalty to God himself. Years later a tape from my preacher brother Reuben gave an order of priorities that I have used numerous times in counseling. God first, your partner next, the children third, then the job, education, the church, and recreation. I'm no longer sure of the exact order, but the first three are the most important.

Since we both were "up in years," we wanted children as soon as reasonable. We were glad when Louise became pregnant about the middle of the year, and she was highly entertained by the kicking in her abdomen. But when she became immensely big, we suspected there were twins. Our doctor was a Dr. Hildegardo Belem, a very good doctor. He sent us to Crato for an X-ray to see if we were going to have twins, but by this time Louise was so big, the X-ray machine did not produce rays strong enough to pass through her! The doctor finally found two heartbeats and declared that there indeed were twins, and they were girls. When the birth pains began, we rushed to Crato to the only hospital in the region and began a long wait for something to happen. It never did. There was no way to know the position of the twins, but there was no way they could ever come naturally in the position they were in. After more than 24 hours of labor, Dr. Hildegardo decided to have them manually extracted, and called in a doctor with a small hand who was able to reach in, straighten out Gene's legs and bring him into the cold, cruel world. Within five more minutes, Duane was also extracted. My nerves had given out, and I was at Charles Hocking's house across the street being cared for when they were born.

Newborn babies are a mystery to me, so Martha Hocking came over to care for them the first night. They were well developed, 9 pounds, 7 ounces and 6 pounds, 11 ounces, and also had strong lungs. All night long they cried and we wondered what was wrong with them. Martha gave them paregoric, and Nestogênio, special milk for newborn babies, anything to try to calm them. When the doctor came the next day and saw the situation, he said, "Those babies are hungry. Give them Leite Ninho!" (a strong milk for adults). Sure enough, when they got a belly full of Leite Ninho they went to sleep and gave no more trouble. The second night was my watch, but with that milk to keep them happy, it was no problem.

Louise had suffered so in the birthing of the twins, she was traumatized and when life returned to normal found it difficult to be a wife again. For a while our relationship suffered until she recuperated more completely from the trauma.

Our first furlough in the States with the twins was problematic in some ways, but a lark in others. We got a good, warm car for winter travel, and went from Pennsylvania to Minnesota in the fall, stayed in the Minnesota area during much of the winter before returning east. Taking twin babies with you everywhere you go isn't easy, but my friends in Minnesota were very accommodating, and everyone loved Louise and her babies.

Before we started out from Altoona, Pennsylvania, having got the car ready for the winter months, and having some special car beds for the twins, I informed Louise we would travel on a certain day. Her reply startled me, for she said she didn't think she would accompany me because her father said we would kill the twins traveling in such cold weather. Louise was three years older than I and accustomed to doing what she thought best, but this was too much for me.

My reply was more or less, "Fine, if that is the way you want it. But be sure of one thing, you will never see me again!" Needless to say, she went with me and seldom opposed my decisions for the rest of our fifty years of married life even though I was often wrong.

When we went on that furlough, I had no certainty as to future plans. I did not qualify for Baptist Mid-Missions because I was not a member of a Baptist church. But after due consideration, and the fact that I had been able to work well with Baptist Mid-Missions missionaries in Brazil, I became a member of Louise's church in Altoona, Pennsylvania, and eventually applied to BMM and went before the council to be examined. This examination is very stressful to most candidates, but I was too innocent to realize this. Frankly, I was not well prepared, and I know that they accepted me mainly because of Louise. One thing I do remember. A lady missionary was present who had known me before and was aware that I had at one time been Pentecostal. In the midst of the exam, she asked, "Mr. Brooks, what do you think of dreams and visions?" Knowing where she was coming from, I hesitated a minute and then came back with, "I suppose that dreams and visions are common to people who eat too much before going to bed." That brought a good laugh, relieved the tension, and the moderator then said, "Now, MEN, do you have any more questions?"

Upon returning to Brazil after our first furlough, my desire was to go into what was known as "church planting," not a biblical term, but very important to Baptist churches in the States. It entailed finding a place where there was no gospel preaching church, moving in, evangelizing, winning men to Christ and forming a church body. All this was new to me, but a real challenge and I had a very good partner to go into this with me. Louise had four years of experience before I came to Brazil, and knew well how to evangelize and relate to Brazilians.

So, in 1953, three and a half years after our marriage, we moved to the small interior city of Icó where there was no evangelical work whatsoever.

Chapter 40
CHURCH PLANTING
(THIS CHAPTER IS DEDICATED TO MY DAD'S FAVORITE BASEBALL PLAYER OF ALL-TIME, TED WILLIAMS)

Choosing a place to work was an interesting procedure. First, it involved much prayer. The necessity of the Holy Spirit's guidance in this choice was obvious, for there were literally hundreds of cities in Brazil northeast at that time with no Gospel work. How to choose the right one definitely depended on His leading.

Barbalha and Missão Velha were two cities in the Cariri Valley close to Juazeiro where we married and lived, both without a gospel testimony, and should have been ideal for us to start our church planting career. But, the Spirit didn't lead that way.

I did go to Missão Velha to explore the possibilities. My prayer was, "Lord, if this is where you want us, make it possible to rent a house." During the time I was there no house was available, and I just didn't feel that this was the place the Lord wanted us. It seemed that the Spirit was saying, "not here!"

A good friend, José, in Juazeiro had previously talked to me about his hometown, Icó. There was absolutely no Gospel work there, a town of about ten thousand population. José's folks lived there still, and he was concerned about their salvation. I found transportation to Icó, riding in a truck that hauled freight from Juazeiro to Fortaleza, and upon arriving there found a Presbyterian family that had a mechanical shop and an open home. They advised me that the Presbyterian pastor from Cedro, about sixty kilometers away, visited once a month, but was an old man and was praying for a younger worker. I then caught transportation to Cedro to see the gentleman. He was thankful for my visit and went back to Icó with me, anxious that I move there and start a gospel church. He had prayed for such and hoped that I would be the answer. We walked the streets of Icó, meeting people that he knew, and preparing the way for me to take his place. I was perfectly at peace with this decision. Later Louise told me that his daughter had studied at the seminary in Juazeiro and was a close friend of hers. She had visited in their home in Cedro.

I had no money to buy a car, and the cars were not easy to find. When I first went to Juazeiro in 1950, two of the missionaries had panel trucks, called "Chevrolet Carryalls." I don't remember any other vehicles in the whole town except for some trucks. But now in 1953 there was a junkman who had an old, very old "junker" going up and down the streets collecting junk. It was a 1927 Chevvy car made into a pickup. The wheels wobbled, it had homemade brakes that didn't "brake" much, and a motor that looked like it may have been used to propel Noah's ark. I bought it for a hundred dollars and got it ready to haul some of our stuff to Icó. Louise and the boys went with the main load in a truck.

The trip to Icó in the rattletrap was an adventure, with practically no brakes, leaky radiator, wobbly wheels, rough roads, a mountain to go over, and maybe one gas station on the whole stretch of about two hundred miles. I recall going down that mountain in low gear, certain that if I should have to stop with brakes I would go over a cliff. But with persistence, faith and courage I finally arrived in Icó safe and sound. I soon had the old car apart to do some reinforcing, better brakes, and generally make it roadworthy, though I do remember that on our first trip to Orós, 24 miles away, to start a work, the radiator leaked so badly I had to stop at almost every farm house along the way to refill it. It was on this trip that I learned that green banana is an excellent ingredient to stop leaks in a radiator, rubbed over the leak on the outside of the radiator. Also, on this trip the twins lost their thongs through the spaces in the loose floorboards.

But the subject is church planting. Great as it was to find one believing family in Icó and to be introduced to a number of friends of the gospel, we soon learned that generally we were not welcome. One dear lady told us frankly, "We do not want you here." She was the baker's wife, expressing clearly the attitude of this almost one hundred percent Roman Catholic community. Our job was not only to preach the gospel on the street corners but also to make friends with the whole city.

This was my first experience in "church planting," so I really had to learn the hard way. We did the usual things, had services in homes, traveled to other nearby communities and cities, passed out tracts, purchased a corner house on the widest street in town and turned it into a church hall, preached faithfully, cared for the sick, brought children to Sunday school, the whole works. After five years we had only 17 professing believers in Icó, and a few more than that in other communities.

I could tell you of some interesting conversions to Christ, but I'll restrain myself and tell but one. An old Catholic farmer, rude and crude, had learned to read a bit. He somewhere got a hold of a Roman Catholic book of Old Testament Bible stories. Upon reading these, it struck him how clearly the book condemned idolatry. I believe it was his sister that brought him to one of our gospel services, and there he was, listening with rapt attention. He came to Christ, was transformed, and eventually all his many children also came. One of them, Irineu, is one of the best Brazilian missionaries I know, and has established a large congregation in the very area where his father lived and where he was born. He has now moved on to begin a work in a mountain where he believes that God has sent him.

There were many interesting experiences I could relate in relation to Icó, but in order not to make this part of my story too long, I shall try to give you a glimpse of the places where and how we were lead. I've told you how the Lord led us to Icó through a friend's pleading. While living in Icó, we were lead to Orós by the invitation of a friendly Presbyterian couple there, also believers in Christ. When we arrived there, we found that the lady who managed the post office was also a Presbyterian believer. She and the couple were our hosts when we first began the work there. It developed slowly, and during the years between our starting the work and our organizing it into a Regular Baptist church 20 years later, a number of seminary students and a few graduates spent time there also. Today there are churches in both of these cities, the Icó church being especially strong.

At this time we also began a work in a small village called Guassussê. Its nickname was "The Hole of

Holy Conception!" It was here that we were chased out by a catholic friar and a multitude of his followers, a story that Louise wrote up for children. That was an adventure that threatened us with death, but God gave us courage and victory. After the Orós dam was built, this village was buried under water, so the folks moved to a new and higher site. It is there that the before-mentioned Irineu, son of the old farmer, has successfully "planted" a large church of about three hundred. By the way, Irineu came to Christ at five years of age one night when I was preaching. Little children CAN understand and believe.

In a future chapter that I intend to title, "Jack of All Trades," I expect to give you a rundown on the varied ministries Louise and I were engaged in together over fifty years, but this chapter is specifically about church planting, so I'll move on. We left Icó after five years, calling a fine Brazilian couple that carried on and saw the work grow. We went on "furlough" to the States in 1958, staying for about six months. While there, we were asked to assume upon our return the directorship of the language school for new missionaries and the pastorate of Central Baptist Church in the state capital, Fortaleza, for one year. Since we had no personal ambitions and placed ourselves at the disposition of the work for any needed labor, we accepted the invitation for that year. I cannot really say that it was church planting although Central Baptist was in its initial stages. As you might presume, the Portuguese language was one of my loves, so it made me happy to be able to help others learn. During the year we dedicated to this service we developed lifelong friendships with the young couples that came to study the language. And I do hope that we also were able to help them spiritually and practically. Our daughter Beth was born there at this time.

While we were in Fortaleza that year, 1959-60, Ruth, the wife of my fellow pilot, Harold Reiner, was found to have an advanced stage of cancer of the uterus, and went to the States for treatment. Soon Harold, her husband was called back because she was not expected to live. We then were asked to assume the work they had started in Assaré, an interior city not too far from Juazeiro where Louise and I were married. We took this as the Lord's leading, and had peace about it. Harold left his four-place Piper Tripacer airplane with me to use for travel to and from the capital to care for the work there and return to my language students in Fortaleza, about a two hour trip. I would fly to a mountain plateau near Assaré where the work there had originally begun, have a Friday night service, and then fly down to Assaré for the weekend. After Louise moved to Assaré, I would fly alone back to Fortaleza on Monday mornings, returning to Assaré on Fridays. I believe Louise was at her happiest and best in Assaré, though I must admit that everywhere we served she was content. I loved to hear her sing as she worked around the house.

Harold never did come back to Assaré, so we stayed for three years, having turned the language school and Central Baptist church over to another very able missionary, Albert Johnson. When we organized the church in Assaré it had forty members.

We went on a six month furlough in 1963 leaving the Assaré church in the hands of a Brazilian pastor while gone, but upon returning were called to direct the Baptist Seminary of the Cariri. So in 1964 very reluctantly we said our goodbyes to the beloved folks in Assaré and moved to Juazeiro to assume the directorship of the seminary.

Our stay in Juazeiro did not keep us from church planting for we were able to use the airplane to carry students to many points in the southern part of the state and also preach on weekends in most of them. Today there are churches in Jucás, Brejo Santo, Barro, Vacaria, Quixará, Campos Sales, Caririaçu, Sousa, Milagres, and probably a few other places that we served with the airplane. It was while preaching in Quixará that the local priest went to get his gun to kill me, but that is ANOTHER story!

We chose to leave the seminary in 1971 to go back into church planting, going to live in Orós where we had started evangelizing in 1953. The church there had been served by seminary students and a single pastor who asked us to come and live there to organize the church officially. Each of these places have special memories of events and occurrences that it would be fun to relate, but since this chapter is primarily to tell of the places we "planted" churches, I'll not go into detail. Our three years here were also happy years. We lived directly in front of the Catholic Church whose priest had been a boy while we lived in Icó back in the fifties. We had no persecution while in Orós and made many friends. We continued to use the airplane to extend the seminary outreach with students.

Our next furlough began in 1974, and for the first and only time we stayed a whole year in the States. It was while living in Dayton, Tennessee, that we received a phone call informing us that our fellow missionary and pilot, Jim Benefiel, had suddenly passed away. He had unknowingly had a heart condition, had been having blackouts, went to the States to care for this, and after a "successful" operation, died of cardiac arrest. At his funeral, his wife pleaded with us to go to Martins in the neighboring state to assume the work that they had left. We had just turned the work in Orós over to a Brazilian pastor, one of our seminary graduates, and had no reason to refuse, so we came to Martins in July of 1975. We usually stayed five years or less in a place to plant a church, so did not expect to stay here more than five years. At this writing I am still in Martins, 30 years later. Louise and I left here for two years to substitute for two missionary couples down in the state of Bahia, and then came back. While here we organized the church, established another congregation, and begun works in two other cities, and also aided Brazilian pastors to begin works in other nearby places.

And speaking of the Lord's leading to places for "church planting," the direction to Martins was special. While we were directors at the Juazeiro seminary, a gentleman came up and asked me if I could fly him to Martins in the neighboring states. I confirmed that I could, but had no idea where Martins was, so got out my navigation chart, located it, and flew him here. We arrived at about midday, to land on the dirt strip just above the city. The temperature was a cool 70 degrees or so, very cool for northeast Brazil, just six degrees south of the equator. He took me down to the city to meet the mayor and get a bite to eat, and I returned home. That must have been back in 1967. A few years later when Jim Benefiel returned to northeast Brazil from the south desiring a place with a cool climate to work because of his wife's emphysema, I Immediately I thought of Martins, and flew over here with him.

Another cool day impressed him with the climate and soon he and his family moved up here to begin a Regular Baptist church. It was his death that brought us here.

The decision to go to Bahia in 1982 was made without consulting Louise. This was a first for me, an obvious oversight, but it was hard for her to accept. She made the best of it, and the work in Bahia in both places where we worked prospered more because of her effort than mine. The first place, Casa Nova, had a fine church hall but only one believer when we arrived. When we moved over to Remanso a year later, there was a small congregation of about 15. While at Casa Nova, we began the development of a youth camp on an island ceded to the mission by the electrical company that built the large 11 km. earth dam just down river. We cleared an airfield and a large area for future buildings there, hiring 30 workers and using dynamite and brush fires to remove large rocks from the airfield.

Remanso had a fairly large organized church, so it was an entirely different ministry. Louise had a great time teaching and enjoying the fellowship of the ladies. Eugene came down from Martins where he had been filling in as pastor and helped with evangelization, flying, and building. He was a great help to us. We worked out in several smaller towns and villages, and

Gene started the construction of a church building in a place called Pilão Arcado, some eighty miles upriver. We had two airplanes to use at this time, Harold Reiner's and ours. We also bought a diesel pickup truck for Eugene. When the missionary couples came back, we all three returned to Martins.

It is not interesting to end this chapter on a sad note, for we have seen quite a number of churches established in which we participated directly and indirectly. However, IF I could do it all over again, I should choose to go back to the biblical style of house churches that one sees in the New Testament. It would be especially effective here in the small cities of the Brazil northeast where people are poor and hardly able to support a church structure such as we seek to impose, with building, lights, water, janitor, pastor, materials and sundry other expenses. My vision would be to establish them on every farm, village, and in city homes where there was an open heart and mind instead of building expensive buildings with foreign funds in the cities and asking folks from all around to "come to church." The present accepted system of church organization with a paid pastor and all the details are not really functional in the small interior cities because of the poverty level. Nor do I consider it Biblical.

Section 1 - Jack of All Trades (but master of none!)

Louise and I were both from poor families. Her father was a bus driver, and she was proud to state that he drove 35 years for Logan Valley and never had an accident. Her humble beginnings made her willing to try her hand at any job, so she served in homes and worked at a store while in school in Altoona. When she became a missionary, she suffered a number of hardships, including hunger, down in the West Virginia-Kentucky area. I imagine this in part made her willing to try her hand at anything that she could do to serve. My experience at the Lake Street Assembly of God, watching the pastor humble himself and do janitor's work taught me that no work was too humble for a man of God. So, between the two of us, we were willing to do any service on the mission field that might redound to God's glory. Since we had no personal ambitions, we served wherever we could.

Louise applied herself to music before coming to Brazil, so she played the piano and accordion quite well. She gave me some instructions on the accordion so that I could accompany hymns when she was unable to travel with me. Between us we were able to do reasonably well when there weren't any really skilled musicians around to do the job. When we were directors of the seminary in Juazeiro I directed the choir while Louise helped teach the four-part harmony and accompany the music. Almost to her dying day we played the organ and piano together for the services in Martins. Louise did some instructing in music to young people in most of the churches where we worked, so that there are skilled musicians here and there who owe their beginnings in music to her dedication.

It was Louise's custom to present a children's story in most of our evangelistic services, and she was very well liked as a young people's Sunday school teacher. At one time here in Martins her class numbered about 24 young people. I was teaching the adolescents at that time. We both enjoyed teaching, and she taught until about a month before her death. We both taught at the seminary in Juazeiro for about ten years altogether. She was a teacher there when the seminary started in 1946, teaching English and music even before she could speak Portuguese. We both taught at the Baptist primary and junior high school in Juazeiro, and I even had the privilege of teaching Portuguese to Brazilian students.

House parenting, if that is a name, was really our first task together. When we married in 1951 we were asked to substitute for the Guy McLains in the Juazeiro primary school dorm, because of Guy's illness. I had never been a parent, of course, and had to establish some rules and regulations with the kids that would function without being too restrictive. I recall that I marked with the boys only one misbehavior that would merit physical punishment. That was fighting, which had been quite frequent. It appeared that the parents who could no longer control their kids sent them to us to educate. If two kids fought, BOTH would get three heavy swats on the bottom with my belt. Once they tasted this pain, they seldom fought again. Louise cared for the girls and resolved their problems. One girl had the habit of having a seizure when she didn't get what she wanted. I was called in to help when she had one of these, so I looked at her, apparently in a seizure of a sort, and told her, "Maria, I'll give you one minute to stop this. If you don't you will get a swat with my belt." Well, she didn't stop, so I raised her up out of the hammock and gave her one swat. When she continued I told her, "Maria, one more minute, one more swat." That ended her seizures, and they never came back. We also established a rule that the students had to eat all they placed on their plates, for most had come from poor homes where the excess food was fed to the pigs. This meant that they filled their plates extra full and ate only what they wanted. We had no other pigs but they soon learned to put only what they could eat on their plates. Generally, it was fun to care for them.

My course in mechanics and further experience in the States stood me in good stead in most of the small interior towns where we established churches. I have always kept a good supply of mechanic's tools on hand, and even today have occasion to give help in difficult situations. Our back yard was a shop or garage for fixing cars in the city of Assaré where we spent three years. I always tried to teach some of the young men in each place we lived, so that when we left, there would be a mechanic who could carry on in my place. I eventually became an aircraft mechanic, as well.

Linguistics became a must for me, for I was asked to assume directorship of the language school in Fortaleza a number of times. The fluency that God gave me in Portuguese placed me at an advantage, so whenever the school became problematic, I was asked to take over. I decided to do the whole language program over, for to me it lacked some important elements to make it easier for new missionaries to learn. In this process, I invited my niece, Joyce Brooks, to come and put the program in shape. Joyce had taken Portuguese at the university in Madison, Wisconsin, and was a very capable person for this job. The program she did has never been substituted. I believe I was director about four times, if not more. While here in Martins, I would fly out to Fortaleza weekly to check on things there.

There was a crisis in the mission in 1964 in relation to the seminary. Louise and I never dreamed, what with the humble preparation for the field that we had, to every become director of the seminary. But when we were asked to do the job we prayed hard and she agreed that we should step in the gap. In our July 1964 prayer letter Louise comments, "For many reasons Pete and I felt led to accept the directorship of the seminary here in Juazeiro although at the present time we still do not know how nor with what we shall carry on this work. There is still a deep yearning and sadness at the work left behind us, but the Lord has given us a peace about it. Somehow He will do what we cannot do." It was strange to me to be other than a simple teacher. I learned about finances, raising funds in the States, investments, legal matters, labor problems, teaching subjects for which I had no preparation, working with many different personalities, student discipline, so many things that I was not prepared for. However, I had a fine teaching staff that gave me good orientation and cooperation. And Louise was always at my side to counsel and correct when necessary. We were there for seven years, as I recall, with a six-month furlough in the middle.

Flying will be the subject of another chapter or two, but since this is the "Jack of All Trades" chapter, it would not be right to leave it totally out. It was the mission's desire that every plane have two pilots. We eventually changed that policy here in Brazil so that each pilot had his own plane, but at that time Harold Reiner was the only pilot, so he asked me to become the second pilot for the plane he had. Brazil suffered a strong communist influence at that time, and the director of the air club in Fortaleza was a professing communist. He did everything to make it difficult for me to get permission from the Departamento da Aeronautica Civil to train and get a license. Eventually, after being denied a couple of times, we bought a torn down trainer, a Brazilian copy of the Piper Cub, and rebuilt it, so that I could train in my own plane. This made it impossible for the DAC to deny me permission to train. I was licensed to fly in 1957, and flew until 2004.

Medical ability was usually expected of a missionary. Both Louise and I learned to give injections, though I could never give intravenous injections because of my color-blindedness (Daltonism). I couldn't see the blue veins!

We were called on for numerous medical tasks. I particularly remember Louise picking maggots out of an old man's hand, and applying some salve. The remaining maggots struggled to get out, because they needed the air.

One certain woman in Icó was expected to die after falling asleep while sewing with a "lamparina" (a small kerosene light) on her knee. She was thoroughly burned after her clothing caught fire. Louise took it upon herself to care for this woman after she was sent home to die and she recuperated. I'm sure there was much prayer involved, as well.

I regard tract distribution as another "trade." Somehow, I had never been trained at this activity until I moved to Martins. Naturally, I had done some tract distribution casually all along, but when moving here, it became a pleasure and a job that I did weekly. In Umarizal, 25 kilometers from Martins, there is a weekly street fair, similar to stateside flea markets, where people gather from over quite a large area. I have never tried to estimate the number of people that come, but I know it is in the thousands. During my thirty years here, with the exception of the year and a half I am retired at this writing, I tried to get to this fair as often as I could.

Some years I estimated that I had distributed close to 40,000 Gospel tracts both there and in the Martins street fair. I had help at times from believers here, making it easier and quicker. After people became accustomed to receiving tracts, they seldom rejected them or threw them on the street. People would come to me and tell me they had a stack of tracts at home and would read and reread them. Giving out tracts this way is very much like Christ's parable of the sower. One never knows the final result, but He does.

Camp work was another of our joyful jobs. Before our mission had any campgrounds of its own, Louise took part in the first camping effort in 1961 while I stayed home with the kids. From that time on either one of us or both would dedicate time to children and youth camps. In 1965 we BMM missionaries purchased a good-sized campground near the city of Iguatu and slowly developed it. It is some distance from the highway, so I took the seminary boys over to open up a road to get there by car. Louise and I and Harold and Joan Reiner had the first youth camp there under very primitive conditions. It has a good sized artificial lake for swimming, cabins both primitive and modern (to us!) on two sides of the lake, a soccer field, volley ball field, large open auditorium, everything a camp needs, besides being surrounded by rocky, wooded hills on two sides. I was a popular camp speaker for quite a few years until the Brazilian pastors pretty much took over. Louise was in charge of camp kitchen a number of times, and always worked well with the Brazilian help. Here is a typical quote from the September 1973 newsletter: "The Brookes' stayed on as Pete was maintenance director for the three camps which followed our Mission Business and Bible conference, and Louise was in charge of the kitchen. This was a real experience for each! It appeared as though everything, including cars, generators, light plant, kerosene refrigerators and such decided to go on strike and break down. The kitchen was a busy place from early morning until late at night as beans and rice, meat and vegetables were prepared on the big wood-burning stove. There were approximately 310 present and we thank the Lord for physical protection and spiritual health for campers and workers."

One of my confessions is that I have never considered myself a scholar. However, studying became a necessity, as I was involved in teaching at the seminary, and also as a conference speaker. My knack for the Portuguese language gave me an "in" with the Brazilian people, so I became a conference speaker involved in traveling to churches and camps often during the year. Louise wrote in the summer of 1979 the following: "Pete has been very busy these months with conferences in Natal,

Recife, Fortaleza, Icó, Iguatu, with Assaré and Várzea Alegre in June. He was the speaker for the Jr. – Sr. banquet of the Fortaleza Academy and we have a special invitation to the graduation service. We are very thankful for the Lord's protection and strength on these trips. Pete had caught a very bad cold making the last several conferences very difficult. Subjects such as eschatology and Pentecostalism were treated as requested by the host pastor or church, requiring research and study that he enjoyed very much." Conference work continued year after year, giving me an acquaintance with many churches and pastors. My 1982 work report reads: "Since our return (from furlough) we have had special meetings in Quixeramobim, Natal, Itaberaba, Fortaleza and Patos. We have spoken at the Carnaval camp at Iguatu, the RN association in Natal, the BGFM youth camp at Poço Doce, and our Regular Baptist camp at Morro Pintado near Areia Branca." Sounds like fun!

The northeast region had a correspondence course offered on our various radio programs. Louise took upon herself the enjoyable task of correcting lessons mailed to her and answering personal questions that often came with the lessons. It was a special delight to her to receive letters from prisoners who had found salvation in Christ through the truths taught in these lessons. Today this course has a large office and stock in Crato on the seminary grounds and sends out thousands of courses all over Brazil, receiving and correcting the lessons and sending diplomas.

And speaking of radio programs, this reminds me that for many years I was a radio speaker. I prepared short messages, usually from five to seven minutes long, for our weekly spot on Transworld Radio, and for other Brazilian stations. These were not sermons, but talks to individual listeners based on incidents and observations that served to awaken interest in spiritual truths. I talked about incidents involving mosquitoes, lizards, snakes, airplanes, most anything that could grab a person's attention for a few minutes. Thus, the spiritual application was more easily remembered.

Missionaries become involved in construction at some time in their missionary career. It was my good fortune to do little of this, but I could not avoid it entirely. In our first work, in Icó in the 1950s we simple purchased two halls and turned them into a big one by doing some truss work and knocking down some wall. But in Assaré in the early 1960s we built a church building with the help of the believers. The width required a long truss that so impressed the mayor that he obligated us to build a small cement column right smack in the middle of the auditorium in order to get approval for the building. Eventually it was removed. When at the seminary, we became involved in several building projects because of the increasing student body. When we moved to Orós in 1971, the church people had begun a building in the form of a cross, a design that one of the leaders had seen on a phonograph record cover. Unfortunately, the foundation was already laid, though the design meant a very limited building size. I pleaded with the men to change the design and redo the foundation, but to no avail. So the building has a very limited auditorium size. From Orós we came to Martins, and I purchased a fine corner property in Martins proper for a church building. When I "retired" at 65 years of age, the U.S. social security system took its good old time to get my retirement going, so by the time they did I had over seven thousand dollars sent me, almost enough to build the building we needed on that property (building is much cheaper here than in the States). Of necessity I have learned quite a bit about building.

It was interesting to become a translator. Chick Tracts had some interesting tracts that had not been translated to Portuguese, so I offered to do so. I did the initial translating and had a team of university students from the local church here correct any "Americanisms" or grammatical errors. There was a couple in Altoona PA that would purchase Chick tracts and send them to me. Our work report for 1993 states, "We receive and mail CHICK booklets to various points in Brazil. Mailing cost per box is about $8.00. Each box contains 1,000. We presently have on hand five titles, ESTA FOI A SUA VIDA, HÁ OUTRO CRISTO, PORQUE MARIA CHORA, OS CATÓLICOS ROMANOS SÃO CRISTÃOS? And A BESTA." While teaching at the seminary a few years ago, a student and I translated a book on missionary radio that is very useful to persons establishing radio stations or programs in foreign countries. Louise would have children's stories in English that she wanted translated, so these gave me an occasional exercise in translating. It is my wish that i had spent more time doing this, for it develops vocabulary and grammatical usage to a high degree.

Oh, yes, I almost forgot. Back in about 1992, the mission in Brazil needed a new treasurer, and for some reason or another I was asked if I would take the job. I consented on the condition that Louise help me. She agreed, so for probably eight years I was treasurer, flying out to Fortaleza once a month specifically for this job. Louise always accompanied me and did a big share of the work.

For a short space of time, I cooperated with the seminary extension program while living here in Martins. I flew to several different places to care for the lessons. As a result of this ministry several young people went to the seminary in Juazeiro and became teachers and pastors. One young lady is on the seminary staff. One of the young men is now an outstanding pastor in Fortaleza.

What you call people that finance projects I'm not sure. Financiers? Louise and I became known as missionaries who financed Brazilian pastor's projects. We purchased cars and motorcycles, financed church constructions, camp projects and personal needs. Of course, we had to raise money from churches and individuals in the States to do this, but since we always sought to live humbly so that Brazilians of any social level would feel at home in our house, we were able to dedicate much of our missionary financing to the Work. Our July 1993 newsletter reads: "We purchased a motorcycle for national missionary Irineu Lopes with money from our vehicle fund plus the help of Alice Stowell, missionary retiree. He was overjoyed at receiving this aid to his ministry. What he really needs, however, is a pickup truck that will enable him to travel more safely and with a group of believers to help in the many preaching points he visits. We want your help toward this vehicle. We have on hand less than two thousand dollars for this, so need another four thousand." It wasn't long before we were able to drive a pickup truck over to Irineu. He still uses it today in 2005.

I think you get the idea that we were involved in a great variety of work in our fifty years together, and of course, "variety is the spice of life." But I believe the title of this chapter is very applicable to us, for we really were never exceptionally talented at anything, but always willing to fill in the gaps. Jack and Jill of all trades, but master of none!

Section 2 - Some Aviation History

(A note to the ladies: This chapter will probably interest you only if you are an aviation fan, so feel free to skip it - you won't hurt my feelings!)

It would be fun to start telling some of the adventures of our flying here in Brazil, but I think that first of all it be well to give a bit of the history and the planes we used. I have already mentioned why and how I got involved, back from 1953 to 57, having to purchase a Brazilian two-place trainer to be able to get my license. In reality, I had already learned to fly and had soloed at Juazeiro before ever doing the course out at Fortaleza, the capital city of Ceará. Harold taught me and soloed me.

Harold Reiner is three years younger than I, arrived in Brazil the year before I did, already married. His first son Tim was born in his house just across the street from ours, one week after Louise and I were married. Tim and his younger brother, Doug, are missionaries in the same area where Harold now lives. My acquaintance with Harold began just at the time he was taking his flying lessons out in Fortaleza in 1951. Harold had an entirely different bringing up from mine, having a very intelligent and enterprising father who taught his boys all about mechanics, carpentry, electricity, even permitting them to make rockets and such things in the garage. Besides being much more intelligent than I, Harold arrived in Brazil with skills I never thought of, what with no fatherly training.

Harold, after taking his lessons, bought an old two-place plane that should have never been permitted to leave the ground. It was called the "Roncador Xingu," named, I believe, after some mountain out in the jungle where the Xingu indian tribe lived. It was an old Aeronca, in bad shape and with a worn out engine, but Harold took it upon himself to fly it in to Juazeiro to put his skills to work in rebuilding it. He made a forced landing in a dry lake on the way, but eventually arrived safely home. We had some interesting experiences in this plane due to Harold's inexperience. When he had overhauled the engine, due to the lack of proper baffles to distribute the cooling air properly over the cylinders, we suffered motor stoppage a kilometer or so from the airfield. The plane had enough altitude to glide exactly to the edge of the field and land, but it was a scary experience.

His second plane was a three-place Piper Super Cruiser, if I have the name correct, a three-place plane, and I have a slide picture of it along side my '27 Chevy the first time it was flown to Icó, probably around 1954.

It was a fine plane, but could carry only 2 passengers, and Harold's vision was to own a plane that could carry seminary students and pastors to places very difficult to reach by ground transportation, and they were many at that time.

It was at that time, about 1956, I believe, that a Convention Baptist pilot, a Rev. Luper, flew a four-place Piper Tri-pacer to Brazil on a tourist visa. He cracked it up on a village street when he got lost out in the state of Maranhão in the evening and landed to save his soul. He approached Harold about rescuing the plane, knowing Harold's knack for mechanics and engineering, and finally traded the plane, sight unseen, for Harold's three-place Super Cruiser. The trip to get that plane out is an adventure that Harold and I want to write up someday before we leave this world! It would take quite a few chapters and won't fit here, but we never forget the adventure.

Rebuilding that Tripacer was a job we undertook in Harold's garage in Fortaleza, and I recall that the women, his Ruth and my Louise, needed a good bit of patience to care for us. When we finally got it flying, we received orders from the DAC to stop flying. It was received from the Convention with the stipulation they get it through customs, but that never happened. The government took it away from us, and for a time the Convention lent us a Navion, a beautiful 4-place ship that Bob Stanley had formerly owned, but eventually gave us a regular Pacer, a "taildragger," in place of the Tripacer. Harold sold this plane and in 1959 flew a brand new Tripacer down to Brazil legally. That plane was destroyed by fire in an accident on a stormy day in Juazeiro in which three lives were lost and Harold and Joan badly burned.

We were living in Icó when Harold and I rebuilt and recovered the Brazilian imitation of the Piper cub. While in Icó, we used this plane for evangelism and flights to Fortaleza. I had a forced landing in this plane, and later stalled it nose first into the ground, miraculously getting out alive. But that story I will save for later. After the accident I stored the wings and fuselage, but some kids, seeing that the bees had built a nest in the stored wings, decided to smoke them out and get the honey, setting fire to the wings, which had a wooden inner structure. Eventually I gave the whole thing, fuselage, wings, and motor, to Harold's son Tim who passed it on to someone else to rebuild.

On our furlough in 1964, I was able to borrow five thousand and two dollars from a friend of Harold's and purchase a brand new two-place Piper Colt. Today just the motor is more than twice that amount. Harold had purchased a new Piper Cherokee, so we flew the two planes down together, in a sense. His plane was about 30 miles an hour faster than mine, so we would calculate the approximate time difference, and I would take off half that time difference before he would so that we would be close to each other for most of the trip, he passing me halfway to the destination. Several times we were over the same spot at the same altitude and never saw each other. Space is enormous when you are up there.

The Colt was a two-place plane with a 105 HP engine, a slightly narrower version of the Tripacer that was supplanted by the Cherokee. Since its forerunner had been a four-place plane, I calculated that with the proper caution and gas loads I could use it as a four-placer. I made a comfortable, light back seat, and flew seminary students with it for about four years with no mishaps. It was a fun plane. I sold it to fellow missionary Charles Smith, who used it for a few years and passed it on. The last I heard of it, it was flying down in São Paulo state.

The Super Cruiser, the pacer, the Tripacer, the Paulistina and the Colt were cloth covered planes, but the Cherokee was aluminum covered, much better for the sunny climate here in this part of Brazil. When I sold the Colt, I purchased a Cherokee in the States, but a Brazilian import company was able to block the importation, so I had to sell it and purchase one through a Brazilian company. As I recall, it cost a bit more than eight thousand dollars. This plane

Ray Reiner and I flew down from the States in 1968.
So, from then on Harold and I were flying Cherokees,
though his had a bigger engine until we installed a 180
hp engine in mine in place of the 150 HP engine.

Just to give you a taste of what my flying was like,
back in April of 1973, our prayer letter states: "This
year we are reaching a new community with the plane.
It is called "Olho de Agua" (a well-spring) and is a
farming community about 15 miles out of Jucás. Our
weekend schedule includes approximately four hours
of flying for the seminary as on Saturdays I fly from
Orós to Juazeiro—a 40 minute flight, take on 4 students
(all of these less than 120 pounds) fly 25 minutes to
Jucás where I leave one, fly 7 minutes to Olho d'Agua
leaving another, go on to Cedro, a 20 minute flight
where I leave a couple, and then return home to Orós.
On Mondays early I reverse the process, leaving the
students at the seminary, and in addition make an 18
minute flight to Brejo Santo to pick up several students
and return them to the seminary. The blessing in all this
is the report of the students when folks accept Christ."

Harold went on furlough and sold his first Cherokee and brought down another one, which he later sold to Benny (James Benefiel who began the work here in Martins) and when Benny died, I purchased his part from his widow, Maxine. That is the plane that I had until last year (2004), having flown it many hours flying seminary students, pastors and sick people to the capital.

I came down from the States with Harold in a retractable gear 200 hp Cherokee Arrow in 1975, the plane he still has at this writing, 30 years later. It is interesting that all of the pilots who used and owned planes here in the northeast have sold their planes and gotten out of aviation, except for Harold, who is still in it for sentimental reasons, by my guess. Even he, talking to me recently, spoke of selling his plane. The high costs and new regulations have made it unreasonable to maintain an aircraft unless one has a very definite need for it. Highway development and good ground transportation have made it possible to get anywhere in a reasonable amount of time.

I believe this is a complete list of the planes Harold and I had and used during our fifty or so years of flying. Harold started earlier, so must have about fifty-five years. Besides us, Benny had a Maule-4 for a while, Tim had a Cherokee Arrow, as did Darrel Haworth and Bill Kettlewell had a Brazilian Cherokee after selling a

Tri Pacer that Eugene rebuilt and sold to him for costs. Benny died, the others all gave up on aviation. The men in Bahia are re-building an ultralight to play around. (Son Eugene gave up teaching in the States and came to Martins to rebuild a Piper Tripacer to help earn his aircraft mechanic's license. He had earned his private pilot's license while in high school at the Baptist Mid-Missions Academy in Fortaleza).

It was mentioned that the mission had a policy that any plane on the mission field should have two pilots. I think this type of thinking dated back to the days when missionaries lived on a mission compound in Africa, sort of a mission village. Here in Brazil, we generally live in separate towns, often very distant from each other. I would imagine that "as the Crow flies" Harold presently lives more than three hundred miles from me in a straight line, about 15 or more hours by car, 2 and a half by small plane. It became obvious that the idea of two pilots per plane was not a workable situation in northeast Brazil, so we worked it out with the mission to each have his own plane.

Also, the mission policy is that the planes, though purchased with funds raised by individual missionaries, belong to the mission and not to the missionary, as do cars. This didn't work in Brazil either because planes owned by an entity could only be flown by pilots with commercial licenses, and we did not have or need these to do our type of flying. So, in spite of mission policy, we were obligated to put the planes in our own names. The following is what I wrote to the mission aviation committee to explain our position:

BAPTIST MID-MISSIONS
BRAZIL AVIATION COMMITTEE
PHILOSOPHY AND POLICIES

I. PHILOSOPHY:

In the early years of Baptist Mid-Missions in Brazil, much time was lost due to primitive modes of transportation and the general difficulty of travel. The first plane was purchased in 1951 as an effort to save missionary time, to reach out farther interior in the evangelistic and church planting ministries and to establish rapport with the nationals in order to gain a hearing for the Gospel, by helping in times of emergency.

Each missionary-pilot through the years has raised funds for purchase and operation of his plane, has used his plane in his personal ministry, has served other BMM people, has preserved and maintained his plane in top condition, and has reported his aviation activities to the regional field Council and to his supporting churches.

Through the succeeding years the parameters and philosophy of flying set by the first pilots have been demonstrated to be sound and successful. This philosophy has continued to guide all of our aviation activities from those early days and remains operational today.

II. POLICIES:

The use of aircraft by Baptist Mid-Mission missionaries in Brazil shall be subject to the following:

A. The pilot-in-charge shall be totally responsible for Financing, maintaining and using his equipment within all legal limits and according to the norms established by the field aviation committee.

B. A missionary's aircraft shall be utilized in his ministries and life according to his needs and those of fellow workers as a piece of time-saving equipment that shall be used conscientiously and carefully.

C. Use of aircraft is discouraged where it is obvious that it will not benefit the mission in the saving of time or money.

D. Pilots coming to Brazil or pilots licensed in Brazil shall initially be permitted to fly as a BMM missionary in Brazil under observation and restrictions of qualified, experienced BMM pilots.

III. PERSONNEL:

To qualify to fly with Baptist Mid-Missions in Brazil, new pilots or veteran missionaries entering aviation shall be considered individually for approval according to pilot certificates and ratings held, ability to work with fellow missionaries, personal attitudes demonstrated, amount and type of hours logged, ability to receive counsel from senior pilots, and other items deemed necessary by this committee.

IV. PROPERTY HOLDING POLICY:

We recognize what might be called LEGAL, MORAL AND PRACTICAL OWNERSHIP:

A. LEGAL OWNERSHIP: Our planes legally belong to us, to SEBMM, or, as has been in some cases, to other third parties.

B. MORAL OWNERSHIP: Baptist Mid-Missions is considered to be moral owner. According to our property-holding policy, the pilot has no personal equity in his plane. That is, he cannot sell it and take the funds out of the work for personal benefit. If the plane should be sold, he may use the money only for other mission projects or personal support.

C. PRACTICAL OWNERSHIP: The pilot that acquires an aircraft for his use, either from another missionary or from another source, is considered for all practical Purposes to be the owner-operator. He must raise the funds for purchase, operation and maintenance, keep the aircraft in top condition, and set up his flight program in accordance with our Brazil aviation policies elsewhere stated.

D. A possible exception to the above occurs when a missionary has invested monies acquired completely apart from his missionary support such as inheritance, sale of personal property in the U.S., insurance, etc. in his aircraft. In the spirit of page 6 of the property holding policy, BMM has established a precedent of restoring such funds to the missionary (as in the case of the Benefields and the Piper Cherokee they operated).

Pete Brooks

Pictured above from left to right you shall see me (Clay Clark), Angelina Clark, Laya Clark, Havana Clark, Aubrey Napoleon-Hill Clark, Vanessa Clark & Laya Clark.

Chapter 41

LIFE OF JESSE (SCREENPLAY AND PLAY)

Life of Jesse

<u>Introduction of Jesse's Family:</u>

(Scene: Sitting at home during the evening. Husband staring into space. Wife working at various chores. Jesse playing with objects on the floor.)

Wife: A denari for your thoughts.

Husband: What? I'm sorry. What did you say?

Wife: I said a denari for your thoughts. You look so engrossed in thought lost that I wondered what you were thinking about.

Husband: Uh, Life.

Wife: Honey, that's a pretty broad subject. What do you mean.....life?

Husband:	Our future; I'm a bit uneasy about it. The Romans are getting harder and harder to please. When Herod wants to build something, he just raises taxes. It is getting to the point where I almost can't and don't feel like I can keep up. I just don't know how I will be able to provide for our family. Prices never seem to go down; the cost of living keeps climbing. And I'm especially worried now that we have another child on the way.
Wife:	Don't worry, dear. I have confidence in you.
Husband:	Thank you. I appreciate that.
Wife:	I know that you will figure out what to do.
Husband:	But, what can I do? Herod is ruthless. He'll do anything to get what he wants, including killing his own family members. And look at me, I'm just a businessman middleman in the sheep business. I don't have any power to fight back.

Wife: Perhaps things will change some day.

Husband: There you go again. I suppose that you
                are going to remind me again about
                the Messiah.

Jesse: Father, what is a Messiah?

Husband: Ask your Mother.

Wife: No, you are the leader of this family.
                You, tell Jesse about the Messiah.

Husband: Oh, all right. But it has been so long
                since we had a prophet that I'm
                beginning to wonder what the truth is
                about the Messiah.

Jesse: What is a prophet?

Husband: I see that this might take a while.

Jesse: I have the time.

Wife: So do I.

Husband:	That's what I was afraid of.........Oh well, I'll try to explain. Prophets are special servants of God. God would choose someone who loved and would obey Him; then God would give them messages to pass on to us. And God used these servants to speak to us by using them as messengers. God chose these men to be prophets because of their love and devotion to Him.
Jesse:	Father, why aren't you a prophet?
Wife:	Yes, dear. Why aren't you a prophet?
Husband:	Never mind. Like I was saying, God spoke to the people of Israel though these men called prophets. When they tell speak us what God said, it is called prophecy. A lot of what they said say is sometimes hard to understand. These prophecies—and almost seems like a riddles.
Jesse:	What is a riddle?

Husband: A riddle is like a puzzle. It is hard to picture what something means until you see everything put together. But it'll makes perfect sense to you when you see all the parts put together once all the pieces have been put in their proper place.

Jesse: Is the Messiah a puzzle that I will see for myself?

Husband: No, the Messiah isn't a puzzle. Sometimes the things said about Him seem like a riddle. The Messiah will be sent to come to us from God to set us free and restore us into a great nation again. He will restore us to a perfect relationship with God and make everything right. Not like this mess oppressive state that we are in now.

Jesse: Will I see the Messiah?

Husband: I hope so. This mess we're in is getting harder and harder to bear.

Jessie: What do you mean by the 'mess we are in?'

Wife:	Your Father is talking about the Romans.
Husband:	That's right. We aren't free anymore.
Jesse:	Will the Messiah get rid of the Romans?
Husband:	I hope so.
Jesse:	Will the Messiah be big and powerful?
Husband:	Like I said, Jesse, I hope so. The prophet Isaiah told us a lot about the coming Messiah. I don't understand some of the things that Isaiah said in his prophecy about the Messiah, but I do know that our God will never forsake us. And I know for sure that everything will make perfect sense when we see the power of the Messiah.
Jesse:	Like seeing the finished puzzle?
Husband:	Yes, like seeing the finished puzzle. Everything will make sense then.

Jesse: Then that is what I'm going to pray for.

Wife: What's that Jesse?

Jesse: I am going to pray that I will see the
            Messiah for myself.

<u>Six Months Later:</u>

[Jesse in the field with other shepherds watching over their sheep]

Shepherd #1:   Jesse! Jesse!

Jesse: What?

Shepherd #1:   Are you awake?

Jesse: Would I be talking to you if I were asleep?

Shepherd #1:   You don't have to be smart mouthed with me!

Jesse: You're right. I'm sorry. I was just thinking.

Shepherd #1:   About your mother?

Jesse: Yes. About her and some other things.

Shepherd #1:   I am so sorry to hear about her death she died. But, at least your baby brother is alive and well.

Jesse: Yes, I know. But, why couldn't I stay with Father instead of living out here in the pastures with you and all these sheep.

Shepherd #1:   Is our company that bad?

Jesse: No, it's not that. I don't mean to offend you. It's just...it's just... that I miss Dad, my family, and setting the table for dinner. Mom said I was going to be her best helper with the baby. But way out here, my little brother won't even know me!

Shepherd #1:   You know your father has a lot of responsibilities. He had to get make sure someone to would care for your brother and still run his business all at the same time.

Jesse: But, what about me?

Shepherd #1:   You have a job, also to do.

Jesse: What is it? To Watch sheep all day?

Shepherd #1: In a word, Yes. It is not as simple as just walking. You're not here just to run around in a pasture all day; this is a chance for you to learn and find out about the family business. And if you want to be really good at it, you must learn about all about caring for sheep.

Jesse: Really? All right. If that is what my Father wants, that's what I'll do. Not that I have a choice in the matter.

Shepherd #1: Ah, but you do have a choice. You can just go through the motions, or you can learn all there is to know. The sheep will recognize your voice and they will follow you. They will depend on you to protect them. What you learn will affect the sheep. And what you learn will determine if you will be prepared to run your family's business when the time comes.

Jesse: That won't happen for a long time.

Shepherd #1: You never know.

[A light begins to glow in the distance]

Shepherd #2:   What's that?

Shepherd #3:   What are you talking about?

Shepherd #2:   The light. That light over there!
(points frantically)

Shepherd #1:   I see it, too.

Jesse: Great. First, I'm supposed to talk to the sheep. Now, the other shepherds are seeing things. This is going to be one long apprenticeship.

Shepherd #1:   Hush. Don't you see it?

Jesse: Yes, I do. And I don't mind telling you that I'm getting just a bit nervous about this.

[Sudden burst of bright lights. The shepherds and Jesse cry out in fear.]

Angel: Do not be afraid. I bring you good news of great joy that will be for all the people. Today in the town of David, a Savior has been born. He is Christ. This will be a sign to you. You will find the baby wrapped in cloths and lying in a manger.

[A host of angels appear and they are praising God and saying]:

Heavenly Host: Glory to God in the highest, and on earth peace to men on whom his favor rests.

[Lights fade back to normal and the angels disappear back into heaven.]

Jesse What was THAT??!!

Shepherd #2 Well, I ain't real sure, but I thought I saw some wings. Do you s'pose them was angels?

Shepherd #3 Angels??! Now why would angels come talk to us?

Shepherd #32: I dunno. What's, So, what are we going to do?

Shepherd #21: We're going to Bethlehem, that's what we're going to do.

Jesse: Now?

Shepherd #1: Yes, now.

Jesse: But what about the sheep?

Shepherd #1: Didn't you hear what the angel said? A Savior has been born in Bethlehem. What could be more important than that?

Jesse: A Savior? Do you mean the Messiah?

Shepherd #1: Yes, that's what I understand it to mean. Very possibly. "Savior" is a word Isaiah uses.

Jesse: This is the Messiah that my Father was telling me about, I just know it! This is great. I can't believe it. I prayed that I would live to see the Messiah. And, now He is here! Forget about the sheep. Let's go. Let's go, now!

[Shepherd 1 shrugs; all exit stage.]

Hours Later

(Jesse and the Shepherds search Bethlehem for the Savior.)

Shepherd #2: Have you had any luck finding that baby?

Shepherd #1: No, but we have to keep asking everyone we see until we find him.

Jesse: How again are we supposed to find the Messiah?

Shepherd #2: You heard what the angel said Din'cha hear the angels? They said, "You will find a baby wrapped in cloths and lying in a manger."

Jesse: Excuse me, I'm missing something here. Are you sure that the angel said that we will know it is the right baby when we find it wrapped in cloths and lying in a manger?

Shepherd #1: Yes. You were there; remember what you heard. Let the same thing that we did Angel's words play back in your head.

Jesse: I know, but I was thinking, aren't plain clothes a bit beneath the dignity for the Messiah to be dressed in plain clothes? And, in a manger? Come on. I think that might be a bit too much stretch.

Shepherd #2: You know what your problem is? You think too much. When was the last time you talked to an angel before tonight's night?

Jesse: That's not the point.

Shepherd #1:   No, the point simple logic is we aren't looking enough—or perhaps in the right places. God sent angels to tell us, humble shepherds, that today the Savior is born in Bethlehem. It is our obligation to see this glorious child follow directions. So, worry about the details pomp later. Today, we are going to find this child.

[Shepherd #3 come running in excited and shouting and out of breath]

Shepherd #3:   I found him! I found him! I found him!

Shepherd #2:   Where's he at?

Shepherd #3:   The last place I looked.

Jesse: That's brilliant. If you had looked in the last place first instead of last, it wouldn't have taken so long.

Shepherd #3:   What, Huh? I don't understand it.

Shepherd #1: Jesse is just playing with you. Tell us the location of the 'last place you looked.'

Shepherd #3: Oh, I get it!.
[Chuckles]
It's that way. Go to that narrow street. Turn right, then right, then right again to the stable.

Jesse: Let me guess. It's the last stable on the right.

Shepherd #3: How did you know?

Jesse: Just a guess.

Shepherd #2: [Motions to Shepherd #3]
Perhaps you should lead the way. Go on, now; show us where.

Shepherd #1: Yes, that may be a wise idea.

Shepherd #3: Okay, then follow me.

(Shepherds and Jesse walk along each wall of the auditorium until they return back to the opposite side of the stage where a stable scene is set up. Mary, Joseph, and Jesus are present. There is some grumbling by Jesse and Shepherd #2 about Shepherd #3 actually remembering the way back to the stable.)

Shepherd #3: See. There they are.

Shepherd #2: Are you sure?

Shepherd #1: He's right.

Jesse: How do you know?

Shepherd #1: Look, see for yourself. It is exactly as the angel said it would be. And, look at the child.

Jesse: So?

Shepherd #1: There is a radiance about this child. It could be no one else. Please, bow down. This is our Savior, Christ the Lord.

[All the Shepherds and Jesse bow down to worship Jesus]

[Mary and Joseph see the prostrate visitors and are startled]

Joseph: Hello. Is there something wrong?

Shepherd #2: No, everything is alright with the world.

Joseph: I don't understand.

Shepherd #1: We are humble shepherds. Last night, God sent angels to tell us about the birth of our Savior.

Shepherd #3: And I'm the one who found you.

Shepherd #1: We'll discuss that later. As I was saying, the angel told us that we would find this glorious child wrapped in cloths and lying in a manger.

Shepherd #3: And that's exactly where he was when I first saw him.

Shepherd #1: We are being obedient to what God has shown us. We have come to worship our Savior.

Mary: Thank you so much. You'll never know how much your words and actions mean to me. This helps confirm to me what God has foretold.

Jesse: If you don't mind me asking, what are you doing in a stable instead of …er… ….'a better place.'

Joseph: I've been asking myself that also.

Mary: It's not your fault. This is all that was available. There were no rooms available in the inn.

Joseph: It was the best I could find after our long trip.

Jesse: Long trip?

Joseph:	Yes. The tax decree that Caesar ordered that everyone must return to his home to register for the census. Since we are from the line of David, we had to leave Nazareth and come to Bethlehem.
Shepherd #1:	What is the child's name?
Joseph:	Jesus.
Shepherd #2:	What's that mean?
Joseph	His name. It means 'the Lord saves!'
Shepherd #3:	Everything the angel said was true. Even his name confirms who he is.
Shepherds #2:	Hey we gotta go. I have to tell everyone Everybody will wanna hear about what happened tonight.
Shepherd #3:	Yea, me to. Yes, we should go. Praise be to God! What a glorious child!

[Shepherd #2 and Shepherd #3 run out]

Shepherd #1   Thank you for allowing us to witness what the angels had told us about. Blessings upon you and this child.

[Shepherd #1 and Jesse exit from the stable]

Jesse: My Father used to tell me about prophets and the prophecies that they gave from God.

Shepherd #1:   What did he say?

Jesse: He said that a prophecy is like a puzzle. Everything will make perfect sense when you see all the pieces put together.

Shepherd #1:   So what happens if you don't have everything put together, like the puzzle your Father mentioned.

Jesse: I don't know. Maybe we should study what the prophets said so that we know what to look for? Next.

Shepherd #1: That's a very good answer. So, tell me, were you bothered that the Savior announced by the angel was found in such an ordinary place like a stable?

Jesse: Yes, I was.

Shepherd #1: Why?

Jesse: Well…a Savior should have good things, and a palace to live in, and be strong and powerful, and, and, and………..he should 'look' like a Messiah.

Shepherd #1: Is that your plan, or God's plan?

Jesse: I don't know.

Shepherd #1: Why don't you study what the prophets said, then see if you can recognize God's plan at work.

Jesse: Okay. I guess you're right. But, I do have a question for you.

Shepherd #1: What's that?

Jesse: Did it bother you even a little bit that the Savior is so small?

Shepherd #1: No.

Jesse: Why?

Shepherd #1: Don't worry. Like all of God's good things, He'll grow.

Song Ideas:

- Write one about prophets?
- Write one about angels?
- "O Come O Come Emmanuel"
- "How Should A King Come?"
- Lanny Wolfe's "Gentle As"
- "Away in a Manger"
- "Such A Strange Way to Save the World"
- "Welcome to Our World"

On Shepherds:

- Shepherd 1 is an educated reader...perhaps a scribe that didn't work out?
- Shepherd 2 is a "hayseed" with a genuine heart;
- Shepherd 3 is spontaneous and sometimes clueless.

Chapter 42

THE BRICKHOUSE (SCREENPLAY AND PLAY)

The Final Chapter

Watch my Dad Living Out His Acting Dreams by Searching for "Thom Clark Brickhouse" in Youtube.

Pictured above my mom (Mary Clark) and my dad (Thom Clark) hold our twins and their granddaughters (Laya & Scarlett Clark). Dad, they are growing up fast. They are both cheerleaders at Metro Christian Academy. Scarlett is hilarious and has an old soul. Laya is an old soul and has an unbelievable attention to detail. They miss their "Pappa Thom."

Chapter 43

1965 NORTHERN LITTLE LEAGUE LINE UP:

- **Dub Kilgo** - Pitcher and Catcher (best curveball in Little League)

- **James Weaver** - First Base / Couldn't make a bad throw to first - caught everything

- **Larry Williams** - 2nd Base / Team comedian

- **Eddie Sherman** - Shortstop/ only irreplaceable part of the team (killed us when he broke his hand)

- **Donnie Snider** - 3rd Base and Catcher (never had a bad day in his life)

- **Ronnie Kimbrough** - Infield/all positions (quick hands - glad he wasn't a pick pocket)

- **Shelby Bradburn** -1st Base/3rd Base (full time chick finder)

- **Tim Hunt** - Outfield / Team supply officer (enough said)

- **Larry Clifton** - Outfield and Shortstop - thought he could shoot dice with the best, until Carlton Kilgo won all his money at the State Finals in Houston / Also a Naval Fire Alarm Specialist

- **Mark Kreuger** - Outfield / head was harder than Sherman's hand /and boy could he hit

- **Donald Scott** - Put him anywhere where there is no poison ivy and he could play

- **Larry Lumus** - Infield/Outfield/Pinch Hitter extraordinaire

- **Dennis (Butch) Roberts** - Infield / all positions - took more pictures than the Japanese team

- **John (Slick) Nemmer** - Outfielder / Thought first-base coaching box was the best location from which to hustle girls and give autographs

- **Thom Clark** - Pitcher / Outfielder / Pinch-Hitter / Tall

- **Jimmy Martinez** - quit team because he would rather go swimming / last heard to be proponent of 8-track tapes and Beta video tape systems

- **Carlton Kilgo** - toughest coach in Little League Baseball / loved him - hated him - always respected him

- **Buddy Snider** - quiet assistant coach / never piss him off or he would run you until you died

That was the 1965 Waco Northern Little League All-Star Team.

To quote Forrest Gump:

"That's all I have to say about that."

"Let us hear the conclusion of the whole matter: Fear God, and keep his commandments: for this is the whole duty of man.For God shall bring every work into judgment, with every secret thing, whether it be good, or whether it be evil."

— Ecclesiastes 12:13-14

(This book was written by King Solomon towards the end of his EPIC wealth acquiring life spent managing his possessions, his kingdom and his relationship with 700 wives and 300 concubines.)

Here is my thesis. The world needs many more fathers (including me) to step up and to unapologetically teach our children about The Bible and how to have a life-changing relationship with our Lord and Savior Jesus. God has a plan for our children and so does Satan. If you and I want to go down in history as the second best father that our children will ever have we must be intentional about teaching our children about the Bible and how to enter a relationship with Jesus.

"Be so good they can't ignore you."

— Steve Martin

(Stephen Glenn Martin (born August 14, 1945) is an American comedian, actor, writer, producer, and musician. Known for his work in comedy films, television, and recording, he has received many accolades, including five Grammy Awards, a Primetime Emmy Award, and a Screen Actors Guild Award as well as nominations for eight Golden Globe Awards and two Tony Awards.)

www.ingramcontent.com/pod-product-compliance
Lightning Source LLC
Chambersburg PA
CBHW010937120626
46554CB00008B/2507